WITHDRAWN

MA

AR 20

SE

A LEARNING APPROACH TO CHANGE

Copyrights and Trademarks

A LEARNING APPROACH TO CHANGE

❖

Ken Griffiths
and
Richard Williams

Gower

Published by
Gower Publishing Limited
Gower House
Croft Road
Aldershot
Hampshire GU11 3HR
England

Gower
Old Post Road
Brookfield
Vermont 05036
USA

Ken Griffiths and Richard Williams have asserted their right under the
Copyright, Designs and Patents Act 1988 to be identified as the
authors of this work.

British Library Cataloguing in Publication Data
Griffiths, Ken
    A learning approach to change
    1. Organizational learning   2. Organizational change
    I. Title   II. Williams, Richard
    658.3'124

ISBN 0 566 07729 9

Library of Congress Cataloging-in-Publication Data
Griffiths, Ken, 1939–
    A learning approach to change / Ken Griffiths and
    Richard Williams.
        p.   cm.
    Includes bibliographical references and index.
    ISBN 0-566-07729-9 (hardback)
    1. Organizational change.   2. Employees – Training of
I. Williams, Richard.   II. Title.
HD58.8.G74   1998   97–26542
658.4'06—dc21   CIP

Typeset in Garamond by Raven Typesetters, Chester
and printed in Great Britain by Biddles Ltd, Guildford.

CONTENTS

❖

LIST OF TABLES

LIST OF FIGURES

PREFACE

Few of us are privileged to be involved first-hand with the reengineering of one of the world's best-known companies. We were: and the company concerned was, and still is, IBM. Because of the fast-moving industry it was in, IBM had to face the challenge of changing itself drastically if it was not to miss the opportunity offered by an emerging marketplace. In this respect IBM was in the vanguard of a period of significant change that occurred not only in the IT industry but also in all forms of organizations and society. Change is apparent across the whole spectrum of our lives. Whether an organization is in the public or private sector, in the manufacturing or service industry, national or international, the need for it to change is being driven by changes in customer demands, new technologies, new legislation, new competitive threats, demographic shifts and many other factors. Furthermore, as the rate of change grows ever faster, a state of change should be considered the norm not the exception – and any organization believing otherwise will find itself in trouble.

The successful enterprises are those that can anticipate and implement change ahead of their competitors. Sometimes the required changes are quite small – almost fine tuning. More and more frequently, however, the severity of the changes involves the training or retraining of a significant number of people, to a degree that goes far beyond normal career development. This is corporate transformation on a grand scale. Another factor is emerging at the same time: the realization that people are *the* key resource in most forms of change. From the 'boardroom' to the 'shopfloor' everyone has to 'buy in' to change for it to be totally successful. This means that a change project, no matter how narrow or broad, is a campaign to win the hearts as well as the minds of those affected by it. This usually requires a change in attitude as well as gains in knowledge and skills. The extent and depth of the impact within these organizations must not be underestimated. These organizations are now the norm; consequently, it is likely that any employee in a modern economy will be significantly affected by business process reengineering or organizational change sooner rather than later.

The expanding role of the training and development function as a prime agent of change leads us to believe that there are three types, or generations, of training and development (T&D).

The first, and the most familiar, is the standard apprenticeship or replenishment type. New intakes are trained to replace qualified people who have left, retired or been promoted. This is 'business-as-usual' training that changes very little over time.

The second generation applies to transformational change projects when, more often than not, T&D becomes the strategic vehicle to achieve that change. This definitely is not 'business as usual'. The training project is specifically designed to achieve the change project's business objectives. By the completion of the project the workforce will have acquired new knowledge, extra skills and usually fresh attitudes. Consequently, the organization will have reached a higher level of capability and competitiveness. Having transformed itself, it will need to maintain this momentum and seek to improve its business capability even further. If it sits back and rests on its laurels, sooner or later competition will leapfrog it.

The third generation of T&D addresses this potential threat. Organizations which have considerable experience of change have found that their staff have developed an appetite for learning. Through encouragement, sometimes financial, people are learning lifetime skills such as problem-solving, teamworking, time management, running effective meetings, communication skills, benchmarking and so on. Empowerment encourages them to take ownership of their work and to seek ways of making it better than their competitors. At this stage the organization becomes a self-developing, learning one, powered by the vitality and creativity of its own workforce. In this regime the role of the T&D function changes from one of training to one of facilitating the learning process.

Whilst a great deal of this book is about second generation training and development, the emphasis throughout is on learning rather than training. In the final analysis the key metric is 'How much learners have learnt', not 'How much trainers have taught'. It is this aspect that led us to the title *A Learning Approach to Change*. The evolution of training and development as a key function in change projects has encouraged some organizations to analyse the factors behind the education process itself; one of these was IBM. In 1987 its International Education Centre in La Hulpe, Belgium produced a compendium of its methodology called the Systems Approach To Education – SATE for short. In this instance, systems meant processes, not computers. The principles laid down in that compendium underline the rationale behind all the main curricula, both internal and external, offered by IBM throughout the world.

The success enjoyed by SATE is due to three key factors. First, it is a logical, repeatable process that concentrates on a comprehensive needs analysis at the beginning of the project. This defines management's objectives and needs and leads to specifications that they can feel committed to as their part of a 'contract' with T&D. Second, SATE recognizes that adults learn in different ways and at different rates. Therefore, the process design of events and courses is key to learning. Third, measurements and evaluation are taken at four different levels to ensure that the curriculum is meeting the organization's requirements.

The logical and structured approach of SATE can be equally useful for auditing an existing curriculum or series of courses – a kind of health check. The methodology can reveal valuable information about many aspects of your current training programme – not least whether it is working or not.

In the first part of this book we introduce SATE in the context of transformational change, together with project management, needs analysis and skills management, in the four chapters under 'Foundations for Change'. How adults learn and how this knowledge can be used to enhance the learning experience are the subjects of the second part of the book called 'Learners and Learning'. The third part discusses further aspects of the SATE methodology as they apply to the design, delivery, organization and measurement of learning. Examples are given of how the SATE methodology is reflected in many of the criteria used for national and international awards. Tangible benefits for US and UK companies underline the link between learning and corporate success in a part entitled 'Delivery, Feedback and Benefits'. In the final part of the book – 'Looking Ahead' – we review organizational trends, and their implications for management, workers and educators. This is the emerging third generation of T&D. The interesting thing is that the principles underlying learning have not changed; if anything, they are more important. Anyone planning such third generation learning needs to be more aware of human psychology, clarity of goals, measurement and a systems approach, just as was required in the second generation. We close the part with a discussion on human resource accounting in terms of intellectual capital and the human balance sheet.

This book should appeal to anyone with responsibility for initiating, influencing, designing or implementing training programmes to support organizational change, and to anyone questioning the validity of current programmes.

Depending on the size and nature of the organization, the content will be relevant to:

○   Executive management charged with planning and achieving significant change, including the sponsor for the change project, who has overall responsibility for its success. The book offers a clear structure to be followed, with checkpoints and examples.

○   General management whose remit includes training and development, whether provided internally or externally. The book offers them, amongst other ideas, a blueprint that they can use to assess the quality and suitability of existing and proposed training programmes.

○   Line management who carry prime responsibility for the continual development of their people. This book gives them insights into the use of a skills management system, the importance of a measurement and evaluation structure, especially level 3 (performance on the job), the value of their feedback to the T&D function, and how they can assess the quality and suitability of proposed learning events for their people.

○   Human resource management (HRM) will appreciate the value of a skills management system and how this can be used both in career planning for the workforce and skills requirements planning for the organization. They should also appreciate the implications of intellectual capital and the human assets register.

○   T&D management, who should be keen to compare their understanding of topics such as project management, adult learning characteristics, measurement and evaluation, skills management systems and T&D organization and responsibilities with those expressed here.

○   Trainers responsible for the design, development and delivery of learning events should find the contents of this book invaluable in either verifying their current approach or giving them new thoughts and techniques that they can immediately put into practice.

○   Consultants who are working in the field of the management of change and who advise their clients on the critical success factors affecting change. This book will underline the importance of the quality and suitability of appropriate learning programmes and give them a blueprint to work with.

○   Managers, trainers and consultants who are keen to take on the new roles of facilitators, coaches and mentors: they should find much in this book to stimulate their interests and point them towards fruitful areas to explore such as creativity and electronic brainstorming.

○   Employees at all levels who undergo training both formally and informally: this book helps them to determine their preferred style of learning, understand why measurement and evaluation are important, appreciate the importance and use of a skills management system, and encourages them to develop lifetime skills that can be transferred from job to job.

O   Academics seeking further understanding of how their teaching institutions can better prepare their students for an effective and fruitful working life.

To help the reader each chapter opens with 'backward and forward links' to the rest of the book so that specific threads can be followed, together with aims for the reader. Each chapter closes with a summary of the key messages and further 'food for thought'.

Despite its important role in the success of most change projects, no one appears to have claimed the high ground for training and development. We don't know why this is, but this book is meant to be a stake in the ground for training and development specifically and human resource development in general. We hope you enjoy reading it.

Ken Griffiths
Richard Williams

ACKNOWLEDGEMENTS

❖

We owe a debt of gratitude to many people, especially our ex-colleagues and ex-students from Entry Marketing Education in IBM United Kingdom Limited who in no small way provided a great deal of the inspiration behind this book. We are particularly grateful to Ronnie Ferguson of IBM, who not only smoothed the way with regard to our use of IBM's Systems Approach To Education (SATE), but also was kind enough to give helpful comments on our original draft. The Systems Approach To Education (SATE) methodology and its associated techniques are the intellectual property of IBM. It is used by IBM's Skill Management & Transformation Practice within the IBM Consulting Group. We are grateful to IBM for giving us their permission to use this information in the writing of this book.

We are also grateful to those people we have worked with in our life after IBM. They not only provided proof that our ideas were sound, but also gave us new experiences to add to our story. Special thanks go to Trafford Business Venture's staff and clients, especially Steve Crowther, Jill Griffiths, Jack Taberner, Tracey Robinson, Chris Randall and Tony Rafferty. We thank Malcolm Brigg OBE for his valuable input on life skills education in schools, and the provision of material for Figure 15.1.

Maxim Training supplied review material for various computer-aided instruction courses that not only helped us to comment on the effectiveness of computer-based training, but taught us more about objective setting and coaching. Our learning is reflected in Chapters 2, 13 and 14, and we thank them for this.

Our thanks also go to Sumantra Ghoshal. He is Associate Professor of Management at INSEAD, and gave us permission to draw on his study of Scandinavian Airlines System which makes up one of our cases in Chapter 1. David Bower, Personnel Director at The Rover Group, presented material for the Rover case in Chapter 1 at a 'distance learning' conference in London in 1993. We acknowledge his cooperation in allowing us to summarize it here, and thank him for his very helpful comments on reviewing it. We should also like to thank The Industrial Society and Andrew Forrest, the Human Resources Director, for giving us permission to reproduce the Carousel of Development in Figure 11.4 and its accompanying notes.

The Investors In People UK government initiative has proved to be a very successful one for the companies which receive its award. These companies have tangible proof of its benefits, and we are grateful to Investors In People UK for allowing us to quote some of them from their booklet, *The Benefits of Being an Investor in People* (REF No. IIP 37) in Chapter 12.

Our thanks also go to Glenda Hall of Warwick University Business School, and Liz Amos of the Foundation for Manufacturing and Industry, for their friendly and responsive last-minute help with the provision of the 'Middle Market' reports referred to in the Epilogue. We received additional help with the review of this section from Liz Amos, Professor David Storey of the University of Warwick and Kevin Delany of Coopers & Lybrand, and we are very grateful for their rapid response and permission to use extracts from their work.

We all learn lessons from life and from those around us, especially our family. Like Jeremy, who needed to live in the Ecuadorian Andes for two months, negotiate with the Ministry of Commerce for a licence to export 1 000 dung-beetles, and to meet and make friends in the bars of Quito whilst waiting: he learned fluent Spanish in a few weeks. (See Chapter 7, 'Putting adult learning characteristics to work': 'Convinced of Need', 'Immediate Application', 'Problem-Solving'.) Like Clare, who invested $50 000 of her bank's money to gain an Ivy League MBA and is now a successful Boston-based management consultant. (See Chapter 16, 'Skills and the human balance sheet', 'Me Inc'.) Discussions with Clare led to much of the thinking behind the later chapters of this book and to the frequent references to Covey's 'Seven Habits'. Like Sandra, who somehow inspired her children to do these things and now tries to do the same for psychiatric patients.

And finally our heartfelt thanks to Joyce, who at times must have felt a little like a midwife attending a particularly demanding pregnancy. Thanks to her patience and care, both parents and offspring are doing well.

KG
RW

PART I

FOUNDATIONS FOR CHANGE

❖

1

THE FRAMEWORK FOR CHANGE

The centre of gravity in business success is already shifting from the exploitation of a company's physical assets to the realisation of the creativity and learning potential of all the people with whom it has contact – not just its employees. Education and training are therefore being seen less as issues of cost, and more as pre-conditions for competitive success.

> Extract from the Executive summary,
> *Tomorrow's Company, An RSA Inquiry,*
> Gower, Aldershot, 1995

BACKWARD LINKS

O   Your own experience and knowledge of change and learning
O   The preface to this book

FORWARD LINKS

O   Managing change (Chapter 2)
O   Analysing learning needs (Chapter 3)
O   Putting adult learning characteristics to work (Chapter 7)
O   Designing and delivering learning (Chapter 8)
O   Measurement and evaluation (Chapter 10)
O   SATE at work – I (Chapter 11)

AIMS

The aims of this chapter are to help you to:

O   Appreciate the role of training in enabling change

O   Appreciate the need for a structured and planned approach to change.

O   Understand the role and strengths of the Systems Approach To Education – SATE.

INTRODUCTION

Whether you are a manager or not, you have probably never been under so much pressure to implement change in your organization as you are right now. You might be dreading the sheer thought of it. On the other hand if you are one of the breed of people who welcomes change you may be exhilarated by it. Whatever your view of change you can find comfort in the fact that you are not alone. Thousands of enterprises around the world are currently embarked on change programmes of one form or another and, amongst their ranks, there probably will be at least one of your major competitors. Now, if that is not enough to make you stir uneasily in your chair, then consider the view that your organization cannot afford to ignore the need for change – it will not go away.

There are many manifestations of change all around us in today's world, most of which we now accept as commonplace, even if we don't understand all of them. These changes were brought about by intense competition; for instance, one enterprise leapfrogging all the others to enjoy a brief advantage until most of the others caught up. The ones that did not catch up are no longer with us – they have either gone out of business or have been absorbed by other enterprises.

One form of change, as yet in its infancy but growing fast and far-reaching in its implications, is mass customization; or how to fashion your products to suit each and every customer in (almost) real time. The following examples are reasonably common ones and illustrate both the concept and practice:

1.   Today's popular computing magazines offer a bewildering array of advertisements by the vendors of personal computers (PCs). Many offer next-day delivery of a system assembled from a range of processors, memory, disk drives, colour monitors, keyboards, printers, sound-boards, CD-ROM drives, fax and modem connections to the information superhighway, operating and application software, and so on. Just pick up the telephone, answer a few questions and, shortly after you've put the telephone down, your system is being built. Provided you call before, say, noon, the PC could be on your desktop the following morning.

2.   In the High Street 'Just Spex' (a pseudonym) literally offer a walk-in

service. One hour after your eye test, conducted by very knowledgeable specialists, you can walk out of the store wearing a pair of
glasses with precision-ground prescribed lenses produced by technicians using high performance technology; a few years ago this
service used to take a week or more.

3.   Other High Street stores offer a one-hour processing of colour print
films, including an extra set of prints if desired. A few years ago this
process used to take at least three working days.

4.   In Japan a customer can walk into a Toyota car showroom on a
Monday morning and sit with a sales representative in front of a
computer terminal. Within an hour or so the customer can choose
the model of car, colour, body style, engine size, instrument layout
and extras, and have that virtual car priced up. If everything is
acceptable, including the financial arrangements, another keystroke
loads that order on to Toyota's production schedule. On Friday of
the same week the customer takes delivery. This is the five-day
motor car. Toyota are working to bring this down first to three days,
then next-day delivery. They are confident that they will achieve
this by the year 2000.

5.   In America the Motorola company offers a similar on-line customiz-
ing facility for its Bandit electronic pagers. In this case the pager is
produced at a plant in Florida within one hour of the final keystroke
and delivery really is the following day on mainland USA.

Why are these examples so successful? On the face of it, it seems obvious.
The first example depends for its competitive success on professionals who
are knowledgeable, skilled in assembly work and motivated. Today's technology is such that soldering the parts in place is no longer needed – they
plug into mother boards or pre-wired slots. A further skill is needed in
pre-installing the operational and functional software, then checking the
assembly out as a fully functional system that does what it is claimed to do.
In the second and third examples the high level of service is achieved by
having the advanced function processing technology on site in the High
Street store. In the last two examples the remarkable achievements are due
to sophisticated computer-based production systems being able to handle a
batch size of one in what is essentially a mass production environment.
Whilst modern communications and information technology systems have
been key factors in achieving this degree of competitive success, they would
count for nothing without the effective training of the people who are
responsible for operating and managing them. There are dozens of successful examples like these, a great many of which touch our everyday lives.
There have been some notable failures as well.

During the 1980s, General Motors reputedly spent $60 billion or so on robotics and extensive computer systems in an attempt to match the efficiency and effectiveness of the leading Japanese car manufacturers. They failed. Not because the technology was inadequate – on the contrary, it was probably the best that money could buy at the time. The project failed because they didn't marry the investment in technology to a corresponding investment in the people who were going to have to operate it as part of their jobs. People are the determinant factor in situations such as this: they need training and time to learn and develop the skills required to master new technology if any significant change is to occur. Equally important, they need to be convinced of the personal benefit of learning new techniques and working with the latest equipment. In other words, they need to know 'what's in it for them'. Happily, General Motors have since learnt their lesson.

In early 1994, a large UK insurance company was fined £300 000 by LAUTRO – the Life Assurance and Unit Trust Regulatory Office – allegedly for putting the public at risk *by failing to ensure its sales force was properly trained.* Over a year later it was reported that another large UK insurance company had made a provision of £100 million against its exposure to the problem of mis-selling personal pension schemes. These two examples are by no means unique.

These cases illustrate some of the consequences of ineffective training. What were perfectly laudable and strategic change projects for these companies failed, at considerable potential expense to their pockets and their reputation. The lesson is clear.

FOUR STUDIES OF TRANSFORMATIONAL CHANGE

So far we hope you will have nodded your head in agreement with our observations. Or, if you haven't, at least you won't have disagreed with any of them. Now let us expand our argument further. Successful change depends on effective training and development, and on getting it right first time. Whilst this dependency is not an absolute one, the contribution made by an effective training programme is substantial enough to make the difference between success and failure. There is ample evidence to support this and, to underline the message, we look at four enterprises in slightly more detail than in the previous examples. This gives us the chance to discuss where each of these companies started from and why they felt they had to do something about changing themselves. We also discuss what their goals were, how they went about achieving these, and what the results were. In some instances, the narrative will describe the kind of people involved in the change and the specific training that was given to them. This will provide a better understanding of what we call 'transformational change' and the issues that have to be faced in the process.

SCANDINAVIAN AIRLINES SYSTEM[1]

Our first example is well known in the academic world of Management and Business Studies. The full case study is rich in content and still evolving. However, we wish to highlight just one aspect of it, at one particular point in time; an important point in time, as it turns out.

When the Scandinavian Airlines System (SAS) group announced their 1986–87 financial results they showed the sixth straight profitable year, their best ever. They also had the highest profit margin in the world of commercial aviation. This was in stark contrast to the situation in 1981 when their operating costs were among the highest in the industry, losses were mounting and they were rapidly losing market share. Much of the credit for this recovery was due to Jan Carlzon who took over as President and CEO in 1981. What he found at the time was an airline that:

○ considered customers a disturbing influence because they, the customers, were always demanding something better

○ was distracted by the latest technology of its Boeing 747s and Airbus A300s

○ contemplated halving the frequency of flights to raise the load factors of these relatively large aircraft

○ operated strictly according to the company's policy manuals which were voluminous

○ did not encourage or reward individual initiative – sometimes the exact opposite

○ not surprisingly, had very low employee morale.

Jan Carlzon reacted very quickly. In a very short time he:

○ replaced or relocated 13 of his 14 executives, as he felt the top team had lost its focus

○ revamped the aircraft fleet mix to meet the demands of increased flight frequency: no 747s or A300s, but nine small turboprop aircraft where previously there had been none

○ scrapped first class and concentrated on the lucrative business class instead

○ improved on-time performance from 85 per cent to 93 per cent – a European record at the time

○ transformed the culture from a bureaucracy to a business that everyone felt committed to

○ emphasized the importance of what he called 'moments of truth' – personal encounters by the workforce with the customer.

He stressed that the customer is not interested in, and should not be affected by, the company's bureaucracy or organization chart. On the other hand, the customer is keenly affected by the efficiency and helpfulness of the check-in staff and the flight crew who are predominantly the only SAS personnel the normal fare-paying passenger meets on a journey.

According to Sumantra Ghoshal:[2]

> Education was considered necessary to reap the full benefits of the new organization, and both managers and front-line staff were sent to seminars. The courses for the front-line personnel were referred to by many as the 'learn-to-smile seminars', but the real benefits probably resulted more from the participants' perception that the company cared more about its employees than from the actual content of the courses.

While there is more than an element of truth in this statement the fundamental reasons for that particular training were quite simple:

O   learning to smile genuinely, especially at people who are your customers or potential customers, is a prerequisite if you want to change from being a technology-led service company to a customer-focused one. Ultimately, 'people buy people', all other things being equal

O   training and development of the right kind helps people to grow and, if people grow, so does the company

O   repairing badly damaged morale.

The new culture gradually took hold and, as it did, SAS stabilized and to a certain extent flourished. While the company has had its share of problems since, including being hit with a devaluation and further weakening of the Swedish krona against its dollar-financed debt, it survives to fight on.

VERNA GROUP LIMITED

Our second example is a contemporary one and tells the story of a medium-sized company that is happily – that's right, happily – climbing the learning curve of 'learning to change'. The benefits and the accolades that they have achieved on their short journey so far has fired them up for more. If ever a company burst with enthusiasm this one does.

Verna Group Limited has its head office and main operating units in Bolton, in the North-West of England. It has another unit based in the county of Somerset, in the South-West of England. Verna Group Limited is the parent company of:

Vernacare: the core business of disposable pulp products and macerators for public and private hospitals, hospices and private care homes

Karomed:	nursing consumables and healthcare equipment
Vernagene:	water treatment and disinfection systems
Vernaware:	ceramic fibre products for high-temperature applications
Vernacare (N America):	promotion of Vernacare Systems in North America and Canada
Carton Carriers:	road transport and distribution.

The Verna Group is a private company that prides itself on having a 'family firm' atmosphere. This is borne out by the number of employees with more than ten years of service. Out of some 250 employees, over 80 have achieved this milestone. Significantly this includes the four Verna Group directors who, between them, have accumulated 92 years' service. These are remarkable figures for a company established as recently as 1964. The Verna Group is essentially devoted to healthcare. Their largest subsidiary, Vernacare Limited, leads the way with its fully biodegradable pulp products for human waste disposal. In addition they also design and manufacture macerators, the units that process the used Vernacare products. The macerators themselves have been awarded the British Standards Institution (BSI) kite mark – a symbol representing quality, safety and reliability.

The company is proud of its record of never having let down a hospital with deliveries. They have a million products in reserve 'just in case'. Not content with that, this reserve is spread across three separate locations – again 'just in case'. This philosophy of 'just in case' is somewhat at odds with the modern practice of 'just in time'. 'Just in case' ties up a fair amount of capital, but the investment is a measure of Verna Group's commitment to its customers. Not only is the Verna Group a caring company, it is also a very successful one and enjoys healthy rates of return on capital employed and turnover. This success is even more impressive when considering that its biggest customer is the National Health Service (NHS). The NHS is by far the largest single employer in the United Kingdom and has an annual budget of almost £40 billion. Like any other enterprise, the NHS is constantly searching for ways to cut costs. Because of the scale of its operations, a saving of a fraction of a penny on a particular item can realize total savings amounting to hundreds of thousands of pounds. Companies which are 'tuned in' to their customers are aware of this, strive for continuous improvement and share the savings with them. The Verna Group is such a company; it has been able to hold its prices for several years and, in some cases, reduce them.

It also realized at an early stage that achieving ISO 9000 accreditation would give it a significant edge over its competitors. Increasingly, accreditation to ISO 9000 standards is a prerequisite to bidding for contracts from government departments and large organizations. Furthermore, attaining equivalent standards within the EU is essential for doing business in some parts of the lucrative European markets. Vernacare has been successful in this respect too and has over 500 macerators installed in 21 countries. Achieving ISO 9000 accreditation does not happen overnight, as it is necessary to train the whole workforce. The Verna Group clearly showed its commitment to the programme by creating and filling two key positions: a training coordinator and a quality assurance manager. The programme began with the training coordinator who was trained in-house by external consultants. Subsequently, 22 managers and supervisors took part in interactive 'Teach the teachers' workshops. The quality assurance manager was trained to British Standards Institution standards; he is also a qualified lead assessor for ISO 9000 accreditation, which enables him to assess formally any other company's compliance to the required standards. The success of the training can be seen in the business benefits that resulted. These included:

> an exclusive five-year contract with the NHS
> scrap reduction equivalent to £100 000 per year
> increased efficiency of £60 000 per year
> productivity gains of £140 000 per year
> plus the very important asset of a newly acquired set of skills for the company.

These newly acquired skills now form the basis of the Verna Group's approach to total quality management – TQM. As Jean Wilson (Chairperson and Chief Executive) said:

> ... we have shown that investing in our people through training produces real benefits. Benefits that are vital for any organization to develop and grow in today's competitive markets. We are reinforcing our commitment to developing our employee potential to meet the needs of the business, by working towards the national standard, Investors In People. I look forward to continued success for the company and all our employees.

And so the commitment goes on. The Verna Group has already got the message about training and is running with it. To illustrate how successful this motivation is, the Verna Group and its subsidiaries have scooped many business awards in 1993, 1994 and 1995:

> Regional Training Award (Employment Department)
> Certificate of Quality and Merit (Royal Institute of Public Health and Hygiene)
> Company of the Year (Bolton Business Awards)
> Exporting Company of the Year (Bolton Business Awards)
> Training for Results (Bolton Business Awards).

The Verna Group may not be a household name – yet! But watch out for it – it intends to be.

THE ROVER GROUP

In the 1950s, 1960s and early 1970s the Rover Group (or British Leyland as it was then known) had a reputation for quality and image and its cars ranked on a par with Jaguar. From then until the early 1990s Rover's reputation suffered badly, along with most other UK mass car manufacturers. This study relates how Rover, with not inconsiderable help from Honda, regained its reputation and its pride, and became a learning organization.

In the 1980s, British Leyland, the nationalized group that Rover belonged to, suffered from a reputation for poor quality. It was not entirely deserved, as some of their models – the Allegro, the Marina and the Ital – were still on the road 10 to 15 years later. Nevertheless, it was their image. Commercial pressures were rising:

O   Competition, especially from Japan
O   Customer choice
O   Supplier power
O   Technology.

Japanese competition

By 1994, the USA Japanese implants totalled 1.75 million units per year. Native USA capacity closure amounted to 1.8 million units per year: the Japanese stole their capacity. By 1994, Japanese implants had reached 1.2 million units per year in the European Union. What will the eventual native closures number in Europe? These effects of Japanese competition should not come as a surprise, because as early as 1979 Matsushita warned the West that they would win and the West would fail because they would get ideas out of the heads of all their employees.

Rover – recent history

The Rover Group was formed in 1986 under Sir Graham Day from British Leyland. The emphasis changed from product/profit to customer satisfaction. Rover became leaner, made a massive investment in total quality management (TQM) and planned to draw the best out of their workforce. This meant a significant change in attitudes to empowered employees, with managers creating a conducive working environment, acting as coaches, not policemen. Empowerment needed to be driven to the lowest possible level. Accountability and responsibility should lie with the person best placed to take a decision. Line managers should deal with people problems, instead of passing them over to Personnel as before.

In 1988, British Aerospace bought the Rover Group from the British government for £270 million. The Rover Attitude Survey that year pointed to:

○   poor communications, lack of leadership and involvement of workers
○   a lack of trust
○   no opportunities for training

yet the job was felt by staff to be important to them.

It was clear that little in the future would be certain. Cars would be different, jobs would be different and ways of working would be different. Processes would need re-examining and reengineering. Processes should:

○   add value
○   have minimum interfaces
○   result in shorter cycles
○   use best practice.

Responsibilities should be focused, not diffuse. At the start of a new vehicle programme, the Project Director should be responsible for everything, instead of responsibilities being spread across design, procurement, manufacturing, etc. A structure should be in place to support processes and reflect the management style, with:

○   a business emphasis
○   product and process focus
○   a trend to lean, flat organizations.

Following a period of association with the Japanese manufacturer Honda, a cross-share agreement was signed in 1990. This extended the cooperation, helping Rover's investment in TQM towards fruition. By 1993, a large part of the transformation was complete and the Rover Group was sold to the German car manufacturer BMW for £800 million. No doubt the future will see further change, this time due to German management influences. But the story of the last decade at Rover will remain as one of significant change and success.

The 'Rover way'

What was the route to this success? What happened in those few years? Rover's Personnel Director, David Bower, calls it 'the Rover way'. The way is through people. In fact, the Rover strategic plan is based on achievement of goals via people. Rover developed four key thrusts (or critical success factors – CSFs) to deliver their vision:

○   reduce break-even point
○   grow in Europe
○   move upmarket
○   extraordinary customer satisfaction.

The last two factors were consequences of being too small a player to address the mass market, therefore Rover aimed to become a niche supplier, commanding a premium price. Hence genuine customer satisfaction was fundamental, not merely a 'nice to have', nor a phrase to trip off management's tongues in presentations. Rover identified nine key business processes:

- Business planning
- New product introduction
- Logistics
- Manufacturing
- Maintenance
- Sales and service
- Product improvement
- Management of people
- Corporate learning.

Competitive advantage

Gaining competitive advantage in the motor industry is possible in many ways:

- By new features – but they are usually easy to copy and the advantage may be ephemeral
- By image – which can be enhanced by clever and expensive advertising, but in the end will always be tempered by reality
- By technology – as with new features, copying is easy and differences are small
- By cost base – note that in the UK in 1994:

	Employees	Vehicles/Year
Rover	34 000	450 000
Nissan/Toyota/Honda	<10 000	350–400 000

The difference is mainly due to the greater proportion of in-house parts at Rover, and their additional activity in design, engineering, sales and marketing compared with the Japanese manufacturers. Nevertheless there is still room for further productivity enhancements. The eventual answer may be customer satisfaction in the chosen niche markets. This will be done through people; it means looking to line managers to lead the change, not to accountants or to the personnel department. The way to do this is to align business and people strategies, to involve everyone and to build on the assumption that, if employees are given opportunities, they will take them.

Change, people and learning

Change needs to be managed through people. The key players need to be champions of improvement, to drive best practices and to consolidate improvements. The cornerstone for Rover in the 1990s was to strive to become a learning organization. There must be a clear vision, clear objectives and values, communicated and agreed by all. Learning must be stimulated by management, but owned by everyone, according to Rover.

All Rover employees have £100 per year to spend on training of their choice – entirely of their choice and often in their own time. They may spend it on Spanish lessons or on learning how to swim. The £100 is a tangible message that says, 'Your company thinks training is important; it thinks you are important.' It also has the effect of making employees in their thirties, forties or fifties used to learning again. These employees may not have had any formal education since school and they need to acclimatize to the new environment, where the vision is for Rover to be renowned for extraordinary customer satisfaction. To emphasize the importance of training and development and to track their progress, employees have their own 'training and development' file which they keep and own.

Rover Learning Business

Rover Learning Business (RLB) was set up in 1990 as a wholly owned Rover company, with an external Board of Governors and an Executive Committee from Rover itself. RLB's challenge is to ensure that learning leads to long-term improvements and to equip a network of 'change agents' round the company. RLB looked at 30 leading examples of 'learning companies', including banks and football clubs. Recognizing that learners have their preferred learning style, RLB provides different media – books, interactive compact disks (CDs), flip charts and so on. At any one time, 8 000 Rover employees will be undergoing RLB training and a similar number doing so in their own time. In all, this is half the company's workforce. Training has jumped up in priority by a factor of ten on line managers' checklists.

Outside the company, RLB supports a similar thrust via Open Learning in their 700 suppliers and 3 000 dealers worldwide. This provides training on:

- ○ Product details
- ○ Total quality leadership
- ○ Selling skills

because to produce a quality car means quality parts, material and supplier service, and to sell a quality car means quality channels. The key across the board is the creation of the right environment for continuous learning and development, and the dangers are complacency and navel-gazing.

The bottom line of learning

So far Rover has calculated benefits of £200 million compared with £6 million invested in training. This 30 to 1 return on investment is equal to that achieved by Motorola in the US, considered by many to be the benchmark in training for results.

Employee suggestions rose tenfold. There are more quality circles and they are finding savings on materials and energy for example. An 'Asset Bank' has been created: it is a networked database called 'GLEN' – Group Learning Exchange Network – where information and ideas can be updated, and thus any employee can add value to the organization. In this way organizations can eliminate waste by recording and sharing solutions and information. GLEN is a visible working example of calling in from the minds of all employees, of never being satisfied, of seeking continuous improvement. In parallel, Rover is a determined benchmarker. It compares itself not just with other car companies, but with anyone with similar processes – an additional benefit of viewing its operations from a process viewpoint. Rover will benchmark internally too. All these actions add up to a powerful corporate learning machine.

Attitude Survey 1992 and the future

In a repeat survey four years after the 1988 one, the categories of communications, leadership and involvement were now all acceptable. There was still room for improvement in the categories of trust and 'my work uses my abilities'. So the story does not end here. Following cooperation with, and influence from, Japan, what will the effect be of adding German experience and influence?

(Further information about RLB, and additional examples of the application of the learning organization concept, can be found in *Implementing the Learning Organization*, Patrick J. Thurbin, 1994.)

IBM UNITED KINGDOM LIMITED

Much has been, and will continue to be, written about IBM's travails and its subsequent metamorphosis. Our own experience relates to the situation IBM United Kingdom Limited faced in the late 1980s, which was replicated in many other countries in which IBM operated. The outcome was a success story everywhere. This was due in no small measure to the uniform implementation of IBM's Systems Approach To Education – SATE – which forms one of the main themes of this book.

The stage for the impending change project was set out in the company's annual report for 1986. In it the then Chairman of IBM UK Ltd, Tony Cleaver

– now Sir Anthony – indicated part of his strategy with the following statements:

> We are determined to increase output per head and, with full co-operation of our workforce, we shall exploit the benefits of our investment in technology.
>
> We are increasing resources available in the field by offering new marketing careers to hundreds of people previously engaged in administration.
>
> Training and retraining of our employees has been given added emphasis.

These statements of direction began to assume a tangible form during 1987. The company needed to put a greater focus on customer care to secure its customer base against the threat from plug-compatible mainframes. It also needed more customer-facing people to work in the growing market for departmental computer systems and personal computers. In reality, this was a double change project: to improve both the defence of one market and the penetration of another.

As the 1986 annual report implied, the increasing use of technology within the company had led to an excess of personnel in staff, administration and on the production line. Many of these people had well-developed professional skills in purchasing, production control, accountancy, business administration and other areas. These kinds of skills were scarce in the field and, properly deployed, would contribute greatly to an improved understanding of customers' needs and add credibility to subsequent business proposals. An internal recruiting campaign for field personnel produced a greater than expected response from this group who were just as keen to start a new career as the normal intake of graduate and experienced hires.

The change project facing the marketing training department was an interesting one. Over a thousand people had to be trained to be effective marketeers in as short a time as possible commensurate with good practice. There was not a bottomless budget for this project, no university-style campus large enough to house this number of people, nor the requisite number of qualified trainers. In addition, the existing curriculum could not cope with this number of people in the timescale required. Nor could it provide the level of knowledge and skills deemed necessary by executive management. To compound the issue, major new product announcements were on the horizon and details about these would need to be integrated into the curriculum and available to the students from day one of the announcements. In brief, marketing training was being asked:

○ to train and qualify 1 000 plus students in two-thirds of the normal time

○ to do so without loss of quality as measured by the rate and calibre of 'qualifying'

○ to handle a student load four times the normal amount.

Amongst the consequences were the needs to:

○   double (to 48) the normal class size
○   double the frequency of courses
○   treble the number of instructors by internal recruitment
○   totally revise the entire curriculum.

Working to the above targets, a special curriculum was devised which allowed an individual to qualify within some 12 months instead of the previous 18 without loss of quality. As a result everyone was cleared through this programme in a little over two years.

The programme was given added meaning in mid-1988 with the announcement of the IBM AS/400 series of mid-range computers. This series was central to the training project we ran. Similar training projects took place worldwide in IBM. In the first 60 days after the announcement, Europe alone sold 13 000 – its forecast for a full year! The AS/400 has since gone on to become one of IBM's most successful products. We cannot prove it, but we suspect a strong link between training and business success in the case of the AS/400.

The success of this project depended on many things, not least the people involved – managers, trainers and learners. We found it particularly beneficial to work closely with representatives from line management, especially with regard to the content of the courses and the standards of performance. Our line management group were seven in number – hence they became known as the G7 group. The project also benefited from the application of a well-founded methodology which covered every aspect of the training programme and which was used throughout IBM in parallel situations. It was that experience that prompted the writing of this book.

THE NEED FOR A METHODOLOGY

There is no disputing the fact that training is a key ingredient in change. It is likely, therefore, that training will figure prominently within the whole project plan – perhaps being a sub-project in its own right. Just as the project is best managed with a proven methodology, so is the training sub-project. A substantial part of a training sub-project is made up of the planning, design, delivery and evaluation of the training programme. To handle such a wide range of key activities it is beneficial to have a methodology, or model, which allows management to maintain control of the process and hence minimize surprises. IBM's Systems Approach To Education – SATE – is such a model.[3]

SYSTEMS APPROACH TO EDUCATION – SATE

The Systems Approach To Education had its origins in a process known as Instructional Systems Design – ISD. It was developed during the Second World War to teach critical skills to military personnel in a simple, efficient way. Since then the process has also been used extensively by governments and businesses, and its methodology validated many times over by research data and high-quality education programmes. Its pedigree, therefore, is excellent.

IBM developed SATE to provide a step-by-step process that begins with the front-end analysis of needs and carries through to the design, development, delivery and evaluation of education courses and activities. It gives organizations which use it a uniform, structured and systematic approach to the total education process. Figure 1.1 (on page 21) shows SATE in diagrammatic form as a system of processes or a model. Although it is not a computer system, parts of it can be computer-based and, at the appropriate points in this book, these will be discussed. Every process and sub-process shown is well known within the education profession and has been the subject of many books. What sets SATE apart from others is its unique combination of these individual processes and their underlying principles and methodologies. There are four of them that stand out as key modules: needs analysis, how adults learn, education delivery systems and measurement and evaluation.

NEEDS ANALYSIS

The first of them is needs analysis. The inputs to the needs analysis process are the essentials needed to achieve the business objectives – the business requirements. These should be defined by executive management and should be clear, numerical, time-based and measurable. They are cascaded and translated into performance requirements. Performance requirements are really a statement of the outcomes needed to achieve the business requirements. Increasingly, these outcomes are a result of an increase in skills; therefore, performance requirements can be further translated into education requirements. The education requirements are the differences between the new skills required and the current skills. These are the skills shortfalls that have to be addressed by the education programme. All of these are discussed in Chapter 3.

HOW ADULTS LEARN

The second key factor in the SATE approach is not even shown in the SATE diagram in Figure 1.1, yet it contains the very kernel of the SATE model –

curriculum planning, course development and course delivery. It is the due importance given to the way adults learn. Not only is learning important, but retaining and reinforcing what is learnt are equally important. SATE recognizes the importance of the learning and reinforcing processes and Chapters 5, 6 and 7 discuss the practical aspects in detail.

EDUCATION DELIVERY SYSTEMS

The third module of the SATE model concerns education delivery systems. There are two types of learner audiences: one is the group audience and the other is the individual; for each of these there are valid delivery vehicles. In the final reckoning the choice of the most suitable delivery system will be decided by a combination of learning objectives, the composition of the audience and the most cost-effective way of delivering the material (see Chapter 8).

MEASUREMENT AND EVALUATION

The fourth strength of the SATE methodology is the assessment and feedback of the actual results against the planned requirements. Each of the three levels of needs analysis provides a convenient checkpoint against which the effectiveness of the training programme can be assessed. A close check can be kept, therefore, on the effectiveness of the programme during and after the curriculum, and changes made accordingly.

SATE defines four levels of measurement and evaluation, based on the work of Donald Kirkpatrick of the University of Wisconsin. Kirkpatrick's four levels are:

1. Student reactions: what did the students think of the course?
2. Knowledge/skill gain: did the students learn what they were meant to?
3. Application: were the students able to use their new knowledge and skills in their jobs as planned?
4. Business results: did the training contribute to the planned business requirements?

Although SATE uses the same levels and definitions, the key difference is that the starting point is *business results* as indicated in our description of SATE above. Therefore SATE measurement and evaluation attempts to start at business needs (level 4), moving via performance needs (level 3) to learning gains (level 2), and last of all to student reactions (level 1). The higher the level, the more important the measurement. The whole measurement and evaluation system should be designed top-down. The measurement system at each level should be designed into the structure of the training processes, from business objective level to event reaction level.

Measuring these reliably is one of the biggest challenges facing management. Yet, they are so important as yardsticks of progress that every effort should be made to record at least qualitative values. Chapters 10 and 11 discuss these matters in greater detail.

The four modules of needs analysis, adult learning principles, delivery systems and measurement and evaluation stand out as the foundations of a totally versatile, robust and proven education model, well suited for use in any change project. Although we have discussed the SATE methodology in terms of its applicability to change projects, its versatility is not limited solely to that particular aspect of business. It also has another potential role to play – that of an independent training health check, as described in Chapter 3.

THE KEY MESSAGES

O   Change is here to stay. Doing nothing is not an option.
O   The cost of getting training wrong can be disastrous.
O   Successful change depends on effective training and development and making it a success first time.
O   If people grow, so does the company.
O   'We have shown that investing in our people through training produces real benefits.' (Jean Wilson, Chairperson, The Verna Group)[4]
O   'Your company thinks training is important; it thinks you are important.' (A Rover belief)
O   Well-defined and targeted training can yield very good business benefits.
O   Business requirements: don't even think about starting a change project without them. It also means that part of the justification criteria would be missing.

FOOD FOR THOUGHT

A class at IBM's International Education Centre in Brussels was dealing with the impact of change in an organization. The instructor illustrated this by asking us to close our eyes, stand on our chairs, rotate through 360 degrees and then sit down. He then asked how we felt. The comments were mostly 'confused, insecure, disorientated, angry', with only a few 'intrigued, interested'. 'That's what it's like for the employees when a business introduces change,' the instructor said.

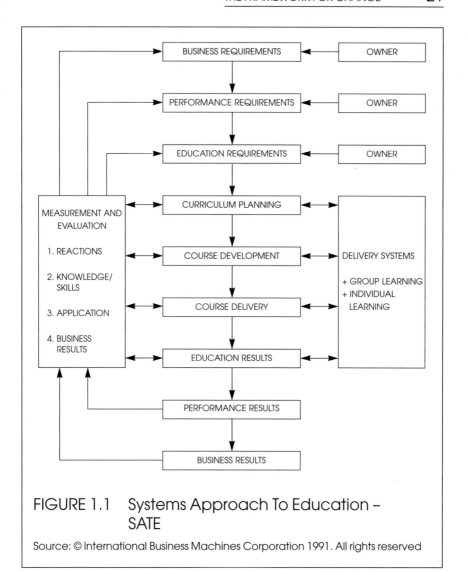

FIGURE 1.1   Systems Approach To Education –
            SATE

2

MANAGING CHANGE

There is nothing more difficult to execute, nor more dubious of success, nor more dangerous to administer, than to introduce a new order of things.

Machiavelli,
The Prince

BACKWARD LINKS

○ The framework for change (Chapter 1)

FORWARD LINKS

○ Analysing learning needs (Chapter 3)
○ Who are the learners . . . ? (Chapter 5)
○ Organizational trends (Chapter 13)

AIMS

The aims of this chapter are to help the reader:

○ Understand the different contexts, causes and parameters of change
○ Understand the move from strategy to plan
○ Understand the definition of project management
○ Understand the hallmarks of a successful project
○ Be aware of the crucial importance of a clear project definition and of a workshop methodology to achieve it
○ Understand the definition of different objective types and how they relate to each other.

CONTEXTS OF CHANGE

Scandinavian Airlines turned round in the 1980s after the injection of a new CEO – followed by a new executive team. IBM moved back into profit in 1994 following the departure of John Akers as CEO and his replacement by Lou Gerstner from Nabisco. Gerstner was the first outsider in history to become IBM's CEO. These two examples of injection change (Eccles, 1994) followed periods of near-catastrophic trading for the two companies concerned.

In IBM UK, prior to Akers' departure, an interesting change took place when Nick Temple succeeded Sir Anthony Cleaver as CEO. Temple had been on assignment from the UK to IBM's European headquarters in Paris, heading a finance function. He was little known to most UK staff on his appointment. Although Temple's appointment looked like a succession change (Eccles, 1994) (an IBM UK senior manager succeeding to the top job), it was in fact an injection change, because Temple's recent career had been in a totally different part of IBM. Previously in IBM UK, the succession change pattern had been promotion from within the ranks of well-known senior marketing managers to CEO.

In a very short time, Temple produced a blueprint for the UK company, allowing many more powers to be devolved to local branch operations. Headcount was almost halved. Thousands of staff took early retirement or voluntary severance, including Temple himself in 1996. By then IBM UK had moved back into healthy profit. IBM's share price by mid-1997 had almost reached $200 (allowing for a share split), from its nadir of some $50 during the Akers/Gerstner transition.

In all, Eccles[1] defines six contexts for top management change.

1.   Takeover (by another organization)
2.   Injection (of an outsider)
3.   Succession (from inside)
4.   Renovation (by existing team)
5.   Partnership (as in a professional practice)
6.   Catalytic (for instance by consultants)

The lower down the scale, the less the power available to the change initiators. Eccles discusses the mechanisms that operate in each case through real-life examples. He makes twelve core propositions about change implementation. Seven of these underpin much of the rest of this chapter (Table 2.1).

He makes two propositions concerning empowerment (Table 2.2).

We shall return to the topic of empowerment as it affects learning in Chapters 13 and 14.

TABLE 2.1   Eccles' Propositions – Change implementation

1	Implementation is not always complicated nor difficult to accomplish
2	Implementation can take place quickly
3	Concentrated power is an aid to rapid implementation
4	A dedicated and unified top management can make things happen
5	Without planning, an organization is handicapped in its execution of strategy
6	The key variable of implementation (assuming that the requisite resources and capabilities are available) is that of obtaining sufficient endorsement for the proposed strategic change
7	Implementation cannot be successfully delegated; sustained senior management involvement is vital

TABLE 2.2   Eccles' Propositions – Empowerment

8	Empowerment does not reduce top management's responsibility for the performance of the organization
9	Empowerment is of little value in times of rapid, radical, frame-breaking change; it works better in more stable circumstances

CAUSES OF CHANGE

Change can be driven by several factors, including one or many of:

TABLE 2.3   Causes of change

people within the organization
success or failure
potential success or failure
external change
client relationships
social factors
technology
competition
growth

Most *internal* changes can be controlled and therefore planned. Some internal changes (for instance, a significant resignation; a shattering accident) may be uncontrolled. However, most of the foregoing causes of change are *external* and, almost by definition, are uncontrolled. So, does the organization concede defeat at the outset and await further developments? With a small, energetic, tuned-in company this may appear to work – the 'one-man band' that always seems to do the right thing and does it quickly. But underneath, certain processes are going on: awareness of the market, awareness of trends, awareness of key technologies and so on. In a larger organization, what can be done to mimic this? We can downsize, rightsize, decentralize and empower in order to divide a large unit into many smaller ones to gain the fleetness of foot of the one-man band. Or we can question why a business process needs so many units in the first place (Hammer and Champy, 1993). Whatever approach we take, the successful organization will have processes in place to detect changes driven by any of the factors in Table 2.3. If no such processes exist then we need a project to deliver them.

PARAMETERS OF CHANGE

Early on in planning for change, certain key questions need to be asked about its nature. These relate in turn to the following parameters:

TABLE 2.4   Parameters of change

RATE	How quickly will the change happen? How soon will its impact be felt?
SCOPE	How big is it? How many parts of the organization will it touch? How many suppliers are involved, and in how many categories? How many customers are involved, and in what markets?
FAMILIARITY	Have we faced this sort of thing before? If so, can we adopt a known solution? Is it totally unfamiliar? If so, who else has done it, if anyone?
STRUCTURE	Is this a well-defined and well-structured change? Do we understand how its effects will hit us?
SIMPLICITY	Is it easy to understand and predict? Do its ramifications take pages to list? Are relationships within the change complex?

The faster, the bigger, the less familiar, the less structured or the more complex the change, the greater the need to manage it. Take just two of these parameters: rate and scope. A small change, happening infrequently, can be handled in flight provided suitable processes are in place. A large change, happening suddenly, will certainly need a special planning effort, with some kind of formal project management. But the most insidious change is one that is small but gradual, and eventually, deadly.

SMALL BUT GRADUAL CHANGE

Take Charles Handy's frog:[2] placed in a pot of water that is slowly brought to the boil, the frog lets itself be boiled to death, even though at any stage it could jump out to safety. What the frog needs is a monitoring and feedback system – a thermometer with a red line at the frog's critical survival temperature, with positive feedback at that point in the nature of a small but effective shock to its rear legs. Organizations can be like the boiled frog. They fail to measure and monitor, even recognize, critical variables. They have no feedback system to provoke action when a variable crosses a life-threatening threshold. The old processes, put in place in different conditions, fail to detect the crisis; new processes are absent.

The moral is: even though a change may appear to score low on the change parameter scales, there may be nasties lurking in the undergrowth. The parameter of familiarity is one that needs particularly careful assessment. It is only too easy to see changes as familiar when they are subtly new, as we note in Chapter 5. Or the same information could be used in different ways, but we carry on using it as before, because we fail to think 'out of the box'. Our advice is that, very early on in planning for change, we need to assess its nature most carefully and to involve different minds with different perspectives.

A-POINTS AND B-POINTS

A useful way of thinking about a change is through A-points and B-points. The A-point is simply the start point: the state we are in today. Many plans fail because no one bothers to analyse the A-point thoroughly. The B-point is the end point: the state we want to achieve. This is a much more popular focus of attention, however ill-defined. We can choose to define each state by whatever means we like, such as:

○   organization
○   facilities
○   image
○   processes
○   business position (revenue, profit, share value . . .)
○   attitudes.

There will be options of routes from A to B. Closer analysis may point to alternative B-points, but first we need a strategy.

FROM STRATEGY TO PLAN

A strategy for change may come about in many ways: it may be dictated from outside (typically in the contexts of takeover/injection changes); it may be developed internally or with outside assistance, formally or informally; it may come about as a result of a completely fresh look at what business the organization is in or the way it does its business; it may even be as a result of a total business reengineering study.

Whichever way the strategy has been formulated, it is likely to have been developed through certain logical phases, such as:

1.	where are we now? (what is the A-point?)
2.	what are our options for the future? (what B-points might there be?)
3.	which can we rule out and which are valid?
4.	what are the implications for the valid options?
5.	what shall we decide to do?
6.	how shall we do it?

A good strategic analysis will start with expansive, unconstrained thinking calling on wide human resources, moving via careful analysis to the chosen course of action. A strategic plan developed from sheer intuition may succeed, but a systematic approach offers better results. When the strategic plan is decided, it is time to define and manage a project to implement the plan.

PROJECT MANAGEMENT

... is not project control. This is most often driven by mass input to a computer that produces vast amounts of critical path analyses including early start dates, late finish dates, floats, Gantt charts, resource allocations and so on. Typically, this information is an approximation of the truth, yet it is taken as gospel, pored over by experts and discussed at length at progress meetings. Such techniques have worked well where the subject of the project is well understood, such as building an oil rig, but they have often failed where uncertainty and novelty are key factors, such as computer projects. This need not be the case. Nor need it be the case with business change projects, which also are often uncertain and novel, instead of being a repeat of what was done last year.

WHAT IS A PROJECT?

To understand what project management really is, we first need to understand what a project is.

A project is a mechanism for bringing about significant change

It has certain characteristics:

TABLE 2.5   Characteristics of a project

It is something different or a one-off
It doesn't fit the normal rules, mechanisms or patterns of activity of the organization
There is usually a 'window of opportunity' that imposes time pressures
It is important enough to justify special efforts and a special approach

The complexity of a project can be gauged by, amongst other things:

TABLE 2.6   Factors affecting project complexity

The number of people affected
The amount of change in attitude needed
The amount of change in job content
The amount of change in culture
The number of decisions needed
How much technical novelty is involved

In the SAS example in Chapter 1, the main elements were:

○   the number of people involved – thousands rather than hundreds
○   the change in attitude needed for success – from technology-
oriented to customer-first. This was the most important factor.

In the IBM example, the main elements were:

○   the number of people involved – over a thousand
○   a large change in job content, from administrator to marketeer
○   the change in culture, from facing colleagues to facing customers.

Most organizational change projects would score very high on the above
'complexity list'. This means that the transformation needs to be carefully

managed, perhaps by different methods from those that the organization has used before. Project management is not a vast super-model predicting the future in the finest detail. There will be detail early on, with early check-points; further on, detail will reduce, but goals and objectives will be clear.

We make no apology for focusing on project management early on in this book. When change is implemented, organizations always manage this somehow, whether formally or by haphazard methods. Those who formalize the process of change will vastly increase their chances of success. In the rest of this chapter we offer a methodology of project management that is not mere process control and can be used at any level in an organization.

It can be applied to:

○   a total change project
○   a detailed project defining training and learning needs
○   organizing a trade fair
○   or anything else with defined A- and B-points.

A good project management system will result in clarity of objectives, effective communications and good teamwork. It will also include risk analysis as an integral part of planning. As change becomes normality and uncertainty becomes the only certainty, organizations which think about and formalize the management of change will lead the field. A brief scan of the Appointments columns of the quality press will emphasize this in terms of the need for project management skills. Such skills are in rising demand as the pace of change increases and will be imperative for any organization to grow in the future and for individuals to acquire for their own career progress.

PROJECT VERSUS PROCESS

At present, the need for learning process tasks in organizations is well understood. There is often less appreciation of the need for softer skills such as project skills, even less of the difference between a process and a project. Organizations will regularly have to change their processes to survive. Even a company with a handful of employees can expect constant and increased competition. No one is immune. Organizations which attempt to change their processes in any significant way by business-as-usual methods risk failure.

Think of a process such as 'getting ready for work'. This is something we do most days according to a very regular pattern; it does not need a formal plan. If snags occur – no milk – then we take coffee without or stick to orange juice. Thus minor changes to existing processes can be handled in flight. A project on the other hand might be 'building a home extension'. It is costed, funded, planned with specialist help, agreed with family, advised (carefully) to neighbours and implemented by a trusted contractor who sticks more or less to a planned schedule. There may be snags along the way, but with foresight gained from experience on the part of the architect or builder, these can be constrained and overcome – that is, they can be managed.

The distinction between process and project is vital. The key point is: *To change a process in a significant way will usually require a project.* What then are the hallmarks of a successful project?

HALLMARKS OF A SUCCESSFUL PROJECT

At the beginning of a project, almost even before it starts, the following should be in place:

LEADERSHIP

Few projects of any significance have gone far without visible and clear leadership – often by one person. Think of President J. F. Kennedy stating the clear goal of the United States of America of safely landing (and returning) a human being on the moon by 1970. Kennedy was already one of the great figures and leaders of the twentieth century. When he set out this goal, the nation believed it. Finances, resources and the energies of individuals and organizations all came together, and the goal was achieved and, furthermore, shown worldwide on live television. With the passing of 25 years since this staggering episode in the history of mankind, we are apt to forget the wonder and amazement felt at the time. What we should not forget is that humanity could organize itself and its resources to manage a project resulting in this historic goal.

In a company the leadership will often be provided by a management group. If the project crosses the entire company, this will be the board or the senior management committee. In any event, the need for authority and clarity are the same as if leadership comes from an individual. If it comes from a group, there must be no splintering or fuzziness at the edges, no grey compromise targets, no weasel words. The troops will see through these sooner than you think.

Life at the top is particularly interesting when the effect of change is to create winners and losers at the highest level. These issues must be addressed at the outset. Eccles, and Hammer and Champy, have ideas on how to achieve this. Ultimately, as in the SAS example, the entire top team may have to change; Gerstner too made widespread executive changes in IBM.

SPONSORSHIP

Whether leadership is provided individually or collectively, a project must have a sponsor. Even if the leader is a single person, that person may not necessarily be the sponsor. Often the lead will be set by the CEO on behalf of the top management team, but if the project concerns mainly one division or one organizational function, then the head of that division or function will be the right person to act as sponsor. The CEO has much to deal with, and a divisional head will have more time to carry out the sponsor's role and will be closer to the issues. Usually, the sponsor will be the person whom the board and CEO expect to deliver the benefits of the change project – the person therefore with the most to gain, or to lose, from its outcome. If you can't identify a sponsor for your change project or if no one will stand up, then do not even contemplate making a start on it.

What then is the role of the sponsor? Primarily, it is to represent the project team (the people involved in the project) to the board and vice versa. Many projects fail because the board members, having appointed a project manager (see 'Key people' later), then sit back and work on the next problem. Sooner or later, the project manager will hit some obstacle and have nowhere to go. The next board meeting will unfortunately be after the next deadline has been missed. No one with any seniority will take on the job of helping the project manager to resolve the issue. When the deadline has passed, recriminations will start. A politically conscious project manager will have scapegoats already identified, and heads will roll. After multiple re-occurrences of missed deadlines, the seniority of rolling heads will rise and eventually the project manager will go. Meanwhile, the project will have slipped far behind. This is why the appointment of a sponsor is vital to stop a project from failing.

To support the project manager properly, the sponsor must have some clout within the organization and be available to the project manager when major issues arise. The sponsor will be committed to the project and demonstrate commitment through personal visibility and promotion of the project. Not every day – that is the project manager's job – but the sponsor will appear to people close to the project as 'their person at the top' who is on their side through thick and thin. The sponsor is someone who can fix problems the project team can't, who can call on resources out of their reach or who sometimes will explain why something really can't be done – but will offer ideas and alternatives.

It will now be apparent that the role of the sponsor is much more than a funnel for communications. In a well-defined and well-managed project, the role may appear to be little more than that of attendance at steering group meetings, but such projects are rare. The sponsor must be prepared to take on this key role of oiling the wheels, fixing, promoting and, above all, just being there when times are tough.

KEY PEOPLE

Besides the sponsor, any significant project needs a project manager who is responsible for the project on a day-to-day basis. The project manager makes things happen and is responsible for achieving the project's objectives. The sponsor does not constrain the project manager's role by constant checking up, yet is there when needed, to help fix issues that the project manager cannot handle for reasons of scope, authority, unforeseen crises or (quite often) internal politics. It is evident that the sponsor and project manager need to work well together. They must have mutual respect and trust, and must always be accessible to each other, even though there will be a formal communication system within the project.

Before the start of the project, the sponsor and project manager must identify the other key players involved. How do they do this? An obvious start is to ask – who will provide resources? If that means money, has it already been sanctioned? If so, how much? What if the amount sanctioned turns out to be too low? What about specialist help? What about other departments affected by the change?

Usually, about three to five key people can be identified in addition to the sponsor and project manager. These must be at a decision-making level appropriate to the size, scope and importance of the project. If more than five or so key people are identified, some way needs to be found to reduce that number, or the whole project should be re-examined. Are we trying to boil the ocean?

BUSINESS CASE

There will be investment in the form of money, people, facilities, resources and time. Right at the outset, before the project formally starts, a business justification for this investment must be on the table. The benefits, preferably based on some form of return on investment (ROI), must be stated. Sometimes, the benefits might be less tangible, but they must still be stated and understood. They must answer the questions, 'Why are we doing this?' and 'What are our objectives?' As Hammer and Champy observe, any business reengineering project must start with a case for action. This is the basis of the 'business case'.

TARGET SOLUTION

Many projects unfortunately start off on a wing and a prayer. There is no business case because no one knows the cost, nor what the eventual solution and benefits will be. There will clearly be extreme situations (the business equivalents of committing to the Second World War) where action has to be taken with little idea of the exact outcome. Yet action must be taken.

But if a business is being run well and critical success factors are being monitored and managed, such extreme situations will be rare. Hammer and Champy give examples, already referred to previously, of companies that have reacted to crises by successfully reengineering their processes, but they also refer to two companies, Hallmark Cards and Wal-Mart, who reengineered from a position of strength, when apparently there was no need to do so.

In most cases, it is perfectly possible for an organization, having recognized a need or an opportunity for change, to spend adequate time on examining a range of solutions and choosing one of them, perhaps with minor variations to be decided during the course of the project, as the target specification for the solution.

FEASIBILITY

The key question is: 'Is the project do-able?' Is it feasible? The target solution has been narrowed down and broadly agreed by the key people, but is it actually achievable? If it needs different skills in the workforce, do they exist or can they be acquired in time by recruitment or training? If new equipment is needed, does it exist in the marketplace and will it perform to the necessary standards of throughput and quality? Can the required funding be raised?

It is an unforgivable planning error to commit to a detailed plan into the future, which depends on an important unknown or which makes a significant untested assumption. If you meet such a situation, look for all possible ways to test out the unknown. Is there a sufficiently close historical parallel? Can we simulate the situation somehow? Can we conduct a pilot test? What shall we do if we have no previous information and cannot simulate the situation? What will the implication be if disaster strikes? Are there other ways of avoiding the dependency? What is the risk?

RISK

Risk has two basic dimensions: probability and impact. Any project of significant worth almost certainly carries some risk. When IBM UK departed, in the late 1980s, from its standard terms and conditions and put together 'Special Bids', a senior manager plotted a graph of the price to the client versus the commercial risk to IBM UK. There was a clear straight-line correlation: the bigger the bid, the higher the risk. To management used to certainty, this was anathema. To the new intake of marketeers (the manager presented this graph in a keynote session at an Entry Marketing Education class), it was highly exciting.

The way to handle risk is evident:

1.   Look for it
2.   Recognize it
3.   Analyse its probability
4.   Analyse its impact
5.   Decide how to manage it. Do we need to worry about it at all? If so, can we reduce the probability or impact? What back-up is there?
6.   Document the above and review risk as an integral part of monitoring the project plan.

In deciding how to manage a risk, the following grid is often helpful.

		PROBABILITY		
		HIGH	MEDIUM	LOW
	H	*****	****	***
IMPACT	M	***	**	*
	L	*	- - -	- - -

FIGURE 2.1   Probability and impact grid

*****   = Ask 'Should we be doing this at all?'

****   = Ask 'This is quite likely to happen, can we afford it to? What shall we do if it does? Do we have time and resources to react?'

***   = *Either* ask 'This is unlikely to happen, but if it does it's serious – probably not enough reason to kill the project, but enough to think of ways round it – what's the next best or what reasonable back-up is there?' *Or* ask 'This will probably happen if we're unlucky, but we can contain the result if it does – what shall we put in the plan for this?'

**   = Ask 'Moderate chance of happening, moderate impact and certainly recoverable – but should we set some cash or resource aside just in case?'

*   = Ensure that the risk is monitored during the project, but otherwise no special effort.

- - -   = Don't worry about this! The project team can handle it.

After a risk assessment before the start of the project or certainly in the very early stages, a formal risk list should be drawn up. Any risk with three stars or more should be regularly reviewed by the project sponsor as part of the formal project review process during its execution. Risks with two stars or fewer can be left to the project manager. Bear in mind, though, that a project never turns out as originally planned and that the H, M, L ratings are dynamic. Part of the project manager's job is to keep a watchful eye on the risk list to see if anything has changed. Any significant movement up to the three-star level or any new risk identified at this level must be brought to the sponsor.

NOW WE'RE READY TO START!

To summarize the hallmarks of a successful project that we have discussed so far, we must have, even before the project formally starts:

○ Leadership: by the relevant top executive or management committee
○ A sponsor: to link the project to the top management
○ A project manager: responsible day to day for the project and for achieving its overall objectives
○ Key people: besides the sponsor and project manager, other key executives and specialists with accountability, authority and a stake in the success of the project
○ A business case: why are we doing it at all?
○ Target solution: roughly, how are we going to set about the solution?
○ Feasibility: is the project actually do-able in practice?
○ Risk: what did our risk assessment reveal?

PROJECT DEFINITION

Instigators of projects have a burning desire to do something

The top man has a brilliant idea, plucks a trusted lower manager out of the organization, sends out a memo to all staff, sends the poor manager out to implement it and returns to the top coterie, checking from time to time how things are going. In terms of the previous checklist, we have leadership (and maybe part of a sponsor), a project manager and that's all. It is hard enough to persuade leaders and organizations to hold on till the checklist is complete without having to tell them that there is yet a final step:

To define what the project is and what it is not

We can then start to plan it in detail (Figure 2.2).

CASE STUDY

The purpose of the morning was to agree on FMSII, the updated version of the Financial Management System.

'This should be pretty easy. I've got another meeting at 11 a.m.', said the

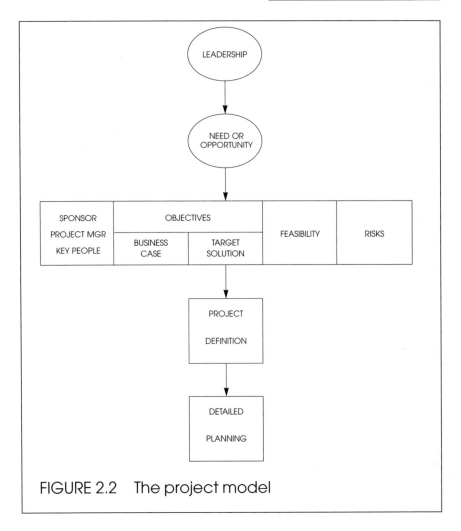

FIGURE 2.2   The project model

finance director (FD). It was 9.30 a.m. and by now everyone had coffee. The facilitator asked everyone to write down their ideas of the project's objectives on yellow stickers. There were four other people in the room – the information technology (IT) manager, the financial applications manager from IT, the most senior works accountant (representing the works sites) and the senior HQ accountant. By 10 a.m. everyone had finished and the facilitator put the yellow stickers on the wall. There were about 100 of them that the facilitator provisionally grouped into areas. There was a long pause; no one wanted to speak first. Then, almost simultaneously, reactions started – 'Why do you want that?' 'I didn't know that's what you expected.' 'We can't possibly deliver that by next September.'

It took until 3 p.m. to agree on the objectives of the project as follows: 'To install an extension to the financial accounting system to satisfy the minimum legal requirements on our company, capable of being updated by HQ accounting staff and available for enquiry/reporting purposes by works accounting staff, using existing terminals and network facilities.'

Along the way, the expectations of works accountancy staff that FMSII would answer all the queries they had thought of already, and those they might think of in the next 12 months and into the distant future, had been put into perspective. The FD had clearly explained that his main concern was to stay within the law. And the IT manager had been given the opportunity to say what could and what could not be done in the time available.

The project was on a sound footing. By grouping the key people together in the same room for less than a working day, the company achieved:

○   clarity (after hard work by the facilitator)
○   realism (after a critical look at each other's expectations via the yellow stickers)
○   agreement (well, they all had a chance to have their say!)
○   commitment (it's too late to go back now).

PROJECT DEFINITION WORKSHOP – PDW

When the business case, target solution and feasibility are agreed and the key people are on board, the next step before project start is, as we have stated, the *project definition*. We recommend that this is done in a formal, rigorous yet challenging manner, by a *project definition workshop – PDW*. We described an example above. The key elements are:

WHO: – The sponsor
        – The project manager
        – The three to five key people
        – A facilitator, skilled in project work and with strong interpersonal skills
WHEN: – After the project is understood and committed in principle
        – Before detailed task work has begun
WHAT: A free debate to achieve
        – Understanding
        – Consensus
        – Commitment.

It might often appear that the 'whats' above are already in place. In our experience, it is usually not so. The above example illustrates this. The chief omission is usually 'understanding': from that, all else flows. It is vital to get all the key players in the same room at the same time.

One exciting thing about such a workshop is discovery. Our experience is that people are motivated for the better by understanding each other's goals, constraints and consequent emotions. This is a necessity for synergy. When we each truly know what the other's goals are and what stands in the way, we will look for ways to achieve both our goals together, to look for win-win solutions. A learning culture will look for ways to promote this. We recommend the PDW technique as an excellent vehicle.

What should be the desired output of a project definition workshop?

1.   A clear definition of the goals of the project, its more detailed objectives and its scope – what is within the project and what is without. We will discuss later the properties of valid objectives. For now, let us remark that the project objectives should answer as a minimum the questions: What have we got to achieve? How will we know when we have finished? How will we know whether we have done well?

2.   The structure of the work: how it will be broken into manageable chunks. Even the largest project, like putting a man on the moon, can be broken down in gradual stages, each of which can be broken down further until individual tasks can be clearly stated and given to responsible, empowered individuals to carry out with 100 per cent conformance. The key words here are responsibility, empowerment and clarity. Already the 1990s' clarion call of 'empowerment' is being devalued as writers latch on to what they perceive to be the current management fad. We see it simply as clarity of (1) end product, (2) bounds of authority and resources and (3) relationships with others: suppliers, colleagues and customers.

3.   Organization and responsibilities: how the teams responsible for the final outcome will be constructed, how they will be led, how they will relate to each other and communicate, and what each team's responsibilities will be.

4.   Management system: there is no doubt that, just as a centrist, detailed planning system cannot work, neither can a free-for-all, laissez-faire project control system. The management system should be appropriate to the nature of the project, the people involved and the nature of the organization. The key elements will be objectives, milestones and review process, for which we offer suggestions below.

5.   Risks and assumptions: we have already referred to the need to recognize risk at the outset. Generally, the higher the pay-off, the greater the risk. The greater the risk, the greater and broader the number of assumptions. There are sophisticated ways of incorporat-

ing risk and uncertainty into project networks by means of probability calculations. Our experience with real projects is that such
calculations can lend a spurious air of accuracy and science to what
is basically a simple set of choices. Our advice is brief: if there is an
element of uncertainty or risk that affects the project so much, then
address it early on by the risk management techniques outlined
above. Do a pilot; find out more facts; do anything to reduce the
risk or uncertainty if the combination of likelihood and impact is
high enough. If after all that there are yet some unknowns, then
document the assumptions and include them in the review process.
If necessary, perform parallel activities, but in the knowledge before
the event that one set will be thrown away when more is known.

Let us look in further detail at three areas: the management system, objectives and benefits.

MANAGEMENT SYSTEM

Detailed planning

This is where PERT, CPA (critical path analysis), resource allocation, Gantt
charts and so on come into their own. This is the stage at which the project
is broken down into sub-projects, with each sub-project specified in terms
of detailed deliverables, tasks, responsibilities, target dates, resources and so
on – the basic units of planning. This is the material for project control, often
mistakenly called project management. Project management has been the
topic of our discussion for the last several pages.

The deliverables: We would, however, highlight one concept from the previous paragraph – the idea of a 'deliverable'. What this means is quite simply
something concrete that can be handed over to someone else – a list of
prospects to call on, an agreed fixture schedule, a completed sub-assembly
ready for trial. It is directly related to the concept of a 'result' as discussed
below. This aspect of planning, especially in an informal situation, is the one
most neglected. Tasks are allocated in quantity – but to what purpose? What
is the intended result of the tasks? What is the deliverable?

Reporting

In most projects, there is far too much or far too little reporting. The main
things the sponsor and the steering group will want to know are:

- is everything going to plan?
- are we meeting our major milestones?
- are there any significant changes since the last review?
- if so, what are the effects (on times, costs, deliverables . . .)?

○   are there any new issues since last time?
○   did the fixes work for previous issues?

The project definition workshop can therefore help by identifying key milestones in the project. These should be:

○   significant project events, usually fewer than 20 and evenly spaced in the project
○   defined in plain language, with a verb in the past tense (e.g. 'new employee handbook issued to all employees')
○   of value for publicity and motivation as well as being of reporting value.

OBJECTIVES

Many projects start off badly because the *objectives* of the project are not clearly defined and understood. Even the word 'objective' itself can be used somewhat vaguely. Is it the same as an 'aim' or a 'goal', or does it suggest something more specific? We offer the following distinctions.

If you ask a general audience to state some typical objectives, they might say: to retire early, to make a million or to rear a good family. These are often called 'aims' or 'goals', but it is useful to call them objectives of intent or global objectives.

Similar objectives relating to business might be: to increase sales, to help the company grow or to downsize. These are global objectives of direction. What all these global objectives have in common is that they lack a specific time measure or, in some cases, a specific measure of success. Such objectives can have high inspirational value and can often be used as mission statements, but they lack the precision needed to drive forward their own achievement. Too often organizations move from such global objectives to a set of tasks that may or may not come together at some time in the future to achieve the desired goal. What is missing?

In our teaching, the acronym 'SMART' is often used to describe objectives. To lead forward to action, objectives need to be:

Specific
Measurable
Achievable
Realistic
Timed

As we have seen, global objectives, quite reasonably, do not have all these properties, so we are now identifying a different type of objective that we may call a specific objective or a result objective. A result objective might be: to recruit ten new graduates by September; to issue to all staff a new pay policy document by the end of the next financial year; or to reduce the over-60 days debt by £20 000 by quarter-end.

At an even greater level of detail, we can define an immediate objective, or a task objective or an activity. Examples might be: to phone 100 prospects daily to tell them about a new product; to call on regular clients, each at least once a quarter; or to organize a departmental meeting monthly. These too are 'SMART', yet seem to miss something – what result are we looking for in carrying them out?

All these types of objectives are linked as shown in Figure 2.3 below.

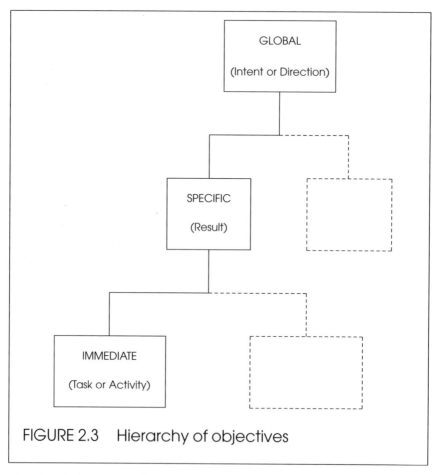

FIGURE 2.3   Hierarchy of objectives

The global objective will point usually to many specific objectives, each of which will point to many immediate objectives. There may be more than three levels. Going downwards, the question 'how' is answered. In reverse, going upwards, the question 'why' is answered. How many workers mindlessly carry on performing tasks without asking 'Why am I doing this?', or 'How does what I'm doing help the organization achieve a result?' If management itself either does not recognize how the objectives it is setting link together to form a unity, or worse still, *does* understand but fails to inform its workforce, how can the workers be blamed for taking inappropriate action when things go wrong or when new situations arise? The workers who know *why* they are doing what they are doing and *how* it fits into the bigger picture have a far better chance of reacting correctly when circumstances change.

Often, the 'result' box is missed out. Management is so keen to see action that tasks are allocated around the company without enough thought as to what *results* are desired. If you cannot break a goal down into 'SMART' result objectives and then break these further down into achievable tasks, how do you know the goal itself is achievable?

BENEFITS

At the conclusion of the project, following celebrations in the case of success or punishment of the innocent and promotion of the non-involved in the case of abject failure, the usual pattern is for all parties to sigh deeply and return to their daily work, vowing never to do it again. The project has finished. Or has it? Why did we do the project in the first place? Remember the business case? We did the project for good business reasons – return on investment. The benefits outweighed the cost. So why not return to the business case and see if the promised benefits have been met.

A project is not over until the benefits have been assessed and compared with the initial target. At the most basic, it is poor business not to check up on the effect of an investment. And how else will we learn for the future?

Figure 2.4 shows the final shape of a project in diagrammatic form.

THE KEY MESSAGES

- ❍ Change is brought about by many causes, internal and external
- ❍ Change is becoming more frequent and faster
- ❍ Good management needs a model to handle change
- ❍ A useful start is to think about the A-point and the B-point
- ❍ Proper project management of a significant change is essential
- ❍ Before starting the project, ensure that:
    – it has a sponsor
    – the key players are selected
    – there is a business case

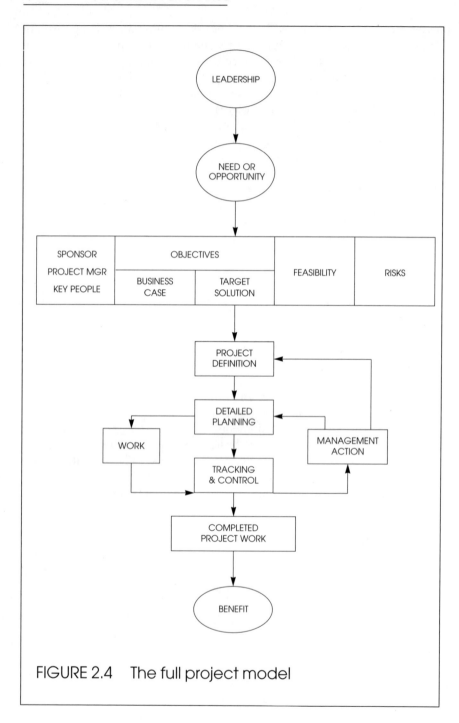

FIGURE 2.4   The full project model

     – there is a feasible solution
     – risks are identified
❍   Clarity of objectives and project definition are key
❍   A project definition workshop is a sound starting point before detailed work starts

---

OBJECTIVES EXERCISE

FOR NEXT WEEK
THINK OF UP TO **FIVE** OBJECTIVES YOU WOULD LIKE TO ACHIEVE.
THESE SHOULD BE MAINLY TO DO WITH YOUR **WORKING LIFE**, BUT IF
THERE ARE ANY TO DO WITH YOUR **PERSONAL LIFE** THAT YOU FEEL HAPPY
TO SHARE WITH THE CLASS, THIS IS OK TOO. BUT PLEASE THINK OF AT
LEAST **THREE TO DO WITH WORK**.

OBJECTIVE 1
_____
_____
_____

OBJECTIVE 2
_____
_____
_____

OBJECTIVE 3
_____
_____
_____

OBJECTIVE 4
_____
_____
_____

OBJECTIVE 5
_____
_____
_____

FIGURE 2.5   Objective setting

FOOD FOR THOUGHT

Set a class of students, or the employees you are training, the 'objectives' exercise in Figure 2.5. See how the objectives relate to each other in the completed exercise. See where the emphasis lies: aim, result or task. Is it different according to each person? What does this tell you about this person? Or about what you should do next?

3

ANALYSING LEARNING NEEDS

If you want one year of prosperity, grow grain.
If you want ten years of prosperity, grow trees.
If you want one hundred years of prosperity, grow people.

Old Chinese proverb

BACKWARD LINKS

O The framework for change (Chapter 1)
O Managing change (Chapter 2)

FORWARD LINKS

O Putting adult learning characteristics to work (Chapter 7)
O Designing and delivering learning (Chapter 8)
O Measurement and evaluation (Chapter 10)
O SATE at work – I (Chapter 11)

AIMS

This chapter should enable you to:

O Review the role of management at all levels in the needs analysis
   process
O Appreciate how needs analysis provides the specification for curriculum design
O Understand how needs analysis defines key reference points in the
   project against which measurements can be made and progress
   judged.

INTRODUCTION

Towards the end of Chapter 2, in the section about the project definition workshop (PDW), we discussed the structure of projects and how they can be broken down into major sub-projects if the degree of complexity warrants it. For a significant change project it is likely that one of the sub-projects would be that of training. It is possible that the training sub-project could justify a PDW in its own right. Certainly this was the case in the IBM example discussed in Chapter 1. Although it was a slightly scaled-down version compared to that discussed in Chapter 2, the PDW was extremely worthwhile in providing a clarity of purpose and a focus on the key objectives and critical success factors (CSFs) involved.

Identifying the main objectives becomes the starting point for a process within the Systems Approach To Education (SATE) known as needs analysis. We deliberately do not give this process the label of 'training needs analysis' for the very simple reason that, under certain circumstances, training may not be required at all. For example, whatever skills are needed can be obtained directly from external sources. This aspect is discussed in Chapter 4 in considering the acquisition of skills. As we shall see, needs analysis follows the hierarchical structure portrayed in Chapter 2 under aims, goals and objectives, and in the same way answers the questions 'How?' and 'Why?'

As well as giving direction to the project, the hierarchy of needs also defines a series of reference points against which progress towards achieving those needs can be measured. This ability to measure progress and to give feedback is crucial in any change project. There can be many people involved who each have a stake in the outcome of the project and they need this feedback to indicate how the project is progressing generally and how their particular aspect of it is affected specifically. Typically some of the key stakeholders and their stakes are:

- ○   Executive management and the overall success of the project
- ○   Line management and their responsibility for aligning the goals of their people with those of the organization
- ○   Human resource management and their ability to assess accurately the skills gaps to be bridged
- ○   Education management and their ability to design and deliver training that closes the skills gaps
- ○   The people undergoing training and their attainment of the next step in their career paths.

We have used management titles here which are appropriate to many organizations and about which most people would have a fair amount of agreement and understanding. However, those titles do not apply across all organizations and in some there may be no such position as 'line manager' nor such a function as 'human resource management'. Though these titles may not always be applicable, there should be people who will have the appropriate responsibilities, namely:

O   responsibility for the success of the project
O   responsibility for aligning the people's goals with those of the organization
O   responsibility for assessing the skills gaps between where the organization is currently and where it wants to be
O   responsibility for bridging those skills gaps
O   and, of course, the people undergoing training.

Depending on the size of the organization these responsibilities may be vested in just one or two people or more, but regardless of the size or nature of the enterprise these responsibilities must be vested in someone. If any one of them is 'un-owned' a shortfall exists, and with it the very real risk of delay or even failure of the project.

For example, we know of one organization where, in a company-wide development exercise, almost all of the line management showed a total ignorance of their people's career aspirations. As a result there was an apparent and wide misalignment of individual and corporate objectives, and the executives' plans to foster a change in the company's culture were shelved for an unspecified period. Needless to say, this lack of ownership by line management created feelings of mistrust and cynicism at the operational level, which will take a great deal of time and effort to dispel. (In a follow-up exercise – in reality a post-mortem – line management claimed that the cause of their ignorance lay squarely with executive management; the line managers' terms of reference did not state that they had to know, let alone understand and plan for, their people's career aspirations! Three months later this company underwent a 10–15 per cent downsizing; amazingly only one of the line managers was dismissed.)

So, as well as answering the questions 'How?' and 'Why?' the hierarchy of needs and responsibilities also answers the question 'Who?' and it is imperative that management be prepared to accept ownership at every relevant level.

With so much depending on the success of the project, the SATE methodology is an extremely valuable tool for management to have in its armoury. It provides a roadmap, a checklist, an audit system and, above all else, it provides a consistency of approach. As shown in Figure 1.1, needs analysis is really the first three elements of the SATE model and is a cascading process of expansion and refinement of objectives which begins at the highest level with business objectives and their requirements. Each level of expansion has an owner or sponsor who takes total responsibility for its achievement at that level. In this way *business requirements* as laid down by *executive management* expand into *performance requirements* as defined by *line management*, which in turn develop into *education requirements* owned by *education management*. All requirements should be clearly stated and measurable whenever possible, for it is this clarity that allows progress to be evaluated at each stage and any necessary corrections made to the training programme. These progress reference points correspond to the four levels of evaluation and feedback that form part of the SATE methodology and which are discussed briefly in Chapter 1 and more fully in Chapter 10. These levels of feedback and their ownership are:

Level 1.   What were the learners' reactions to the training? It is the responsibility of education management to gather and assess this data.

Level 2.   What new skills and knowledge were learnt compared with the education requirements? It is also the responsibility of education management to gather and evaluate this data.

Level 3.   How well were the new skills and knowledge used to improve job performance compared with the performance requirements? It is the responsibility of line management to gather and evaluate this, with assistance from HRM and education if needed.

Level 4.   How did the training programme overall impact the business results compared with the business requirements? It is the responsibility of the sponsor to gather and evaluate this, again with some help from HRM and education if needed.

We have indicated above, and elsewhere in this section, the involvement of human resource management (HRM). If your organization has such a function or its equivalent, we strongly recommend that you involve them at a very early stage in the needs analysis process. The HRM function has a great deal of work to do in setting up a viable skills management system (SMS). Without such a system skills profiles, skills gaps, people development and career planning will be difficult to track and administer once an organization grows beyond a certain size. The skills management system is discussed in Chapter 4. Now let us go on to describe the needs analysis process in detail.

BUSINESS REQUIREMENTS

Business requirements can mean different things to different people. In the following passage we give our views of business requirements and put them into context with vision statements, mission statements and their like on the one hand, and the various types of objectives we discussed in Chapter 2 on the other.

Martin Luther King's 'I have a dream ...' was a vision statement. He was able to paint a picture in words of the kind of America that was possible if everyone shared and strove for the same dream. It was also an objective of direction. Generally we can say that a vision statement frames a mental image of the future and provides direction and focus with which employees can align. In this respect vision statements can also be classed as objectives of intent or direction.

Mission statements, on the other hand, deal with today's world, with reality and what is – not with what may be possible at some unspecified time in the future. Generally they are statements about what business the organization is in. For example, Levi Strauss's mission statement reads, 'To sustain responsible commercial success as a global marketing company of branded casual wear'.[1] However, this can also be seen as an objective of intent.

Vision and mission statements are usually the province of executive management. The statements provide an organizational identity and business direction and they play an important part in strategy development.

Goals generally describe ideal states to be achieved, guide day-to-day decisions and actions and are consistent with the mission statements. J. F. Kennedy's statement that the United States would '... put a man on the moon by the end of the decade ...' could be seen both as a goal and as a result objective.

Some objectives on the other hand:

O   focus on critical organizational issues and milestones
O   describe activities to be accomplished to achieve goals
O   identify dates when specific results are to be accomplished
O   are measurable, so that progress can be assessed.

In this respect they are SMART and usually can be viewed as task or result objectives (see Chapter 2 for a definition of SMART objectives). We believe that this view of objectives aligns very well with SATE's expression for them – business requirements. It also helps to put them into perspective with respect to other strategic corporate statements of direction. Business requirements are defined at the top of the organization by executive management. They must give clear, measurable objectives which state the desired outcome of the change project and ones which they can commit to wholeheartedly. We note with interest that the importance of the SATE principles of clearly stated business requirements and commitment from everyone, especially at the executive level, is underwritten by the guidelines of various quality bodies. For example, the UK government's 'Investors In People' initiative has this to say about commitment:[2]

> An Investor in People makes a public commitment from the top to develop all employees to achieve its business objectives.
>
> Every employer should have a written but flexible plan which sets out business goals and targets, considers how employees will contribute to achieving the plan and specifies how development needs in particular will be assessed and met.
>
> Management should develop and communicate to all employees a vision of where the organization is going and the contribution employees will make to its success, involving employee representatives as appropriate.

The international guidelines for quality management systems – ISO 9000 – ask for clear statements about what the organization is aiming to achieve, how this is to be done and how it will be monitored and improved. The British Quality Foundation and the European Foundation for Quality Management in their assessment criteria for policy and strategy ask for: 'The organization's mission, values, vision and strategic direction, and the manner in which it achieves them'. Further sections address how policy and strategy are the basis for business plans and how they are to be formulated, evaluated and improved.

The US government's initiative in quality is the Baldrige Award, and part of its assessment criteria is concerned with business plans and goals for both short and longer term. It is looking for key requirements and key performance indicators, together with evidence showing what resources have been committed to training and development, for example. It also addresses key business requirements and is looking for clear, unambiguous statements such as, 'We will be the number one supplier of brass widgets in the automotive industry by the year 2000.'

As mentioned previously in this chapter, and discussed in Chapter 2, a key criterion for successful projects is that their objectives, or business requirements, should be 'owned' by one specific executive who carries total authority and responsibility for their achievement, that is, a sponsor. As far as the training project is concerned this sponsor:

○   Owns the business results
○   Owns the human resources needed to achieve the business results
○   Owns the budget for the project
○   Can commit line management's involvement in the training programme before, during and after the training
○   Will take responsibility for authorizing the training programme
○   Will accept partnership in assessing the impact of the training on the business results – level 4 feedback
○   Has a great deal riding on it and will be very upset if, for one reason or another, the training project fails.

Although training may be only a limb of the total change project, its contribution to the final outcome makes it inevitable that it will receive a significant share of the sponsor's attention.

PERFORMANCE REQUIREMENTS

Performance requirements is the second level of needs analysis and, in a conventional organization, it is generally the responsibility of a different group of people from those involved at the business level. Because of this transfer in responsibility it is known in business process reengineering as a 'hand-off' – a wonderful opportunity for things to go wrong, objectives to be attenuated almost to the point of extinction and messages to be distorted as if they had been through an encryption process. At the outset, it is absolutely vital that nothing should be lost in the transition from the business requirements phase. The simplest methods are usually the best and a plain, clear document with the business requirements written out in full will normally prove sufficient.

The process of developing the performance requirements generates a great deal of information. The nature of this information is such that any misinterpretation of it could jeopardize the business objectives and possibly the business itself. If that sounds overly dramatic it is meant to, and as you read on we are sure that you will come to agree with us. If we fail to convince you, though, please re-visit Chapter 1, where we discussed and gave examples of the cost of getting it wrong.

The responsibility for this phase, and the onus for ensuring no mishaps occur, lie squarely with line management, assisted where necessary by human resource and education management. One of the key outputs is line management's definition of the job to be performed if the business requirements are to be met. This job performance is a description of the tasks that a competent person should be able to do and the degree of autonomy that the job involves. In addition, line management need to define the acceptable standards of performance for those tasks. This requires a definition of the skills, knowledge and attitudes needed to perform each of them, the skills profile and the minimum level of accomplishment. Where possible the skills should be identified as core skills and non-core skills, or given some order of ranking in importance. This will help, for example, with the wording of any job advertisements and, later, with the design of the training curriculum. Line management also need to decide how many people are needed with the preferred skills.

In addition, line management need to generate a description of a scale of competencies for the job, so that a career progression can be drawn up and discussed with interested employees, with potential recruits at interviews or for guidance to agencies supplying contractors on assignment. There is a direct relationship here between competence and the speed of meeting the business requirements. A specialist with a great deal of experience would be expected to perform the tasks more easily and quickly than a newly trained person.

At the end of this phase four important outputs have been generated:

1.   a definition of the skills profiles needed to meet the performance requirements, together with levels of attainment
2.   a view about how many skilled people will be needed
3.   the definition of a career progression for people with those skills
4.   an agreement on how to derive valid level 3 feedback data.

Conditional decisions can also be made about how the new skills are to be obtained. The choices here are:

1.   to train existing employees
2.   to recruit experienced people
3.   to use contractors with the required skills profiles.

The decision about choosing option 1, 2 or 3, or a combination of these, is not a simple one. The answer to the question, 'Have we got enough people with the right entry skills to undergo training in the right timescale?' will affect how much recruiting activity there will be or how much outsourcing will be undertaken. There are pros and cons for all of these alternatives. Which ones are important for your organization will depend on your specific circumstances and, in considering the options, some of these factors will be more relevant than others. The choices and their pros and cons are discussed in greater detail in Chapter 4.

EDUCATION REQUIREMENTS

This is a further hand-off to another function – education – but as this function was involved with the generation of the performance requirements, the chances of any mishaps occurring should be considerably less. Although this phase involves mainly education management, there should be assistance from both line and human resource management at the appropriate points.

There is now a need to know what the potential audience for training and what their specific skills are. This will define the current skills profile. The planned skills profile is already known from the previous performance requirements phase. The difference between the two is the skills gap that has to be closed to meet the business requirements. The information needed about the learners is:

O   Who they are and where they are
O   What skills they have got and at what levels

O   What experience they have had and at what job level
O   What education and training they have had and their results
O   What their attitude is to training.

Getting information like this can take a great deal of time and effort, but it is worth it. As we shall discuss in Chapter 4, this is essential data for inclusion in a skills management system. Having acquired this information the skills gap should now become evident. This should be stated in impersonal terms, giving only the number of people with the relevant skills, knowledge and specific levels. This information can be supplemented with input from line management about the overall training requirements of individual employees.

Line management are now better placed to make the decision left over from the performance requirements phase – how best to close this shortfall in skills; retraining, recruiting or sub-contracting. Education management can subscribe further input to this decision with information on the availability of suitable courses. This would include information about available classroom courses, self-paced learning events, individual coaching sessions and their like, in terms of content, duration, capacity and cost to run. This not only helps to make this particular decision, but is also valuable input into any cost-effectiveness analysis that needs to be done.

Having made the decision about the acquisition of the necessary skills, the education requirements can now be decided. These will address those skills, knowledge and attitudes which are selected for inclusion in the training of existing personnel or new hires. The key to this selection is in deciding which of the required skills the learners currently cannot perform to the required standard. Skills that they already have or those which do not contribute to the performance requirements should not be included. For experienced hires there will probably be a need for an induction course, and perhaps product and service courses as well. At the end of this phase of needs analysis, the knowns are:

O   who and where the learners are
O   the number, calibre and timing of any new hires
O   the current skills, knowledge and attitudes of all learners
O   what other skills, knowledge and attitudes they need, and by when
O   the availability and suitability of existing courses and learning events
O   how levels 1 and 2 feedback are to be obtained.

RETURN ON INVESTMENT

No self-respecting manager would commit to an investment of any kind without an analysis of the costs and expected benefits. Investing in a training programme is no different. Management can only feel committed if there are multiple dollars in benefits for every dollar spent. Even in a customer-driven organization training has to be justified in terms of the return on investment – ROI.

Both Motorola (US) and the Rover Group (UK) claim an estimated ROI ratio of 30:1. Some of the specific Motorola benefits include a cost reduction of $3.3 billion, a doubling of sales per employee and an increase in profits of 47 per cent over the period 1987 to 1992.[3] No doubt there are other companies that enjoy a similar performance. For instance, Honeywell's Canadian factory introduced an adult education and job training programme called 'Learning For Life' in the early 1990s.[4] Since then, productivity has increased by 40 per cent, work-in-progress has decreased by 60 per cent, the cycle time of order to delivery has halved, and rework and scrap rates have halved. Just how much of these benefits are directly due to training and how much are due to training acting as a catalyst for other 'multipliers' is debatable without specific evidence. However, consider the testimony of the following two examples.

According to a survey published in the USA[5] based on the replies of 125 middle managers in the information systems function of large corporations, untrained users (of information systems) will take three to six times as long to reach the same level of proficiency as trained users. In addition, formal training and support costs about $1 400 per trained user, while an untrained one will absorb between $3 000 and $5 000 to reach a comparable skills level. Multiply these figures by the number of untrained users on a given application, and the cost of not training becomes starkly obvious.

On a similar topic an article in the *Wall Street Journal*[6] stated that whilst 90 per cent of all employees had access to computer terminals, more than a third felt they didn't have adequate skills to use them. Among the reasons for this were:

- Some companies don't offer formal training
- People can't afford time off from their job to be trained
- They get help from the help desk when they're stuck
- Failing that they get help from the office whizz kid instead.

This severe shortfall in skills is hindering reengineering efforts to gain productivity through new procedures and processes. The hoped-for increase in productivity is lost as organizations end up spending more on help desk support and lost productivity from employees who are busy teaching others how to use their computer terminals. Companies will never get the return on investment they expect if they don't invest in training in the first place. These are both solid examples of the case for training, where the level 4 feedback – the impact of training on business results – is clearly apparent and justifies the expenditure.

In general, the development of a reliable methodology for measuring ROI would include the following:

○   precise and clear needs analysis that measures the skills gaps
○   identifying the key indicators that can be used to assess progress
○   tests to measure knowledge and skills gained during training (levels 1 and 2 feedback – reaction to the course and knowledge and skills gained, respectively)
○   indicators to assess how training is applied on the job (level 3 feedback – application of the knowledge and skills to improve job performance)
○   the ability to measure the impact on the business results (level 4 feedback – how the training has improved business performance).

The needs analysis will determine the size of the skills gaps. The education function, or its equivalent, then needs to decide whether to design a new training programme, adapt an existing one, buy one in or outsource all of it. This analysis also involves determining which one is the most cost-effective to implement. They should then recommend a specific solution, a cost and a schedule. At the same time line management should be investigating likely savings and be prepared to underwrite them. If this proves difficult to do they should consider consulting such bodies as the European Foundation for Quality Management, the British Quality Foundation, Investors In People UK (or similar groups in other countries), for guidance. These bodies possess a wealth of information about the actual benefits that similar organizations have achieved. Another potentially rich source of information is benchmarking. Many of the leading organizations are very willing to share their training and development philosophies, experiences, methodologies and findings. The outcome from this analysis should then be included in a summary report to the sponsor.

SUMMARY REPORT

This report can be produced by any of the management groups on the project providing they have been continuously involved. The main recipients would be the project sponsor and others with a need to know. The report should include:

1.   *The business requirements*: prioritized to focus the readers' attention on the prime drivers, together with recommendations for gathering level 4 feedback.
2.   *The performance requirements*: including required skills profiles, standards of performance, number of people required, career opportunities and level 3 feedback mechanisms.

3.   *The education requirements*: who and where the learners are, their current skills, knowledge and attitude level; what additional skills, knowledge and attitudes they need, and by when; the number, calibre and timing of any new hires; the availability and suitability of existing courses and other learning events: levels 1 and 2 feedback methods.

4.   *Critical success factors*: potential 'show stoppers' identified during the analysis that should be included here in order of declining severity.

5.   *Return on investment*: where it is called for, and including as many alternatives as possible in the analysis.

6.   *Recommendations*: these should include a training solution and suggested commitments by the sponsor such as providing subject matter experts, personal involvement with the training, supplying keynote speakers on induction courses, plus actioning the next step.

At the beginning of this chapter we described the needs analysis process as one of the most important phases of a change project. At its completion all the necessary information is available to go on to the next stage of SATE, that of curriculum design as described in Chapter 8. If needs analysis has been part of a training health check it will have produced a very helpful template which can be used to audit a current or planned training programme.

A TRAINING HEALTH CHECK

Millions of dollars are spent on training each year by well-meaning organizations. To the best of our knowledge very few of them go to any great lengths to find out whether this money is well spent or not, and what kind of return on investment (ROI) it generates. This is in complete contrast to both the Rover Group and Motorola, for example. Whilst SATE does not supply these ROI figures directly, one of its most valuable uses is in providing management with a 'health check' of any ongoing or planned training programme, whether it is for a change project or otherwise. In this, as well as its more normal role, the use of the SATE methodology yields valuable information on which a business and financial assessment can be based.

It costs good money, straight off the bottom line, to finance a successful training programme. It costs even more money, again straight off the bottom line, if it is wrong or non-existent. It is worth taking the trouble to find out which of these best describes your organization's current training plans.

All or only a part of the following checklist need be used to suit your specific circumstances. Whichever you choose, it will highlight any important omissions and thus help avoid any nasty surprises. If your training programme is aimed at a large change project, consider using the full check-list. For other projects we would suggest that, as a minimum, you should check that the training programme has a sponsor, that it is justified (needs analysis), that it will more than pay for itself (ROI) and that you will be able to measure its success (feedback and evaluation).

CHECKLIST

1. Is there a recognized sponsor with the requisite authority for this programme?
2. Are business requirements in place to justify this training pro-gramme?
3. Have these been developed by, or agreed with, senior manage-ment?
4. Have they been translated into performance requirements by line management?
5. Have education requirements been developed?
6. Is there a clear understanding of the skills and knowledge to be taught, and to what level of competence?
7. Do line management agree?
8. Are all requirements so defined that meaningful feedback and evaluation can be done at the appropriate points?
9. For an ongoing training programme is this feedback process already in place?
10. Does the training programme show a good return on investment (ROI)?
11. In light of your analysis so far, does it make sense to continue the programme in its present shape and form?

This is a high-level checklist and it should provide key answers for manage-ment's attention. One negative answer should set alarm bells ringing: two negatives call for an urgent review.

THE KEY MESSAGES

○ If the project does not enjoy the total commitment of executive management, it is probably doomed to failure.
○ The importance of the SATE principles of clearly stated business requirements and commitment from everyone is reflected in the guidelines of national and international quality bodies.
○ Management can only feel committed if there are multiple dollars in benefits for every dollar spent on training.

○   SATE methodology can yield valuable information on which a business and financial assessment can be based.

FOOD FOR THOUGHT

Those organizations that either fail to understand the need for change, or are inept in their ability to deal with it, will fade and fall behind, if they survive at all.

Rosabeth Moss Kanter, *The Change Masters*,
Simon & Schuster, New York, 1983

4

SKILLS AND SKILLS MANAGEMENT

At any given moment an organization is a unique collection of skills, talents and experiences that are in the minds and muscles of its workforce, and a body of information relating to its products, internal structures and its business relationships.

Those skills, talents and experiences bear upon that information – analysing it, packaging it and using it to improve the firm. To do this requires basic skill levels and career-long training and retraining of all employees.

Davidow and Malone, *The Virtual Corporation*, HarperCollins, New York, 1992

BACKWARD LINKS

○   Analysing learning needs (Chapter 3)

FORWARD LINKS

○   Organizational trends (Chapter 13)
○   Skills and the human balance sheet (Chapter 16)

AIMS

This chapter should help you to:

○   Understand the need for, and the operation of, a skills management system
○   Appreciate the choices available to management in acquiring necessary skills and the advantages and drawbacks of those choices.

INTRODUCTION

In this chapter we shall discuss skills, skills profiles, skills management and the various ways of acquiring skills from an organization's point of view. We also conduct some arithmetic exercises, using hypothetical scenarios and simple skills profiles, to illustrate the kind of forecasting and planning that can be achieved with a skills management system.

SKILLS MANAGEMENT SYSTEM

We have mentioned in Chapter 3 the role of a skills management system – SMS. Many of the detailed questions about skills profiles and learner demographics can be answered more easily with the help of such a system. Our own experience, and our research for this book, indicates a growing awareness amongst management of the value of an SMS in the development of their people and, through them, the business. Furthermore, any organization seeking awards or accreditation from any of the various national and international quality institutions would be well advised to have some form of SMS, otherwise it may prove difficult to demonstrate to what extent the workforce is being trained and developed.

In this section we discuss some of the main facets of an SMS. As skills management is a big subject, and growing by the day, we do not intend to go into too much detail except where we feel it might help understanding. However, one thing we would like to make clear at the outset is our view regarding the privacy of the information held in an SMS. We believe fervently that this should not be a secret database, held and developed by management and their staff behind closed doors, unknown to all except a favoured few. Its existence should be known by everyone in the organization and each employee should have an up-to-date copy of their personal record as a right. This information should be private and confidential and never disclosed to third parties other than those with a need to know.

THE AIMS AND USES OF A SKILLS MANAGEMENT SYSTEM

Setting up a skills management system can be a relatively easy but sometimes lengthy task, depending on the number of employees and the amount of detail required. The system has to be defined, and the initial data has to be entered and checked. Experience shows that the people best equipped to do this are the employees themselves. Provided they understand its purpose and criteria (see the preceding paragraph), they usually make a thorough if somewhat self-effacing job of it. Line management then have the chance to adjust the information one way or the other. The end product is a skills inventory of the organization – a human assets register. The operational aims of such a system are to provide direct assistance in the following areas.

Self-assessment

The first step in the process is to develop a current skills profile for each employee. The input to the system should be designed so that people can easily record their skills, knowledge and attitudes, together with their assessment of their competence level in each of them. They should differentiate between those skills that they believe are central to their current job position and those that are peripheral. Previous experience, academic qualifications and training courses already attended should be included, especially those resulting in a recognized certification. In fact, it is almost impossible to decide what to leave out at this stage. Most of the information about what people think about themselves has value of one kind or another.

TABLE 4.1 A general skills matrix

Skills level	Definition	Experience	Knowledge	Education	Title
1	Assist others on a limited basis	No direct	Conceptual	Informal or introductory	Trainee or apprentice
2	Execute or perform with assistance	Limited	General	Entry level or qualified	Junior or journeyman
3	Execute or perform, no assistance	Practical	Applied	Advanced or qualified	Senior
4	Give specialist advice and lead others	Extensive and/or competitive	Abundant and judgemental	Completed all and/or could teach others	Expert or specialist

The simple matrix shown in Table 4.1 is an aid to deciding skills levels. It defines four levels of skills in terms of experience, knowledge and education, with the skills levels ranging from 1 = trainee or apprentice to 4 = expert or specialist. The matrix is used as in the following example: 'I have a skills level of 3 and I am a senior ... I can execute or perform without assistance because I have practical experience, applied knowledge and advanced or qualified education.'

If it is not obvious to some employees what skills levels they currently enjoy and their job title doesn't help to resolve it, they should err on the side of the lower skills levels. Their managers will always provide a second opinion, as we shall discuss in the next section.

Management assessment

This means the managers' assessments of the foregoing information for each member of their staff, together with the managers' views about possible career paths and the next planned developments. The managers should verify which skills are the central or core skills, adding those that have been missed by the employees. This independent assessment by the managers could form the basis of a meeting with each employee, where differences in grading and career development can be discussed. At the end of this exercise there is a comprehensive skills profile for each individual, including managers.

Figure 4.1 is a simple histogram representing a typical skills profile. It shows skills levels against the four most important central skills of a person's job. As part of a career development plan, management can arrange training

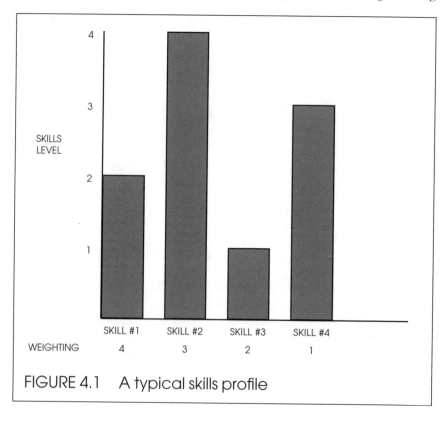

FIGURE 4.1   A typical skills profile

and projects to increase the levels of skills #1 and #3 by one level, by a certain time.

We can take this a stage further by assigning weightings to the four skills. So, for example, skill #1 could be given a weighting of 4, skill #2 a weighting of 3, skill #3 a weighting of 2 and skill #4 a weighting of 1. Thus, a top expert having a skills level of 4 in all four skills would 'score'

$$(4{\times}4) + (4{\times}3) + (4{\times}2) + (4{\times}1) = 40 \text{ units}$$

We could assign ranges to the various levels as follows:

Trainee	=	0–15 units
Junior	=	16–25 units
Senior	=	26–35 units
Expert	=	36–40 units

The example given in Figure 4.1 has a current score of 25 (junior), arrived at as follows:

$$(2{\times}4) + (4{\times}3) + (1{\times}2) + (3{\times}1) = 25 \text{ units}$$

with education planned to take it up to 31 (senior), by increasing skill #1 by one level and skill #3 by one level. The relevance of this will be seen in the following items on staffing and composite skills profiles.

Staffing

Given the need to identify people who have a certain skills profile, the SMS would be able to provide a list of candidates who meet the qualifications or are close to meeting them. For example: 'List all people who have a minimum skills level of 2 for both skills #1 and #2.' Or, 'How many people have a skills score of 30 or more?'

In putting together a team to staff an upcoming project, for example, the SMS can be used to find possible team members, experts or seniors, with specific central skills and certain 'soft skills' such as the ability to lead a team, or be an effective team player, have well-developed report-writing skills, or be able to run effective meetings. The same principle would apply in satisfying customer requests for specific skills. This whole area of 'soft skills' is receiving increased attention from many areas of management, especially human resource development. We notice that more and more companies are investing time and money in providing their people with these kinds of skills. We believe that the successful deployment of these kinds of skills across the whole workforce will give organizations a critical competitive edge. For example, if every customer-facing employee in your organization could make a confident foil or slide presentation to your (their) customer, follow this up with a comprehensive letter summarizing the main points and agreed actions, then effectively chair subsequent planning and review meetings, this will definitely give your organization an edge over your competitors – provided, of course, they are not doing the same. If they are, it's even more important that your organization should be following this route! The theme of soft skills is discussed further in Chapter 13.

Composite skills profile

This is extremely useful for general human resource planning.

TABLE 4.2   Sample unit skills requirements

	Skills available	Skills needed	Skills difference	Per cent
TL	89	96	–7	–7.9
P	138	177	–39	–28.3
D	144	132	+12	+8.3
W	65	96	–31	–47.7
S	88	102	–14	–15.9
Total	524	603	–79	–15.1

TL = Team leader   P = Planner   D = Developer   W = Writer   S = Support

Consider the example shown in Table 4.2 which shows a matrix of available and needed skills profiles for a mythical unit comprising team leaders, planners, developers, writers and support personnel. At this level of detail the matrix does not show which skills are needed for which job, only if there is an excess or shortfall. The information is impersonal and stems typically from a management planning exercise. An aggregation of similar information across the location for identical or similar jobs would indicate where load balancing was possible, or where major training or recruiting was required in the light of the organization's requirements. The next step would be to gather information at an individual level and would consider specific skills profiles by job type. This example and its attendant processes, while being similar to that discussed under 'Performance requirements' in Chapter 3, are applicable to periodic personnel planning, or in assessing the feasibility of taking on new or additional work.

Our next example is slightly different. Assume that in a department of, say, ten people all doing the same job, the composite skills profile is 250 units, an average skills profile of 25 units. Tackling a change project or the possibility of doing higher-calibre work would mean raising the composite profile to 300 units. What we are seeking is a growth in composite capability of 50 units, assumed to be mainly in skills #1 and #2. While this exercise seems mathematically simple enough, there is an intriguing twist to it. People leave, people join, people get promoted and move out of and into the unit. To take account of these possibilities, it would be helpful to know what flexibility there is in meeting the new skills requirements. Theoretically, there is more than one way to achieve the new composite profile. For example, consider the following. Initially, there are ten people in the department with a composite skills profile of 250, an average of 25 units each. The requirements are for a composite skills profile of 300, which is a 20 per cent increase overall. Mathematically this can be achieved in at least five different ways:

Case 1. 10 people × 30.0 each = 20 per cent increase each, or
Case 2.   9 people × 33.3 each = 33 per cent increase each, or
Case 3.   8 people × 37.5 each = 50 per cent increase each, or
Case 4. 11 people × 27.3 each = 9 per cent increase each, or
Case 5. 12 people × 25.0 each = no increase.

Case 1 represents numerical *status quo* in terms of the number of people in the department. There may be a transfer of people in and out, but the net effect is the same and ten people would require extra training to get them to an average skills level of 30 each.

Case 2 may reflect a promotion out of the group, with the option to see how the nine-strong department could handle the new work with their increased capability and, of course, their cooperation. Success in this instance should have a positive effect on their career progression.

Case 3 represents the loss of two people. This would seem to place too great a demand on the remaining eight people, as it means a 50 per cent uplift in their individual capability on average. However, if these eight people could get anywhere near the output level required, then their careers would be very promising indeed.

Case 4 allows for one extra person to join the group, perhaps as a planned career progression. Providing that that person's skills profile is about 27 or 28 units, the rest of the group need to upgrade their capability by only 9 per cent on average.

Case 5 shows an increase in the departmental strength of two people. Provided the newcomers were as capable as the existing staff, no further training would be necessary. Note that this solution means skills stagnation as far as the existing group members are concerned. Is this what they and their organization would wish – skills stagnation? It is highly unlikely, so on the face of it the viable alternatives are Cases 1, 2, and 4.

However, an increase in the number of people (Case 4) invariably means an increase in the time spent on communicating and managing, whereas a reduction in numbers (Case 2) simplifies communications and allows time for more focused management. This applies even more to Case 3, which we all but dismissed as being too demanding on the workforce. On the other hand, in an organization that genuinely believes in stretching its workforce, with commensurate rewards, Case 3 is a very attractive solution. Unfortunately, this approach of reducing headcount by 20 per cent and asking the remaining 80 per cent to produce 50 per cent more is equally attractive to those organizations which are cutting costs through downsizing. Fear for their jobs among the remaining employees is not enough to result in the desired increase in productivity. In fact, fear and anxiety probably have a negative effect. Nevertheless, productivity gains of this order, and greater, can be achieved in the positive and cooperative environment of business process reengineering (BPR), which in turn means that an additional set of skills have to be learnt. We have more to say about downsizing and associated topics in Chapter 13.

But what does all of this mean for re-skilling? From the training department's point of view:

- Case 1 means a training load of ten people, needing a skills upgrade of five units each – a training load of 50 units;
- Case 2 gives a training load of nine people needing a skills upgrade of over eight units each – a training load of 75 units;
- Case 3 means a training load of eight people with a skills upgrade of 12.5 units each – a training load of 100 units;
- Case 4 gives a training load of 11 people with a skills upgrade of just over two units each – a training load of 25 units.

These represent four different training courses, depending on the chosen option. It is worth noting that for those organizations contemplating downsizing, Cases 2 and 3 indicate that a significant training effort is needed if this strategy is to be effective. Case 5 doesn't involve training at all.

We realize that most of the foregoing is arithmetic and averages, and that life isn't really like that. We deal with people and individuals who don't have an average skills profile. They have their own skills profiles and their own aspirations: their individual record on the skills management system would show that. What we were doing here was demonstrating, albeit at a macro level, some of the ways in which an SMS would be useful to both management and employees.

Education planning

Education planning should reflect the results of the needs analysis exercise and produce the plan to close the skills gap. At the very least it would show which skills are to be upgraded and the anticipated levels of performance. It should also show whether new central skills are to be introduced. This means that the published descriptions of training courses and events should indicate which skills are being addressed, the expected entry level of those skills and what the planned exit skills levels shall be. They should also indicate if completion of the course results in a recognized certification or credits towards one. Certification provides a tangible result of training. Additionally, it can help to justify the cost of training and it makes employees more valuable. It is a way of recognizing skills and it could differentiate your organization from another in an otherwise equal situation. Given the choice, customers usually opt for a certified or accredited supplier. For example, most of us usually have our motor car serviced by authorized or certified garages, rather than entrust it to anyone just because they happen to be 'very good with cars'. Additionally, the SMS should be able to provide a list of those people who are to receive this training. This also becomes valuable input to the training department as they are now dealing with real people, not just numbers.

At the conclusion of this work, what is available to the organization is an inventory of skills, knowledge, attitudes, capabilities and a host of personal and departmental information – in short, a human assets register. This is discussed further in Chapter 16.

Some of the examples we gave earlier implied a skills management system having a degree of sophistication beyond the normal capabilities of a manual, paper-based system. However, for a small organization with fewer than, say, ten employees, a manual system could be quite adequate. The arithmetic only becomes cumbersome beyond a certain size, which is probably about 50 or so people. At this point a computer-based system has its advantages, especially if there are to be many 'what if' exercises or queries such as 'How many people are expert planners, have good presentation skills and can speak French?' There is a spread of solutions that support a skills management system. These range from sophisticated host computer systems through to systems running on personal computers (PCs). There is no doubt that as people become more computer literate more PC-based software will become available in this area. In fact, anyone with a modicum of PC expertise and some knowledge of spreadsheets and databases should be able to develop a system tailored for their own organization which would serve their purposes well. At the same time, the humblest card index system can also provide a wealth of information. Provided the data is kept up to date, the analysis of that data is just the same as it is for computer-based systems; it just takes longer to get to the answer. On the whole, we detect a move towards the PC-based approach.

The skills management system we have proposed here is quite a simple one in terms of skills profiles, levels, people's titles and capabilities. In practice an SMS can be very sophisticated in terms of the range of data it stores, what it can do with it and how it can be accessed. Don't be inhibited by all of this. Whatever you believe your organization needs, and can take advantage of, there is always a supplier who can help you attain it and at a reasonable cost. Just be clear about what you want to accomplish now and in the future, and don't deviate from it.

THE ACQUISITION OF SKILLS – THE CHOICES FACING MANAGEMENT

We promised we would return to this topic when it first arose in Chapter 3. There we said the options were: 1 to train existing employees, 2 to recruit experienced people or 3 to use contractors with the required skills profiles. The decision sometimes seems an easy one to make. When the skills analysis shows that the necessary skills can be acquired in the right time and in the right quantity by further training of the existing workforce, the answer seems obvious – choose option 1. Equally, when the skills analysis shows the opposite picture the decision seems just as clear; you must look outside the organization for some or all of the new skills – choose options 2 or 3, or a combination.

As always the best decisions are those made when all the nuances of the situation and the arguments for and against are known and understood. This is especially true of this decision, as the acquisition of the right skills, in the right quantity and right time frame is one of the critical success factors (CSFs) in meeting the business requirements. What follows are our views on the pros and cons of these three choices. Whilst not claiming them to be exhaustive lists, we have tried to include the factors we consider relevant to the decision.

There are three ways of acquiring the requisite skills. These are:

Train existing employees

In other words train and retrain the current workforce whenever necessary. The arguments in favour of this solution are:

○   The employees know the organization and its culture, therefore no induction course will be necessary.

○   The organization knows the individual employees in terms of skills, knowledge, attitudes, behaviour and career path – therefore skills management will be easier to administer.

○   The organization also knows the workforce in terms of their individual learning ability, style, aptitude and attitude – therefore course design will be more readily customized.

○   Through association, client-facing employees will know and be comfortable with the organization's clients and vice-versa.

○   Their interpersonal network (grapevine) will be well established

and operating to good effect both for the individual and the organization.
- ○   Their role within any team environment will be established.
- ○   Loyalty to the organization and its goals will be one of their major
  personal strengths.

The arguments against this solution are:

- ○   Some employees will be fixed in their ways and resist change or
  more specifically resist being changed.
- ○   They may prolong a *modus operandi* that is inappropriate for the
  prevailing and future business conditions. How to handle this attitude requires a further management decision that is really beyond
  the scope of this book.
- ○   Significantly, the opportunity is lost to absorb new ideas, extra
  experience and fresh attitudes from experienced recruits or contractors.

Recruit experienced people

Despite the glut of downsizing, this solution may not be easy. The best
people have either become self-employed, work for organizations which
specialize in sub-contracting or have been snapped up by smaller companies wishing to gain experienced employees.
    The arguments in favour of this solution are:

- ○   The new hires would need a minimum of training. All they might
  need is an induction course as (presumably) the required skills are
  already in place.
- ○   They come with a wide range of experience and new ideas, and
  quite rapidly begin to make an effective contribution to the organization.
- ○   Their arrival can act as a catalyst for existing employees. This would
  apply especially to the doubters and resisters to change, and may
  just be the spur that some of them need.
- ○   They can act as role models, and provide positive benchmarks for
  other employees to aim at. This is particularly relevant in career
  management.
- ○   Because skills and attitudes rub off on to colleagues they sub-
  consciously 'teach' others, almost by osmosis.
- ○   With the right attitude and approach they can formalize this process
  and actively train other members of the team or group.

The arguments against this solution are:

- ○   It can be very expensive to recruit the right skills. House moves can be involved and the existing pay structure compromised to get the right people.

○   This latter point can be a source of resentment and friction with the current workforce and needs very careful handling.

○   The newcomers may not readily absorb the organization's culture. A shallow learning curve here will delay and reduce their potential effectiveness.

○   Until a reasonable time has elapsed – two or three years – there must be a doubt regarding loyalty. If your attractive package enticed them away from their previous employer, what interest will an even better one create from another organization?

This last section highlights the importance of interview and selection standards and techniques. More and more organizations are sub-contracting this work to specialist companies who take responsibility for advertising, initial interviewing and drawing up shortlists. Only the final interviews and selections are conducted by the prospective employer.

As a slight digression (but only slight) there is a trend for sportspeople and athletes, even average ones, to employ agents to plan and oversee their careers. In this respect they are taking a lead from tennis and golf professionals who have been doing this for years. Agents do not owe loyalty to anyone except their clients and, of course, themselves. Consequently, there is a growing tendency for these agents to plan their clients' careers to the extent that it is the agents who suggest when it is time for their clients to seek fresh pastures and increased earnings, thereby gaining the agents further fees. For example, the soccer transfer market within Europe over the past five years has seen an explosion in both the size of transfer fees and the wages paid to the professionals involved, and it has more than once called into question the whole role of players' agents. This leads to the intriguing question: how long might it be before individual employees engage an agent to oversee their careers? One can argue that this is what unions do already and, to a certain extent, that would be correct. But, with the best will in the world, unions cannot look after each individual member's career. So, in the future those final interviews may well be conducted not only with the applicants but also their personal advisers.

Another increasing trend in employment practice is to engage people on fixed-term contracts for a specific number of years, typically four or five. This ensures that the organization has a steady replenishment of new blood, the right skills, experience and ideas. In exchange the new recruits have the opportunity to work with different organizational cultures, systems and people, thus helping to sustain their vitality and marketability.

Use contractors with the required skills profiles

This option is proving to be a popular choice with many organizations and the number of consulting firms offering a wide range of skills and talents is growing steadily.

The arguments in favour of this solution are:

O   The companies offering contract staff must keep their people's skills relevant and up to date if they are to succeed in the marketplace. Thus, there will be companies which have staff who are knowl- edgeable in the quality movement, ISO 9000, total quality manage- ment (TQM), Investors In People (IIP) and so on. They will also be skilled in techniques such as statistical quality control (SQC), problem-solving, benchmarking and brainstorming.

O   As with experienced recruits, contract people bring a wide range of practical knowledge and experience gained on a variety of projects for a number of clients.

O   Because of the range of skills available, organizations can be quite precise about the calibre of the people they would like on the pro- ject, even to the point of requesting specific individuals.

O   As they are not employees of the organization, the contract staff's advice should be objective, not subjective.

O   Since there is no time spent on recruiting and training, the contrac- tors can begin work and be productive almost before the ink is dry on the contract.

O   Some of their expertise and knowledge should rub off on to the organization's employees working in the same team or group.

O   The contract is for a specific period or project. Thus there is no long-term commitment to the contractors as there is to full-time employees.

The arguments against this solution are:

O   This solution can be quite expensive – contract staff do not come cheap.

O   Understandably, the contractors will have no loyalty to the organi- zation which has engaged them beyond the terms of the contract. Whilst they will complete the contract, they are unlikely to 'go the extra mile' that full-time employees would.

O   The contract staff may not understand the organization's culture, aspirations or customer base. Hence, there are possible exposures in these sensitive areas.

O   The contractor may go out of business before the project is com- pleted.

O   Key contract personnel may resign and leave the project overnight.

○   Ultimately, the responsibility for the success or failure of the project rests firmly with the hiring organization, not the contractors.

Hammer and Stanton[1] have some relevant advice to offer, in respect of choosing consultants: 'Ask them to give you five articles to read, five seminars to attend, five other clients to talk to. Then do your homework. The investment in time and energy will more than pay for itself.'

THE KEY MESSAGES

○   Skills management is indispensable if the organization is to meet its business requirements.
○   The human resource role of an SMS is to shape square pegs and round pegs to fit the right holes.
○   Once a skills management system has been built, what is available to the organization is, in short, a human assets register.
○   On the face of it downsizing means a greater training load, not less. This affects both trainers and learners.

FOOD FOR THOUGHT

We have found what we believe to be the distilled essence of competitiveness. It is the reservoir of talent and creativity and energy that can be found in each of our people. That essence is liberated when we make people believe that what they think is important – and then get out of the way while they do it.

Jack Welch, GE's CEO

PART II

LEARNERS AND LEARNING

❖

5

WHO ARE THE LEARNERS . . . ?

Q: 'How many psychotherapists does it take to change a light bulb?'
A: 'Only one. But the light bulb really has to want to change.'

Anon

BACKWARD LINKS

O   The framework for change (Chapter 1)
O   Managing change (Chapter 2)
O   Theories of psychology and behaviour

FORWARD LINKS

O   . . . And how do they learn? (Chapter 6)
O   Putting adult learning characteristics to work (Chapter 7)
O   Organizing learning (Chapter 9)
O   Measurement and evaluation (Chapter 10)
O   Organizational trends (Chapter 13)

AIMS

This chapter aims to help the reader:

O   To be aware of certain features of the human mind which affect learning
O   To understand how various theories of psychology can be used to derive some principles of how adults learn.

INTRODUCTION

People are a key resource in any organization, especially at a time of change. Chapter 2 has already underlined the need for good communications amongst the people affected and the setting and accepting of clear, measurable and achievable objectives. Sadly, a structured and planned approach to change is sometimes thought of as being 'too clinical', 'unrealistic', 'lacking allowance for people's feelings' and so on. We have invariably found the opposite with successful projects. Change projects managed in an irresolute way, with vague goals peppered by sporadic and often inconsistent messages from the top, lead to staff disillusion and to project failure far more often than those which are clearly communicated and structured. However, we would not wish to leave the reader with the impression that a change project can ignore people, their feelings and their attitudes. How participants in a change project perceive the need for change, how they prepare for it and, afterwards, how they react to it, all fundamentally affect its chances of success. These people are almost exclusively adults. During a change project they will have to gain much new learning.

Adults learn both formally and informally. This chapter and the next will look at how learning generally occurs in people, especially adults. The propensity to learn differs markedly in people, and can depend on age, motivation, personality or the learning situation itself. Adults come to any learning situation with prior knowledge, skills and experience. They come with formed personalities, existing patterns of behaviour and attitudes they have developed over the years. They have built up obstacles to learning. 'I couldn't possibly stand up there like you do and face a class. I've been asked to be best man plenty of times but I've always turned it down – I couldn't possibly give the speech,' is a typical statement. In addition, adults come to any formal learning situation with expectations. Sometimes these are negative: 'I don't need to know this' or 'I can't possibly learn this – I was no good at school.' When we attempt to provide learning opportunities for staff in an organization, especially at a time of change, we need to be highly aware of the characteristics that will govern successful learning.

Modern psychologists, physiologists and others have been investigating learning for the last century. Early on in this period the American, Twitmeyer, and more famously, Pavlov, published results concerning one form of learning called 'classical conditioning'. Since then theorists have added to the body of thought on what is a complex area. We shall briefly review the main theories, build on them from our own experiences and derive 13 principles governing the way adults learn. In Chapter 6 we shall condense these to seven adult learning characteristics. Along the way, we shall touch on one of the elements of learning in people – human personality. This is of double importance: first, our personality can affect how people choose to learn – or even if they choose to learn at all; secondly, an understanding of how people behave and why, and how they relate to each other in groups, is part of necessary learning for everyone. It is particularly important at a time of change. Change often reveals aspects of personality that can be hidden in the routine of stable conditions. It is of special importance in developing a team approach, which we shall discuss further in Chapter 13.

STARTING WITH THE BRAIN . . .

Human learning is complex. It is a subset of how the human mind itself works, which in turn is a subset of how the human body as a whole works. We understand many of the physiological processes that take place within the human body and how some of these involve the brain (assuming for the time being that this is the primary seat of what many people call the 'mind').

In the cerebral cortex of the brain, where man's higher functions tend to operate, there are of the order of 100 billion cells and some million billion connections (synapses). A cell plus its synapses form a neuron. If you counted one connection per second, it would take over 30 million years to count all the connections in the brain. This ignores the multiple combinations of paths between neurons which a simple thought (such as you reflecting on this sentence) or a sensation (such as you being aware of holding this book) might take. The number of such possible 'firing patterns' in the brain is greater than the number of particles in the known universe. The chances of working out how the human psyche operates based on a careful analysis of the behaviour of each neuron seem to us to be slim in the extreme. This is why psychologists have turned to models.

MODELLING

Modelling is a very common scientific technique. After Sir Isaac Newton proposed his Laws of Motion, scientists thought they could predict the future. If the universe was made up of particles that collided with each other like little billiard balls, and if Newton's Laws predicted the outcome of each collision perfectly, then the universe itself was completely predictable. Unfortunately, this simple model is not an accurate representation of nature. Einstein showed that, when applied to extreme speeds and distances in the universe, Newton's Laws were false. Heisenberg stated in his Uncertainty Principle that the model of a very small nuclear particle as a billiard ball was also wrong. A nuclear particle can either have a known position or a known velocity at any one time, but both cannot be measured with certainty at the same time.

Nevertheless, Newton's Laws represent reality well enough for them to be useful and sufficiently valid for most calculations in the world. A billiards player will unconsciously apply Newton's Laws and will ignore Einstein's Theory of Relativity and Heisenberg's Uncertainty Principle. The player's 'model of the world' is quite accurate enough for the purpose of the game. A more advanced player will, through intuition or teaching, extend this model by including the effect of friction and will learn to apply 'side'. But the player's need for the concepts of relativity and uncertainty will remain at zero. Not so in the case of the cosmologist or the nuclear scientist. Their 'models of the world' must include these concepts.

A further need for models arises from complexity. Even if Newton's Laws were true, it would require innumerable calculations to forecast the future. What might in principle be possible is not so in practice, therefore simplifications must be made. In science, a 'model' usually means a 'set of equations'. One set of equations might be used to examine the behaviour of elementary particles, smaller than the atom; another set for the behaviour of atoms in a gas or a solid. And so on via planets, stars, galaxies to the universe itself. Each 'model' is as correct as current research permits. Each corresponding 'set of equations' is governed by the laws of mathematics and logic. Each produces conclusions which can be tested by experiment. Each 'model' may be correct as far as it goes, but does not, and cannot, represent a total picture of the physical universe.

In the same way we encounter different models of the human psyche. They will handle it at different levels (from neurons to personalities) and at the same level in different ways (various learning theories). We shall refer to some of these models in the rest of this chapter. Like models of the universe, they are deficient in many respects:

O   they are probably wrong to some degree
O   they are a simplification of reality
O   they usually view one level of a complex hierarchy or one aspect of a broader system.

However, if they produce useful conclusions which can be compared with reality. they can be adopted pending something better. If they make correct predictions of new outcomes, then they are of even more interest.

DE BONO'S MODEL OF THE MIND

In *The Mechanism of Mind*,[1] Edward de Bono offered a model of the mind that has proved useful to us. Imagine a shallow dish containing a table jelly that has set. The horizontal surface of the jelly represents the virgin memory-surface of the mind. Let a spoonful of hot water (representing an incoming pattern of information) be poured on to this surface: it will dissolve an amount of gelatine. Then pour this off: a hollow results, representing the record of the incoming information. Add a second spoonful of water, let it settle, pour it off. Repeat this sequence with a third spoonful, a fourth, a fifth and so on. The result will be a surface full of depressions, perhaps overlapping, perhaps forming channels. They may be of different depth, where the flow of hot water into an existing depression has deepened it.

Now imagine the jelly-surface thus created, with all its depressions, to behave like an elastic sheet that has a gradual but inexorable tendency to stretch level, as though the jelly-surface was trying to return to its original flat state. This represents the 'tiring' effect of memory. The combination of creation of depressions and this tiring effect completes de Bono's simple model of his 'special memory-surface'. The final part of the analogy is that the flow of each new spoonful of water (representing a new incoming pattern of information) may move into an existing depression, or down a channel connecting existing depressions, to the lowest point it can find. This flow represents thought. De Bono calls the channel thus created a 'd-line'.

Several properties follow which have importance for learning:

1.   New patterns falling across old ones tend to reinforce the old ones. This leads to two important adult learning principles: association and building on previous experience.
2.   Once depressions and channels are established, they become difficult to alter, hence learning blocks.
3.   Because depressions can be linked to form a channel, an arriving pattern may lead to a long thought flow ending far away, causing a 'red herring' response from the hearer.
4.   If the same pattern is presented to different people there may be different outcomes. Think of Leeper's famous 'ambiguous lady' picture. If this picture is shown to an audience for the first time, some see an old lady and some a young lady. Leeper showed one audience a less ambiguous version of the picture, emphasizing the 'old lady' aspects, and a second audience a version emphasizing the 'young lady'. In each case, they then interpreted the ambiguous picture as the type of lady already shown to them. Trainers need to be constantly aware that the same information presented to different students in a group will be interpreted in the light of their different previous experiences. They may therefore come to different conclusions. A good trainer will harness such variation in experience to widen learning for everyone.
5.   The order in which the patterns arrive is important. If the same set of patterns arrives, but in a different order, a different final 'mould' is left behind. This effect shows how the order in which things are

learned can influence the outcome. A good trainer will take this into account in designing learning events. See Chapter 7 for an example.

6. Due to the 'tiring' effect, the shallower depressions will disappear first. Therefore if a new pattern arrives which overlaps an existing one, it will part-reinforce the existing one, and part-establish itself. However, the memory-trace (depression) it has created for itself will tend to disappear while the existing one remains. The special memory-surface has in effect *selected* what it wants from the new pattern and ignored the rest. The learner can be too keen to make the new information fit the old. When using the adult learning principle of 'building on previous experience', a good trainer will be aware of this danger.

7. Because of the 'tiring' effect, new knowledge needs to be re-inforced soon. Otherwise the useful depression in the memory-surface will relax to the original flat surface, and the knowledge, skill or behaviour will be forgotten. Therefore the student must be given the opportunity to exercise new knowledge straight away, via exercises, tests, role plays or in the real world. This adult learning principle we shall call 'immediate application'. The application of new knowledge could take the form of seeing, hearing, talking or doing. The more active the participation, the better. We shall call this principle 'active participation'.

D-LINES

A set of connected d-lines represents a chain of thought. Imagine liquid pouring down a set of connected channels, like the Colorado river deepening its valley to produce a Grand Canyon of the mind. Yet de Bono shows[2] that *by entering a set of d-lines at an unusual point* the sequence of flow (thought) can totally alter, with a totally different conclusion. When faced with a mental block, *start somewhere else!* We are all familiar with sterile discussions where the other party seems to have a fixed set of ideas and, whatever evidence we introduce, we are met with the same train of 'logic' and the same conclusion.

Those d-lines are extremely important. As a baby we have relatively few, our memory-surface is an unetched plateau. The synaptic connections in our cerebral cortex contain millions of possibilities. As we age, these reduce dramatically. The more possibilities we keep open, the more flexible our thinking can remain. Flexibility, resourcefulness and avoiding preconceptions are key attributes in this changing world.

APPROACHES IN PSYCHOLOGY AND CONCLUSIONS FOR LEARNING

Over the last century, psychology has progressed on many fronts and much new knowledge now exists as a result about how people learn. Approaches have ranged from treating the human being as a physiological/neuro-biological entity where the physical behaviour of the brain is dominant to one of treating the human being as a free, rational and self-determining whole. These approaches may be divided as follows.

1.   Neuro-biological
2.   Cognitive
3.   Behaviourist
4.   Psychoanalytic
5.   Humanistic

Sometimes, adherents of one approach may have followed it too earnestly for our liking. It seems to us that all of the above approaches have something to offer in explaining the human condition. One attraction of de Bono's model, apart from its simplicity, is that it bridges many of these approaches. It is largely cognitive in nature, but it can be applied to human phenomena such as insight, humour and myth-making as well as applications to learning such as those mentioned earlier. However, no one model could be expected to explain the myriad of facets of human behaviour. Therefore we shall now briefly summarize the main conclusions of the above approaches to psychology as they apply to human learning. We shall discuss the first three approaches in the remainder of this chapter, and the last two approaches in Chapter 6. We shall continue to draw essential principles for how such learning occurs.

NEURO-BIOLOGICAL

The variety, quantity and sheer versatility of the elements of the human brain, its connections and its peripheral units are staggering. Think of the central nervous system and its interfaces with the brain. If you slip a disc you may suffer for years from *referred pain*. This syndrome can tell you that you have severe leg pain, ranging from numbness, via pins and needles, to a chronic burning sensation when nerve-endings near the primary disorder are disturbed. The sciatic nerve (the longest nerve in the human body) connects the base of the lumbar spine to the little toe. Sciatic nerve-root damage after a disc episode can convince you that your feet do not exist any more and that your legs are on fire.

When a six-stone (40 kg) female anorexic looks in a mirror at herself, she sees herself fattening when in reality she is starving to death. The collusion of the central nervous system and the brain results in lies – lies that are obvious to the observer, but not to the unfortunate subject. In the psychology of learning, neuro-biological effects have received less investigation and exposure than other approaches that we shall shortly discuss. The connection between learning and boredom, anxiety, excitement and ecstasy is still mysterious.

De Bono's memory-surface may be an over-simple starting point. The Nobel Prize-winning biologist Gerald Edelman[3] advances a Darwinian model of the mind. Edelman questions the black box computer model of the mind which cognitive models often seem to imply. In a real brain, cells move around, die and reconnect, forming a computer whose parts constantly change. At birth, the brain is ready to interact with the outside world. Imagine a pram-bound baby feeling at random for space for its rattle or for its mother. Successful signals transfer back to the brain stem, the seat of ancient value systems – food, sight, feel and perhaps emotions that we call pleasure, love or fear. Edelman's theory implies selection from the vast number of potential firing patterns (potential thoughts and actions), those which produce useful behaviour. Neurons that happen to be firing are then strengthened, echoing de Bono's model. The determining factor with Edelman is the value system, which sends chemical signals to the rest of the brain to perform the strengthening of connections. Unused or unstrengthened connections meanwhile wither.

The satisfying and unifying feature about Edelman's theory is the connection between logic and emotion, between thinking and feeling, via a virgin memory-surface with a vast library of underlying patterns ready to fit complementary patterns from the outside world, then to signal satisfaction to the primal brain. We could leap from here to the fifth approach to human psychology (humanistic), but we will travel there more gradually.

COGNITIVE PSYCHOLOGY

Historically, psychology was divided into three components, 'cognition', 'conation' (or 'motivation') and 'affect' (or 'emotion'). Even today, cognitive psychology tends to avoid the topics of motivation and emotion. Nevertheless, it has provided a vast number of important conclusions for learning. Cognitive psychology concentrates on the processes involved in attention, perception, learning, memory, language, concept formation, problem-solving and thinking. We will extract from recent research those aspects which are important for learning. We will find many parallels with de Bono's model, which is most closely related to the cognitive approach, for instance Bruner and Postman's experiment.

In 1949, these researchers presented what were apparently conventional playing cards very briefly to subjects. When black hearts were presented, some claimed to have seen purple or brown hearts. What we think we see is a mixture of what actually is there, plus what resides in our mind from previous experience. The special memory-surface distorts the truth.

In the chain stimulus → attention → perception → thought → decision → response, something is happening in the 'thought' area and maybe on either side, to make sense of the incoming pattern (stimulus) and to make it fit with what we already know.

Parallel processes and basic skills learning

The above chain implies that this process is serial. However, with practice processes can be carried out in parallel, when you drive a car for example. But such outcomes may not happen overnight. What the trainer needs to do is to break a complex task up into parts and ensure that the student is comfortable with each part before putting them together again. This process leads to another adult learning principle that we shall call 'whole-part-whole sequencing'; it also emphasizes the need for basic skills training. If people are not confident about basic competencies, for instance in mathematics or simple science, then many more complex skills will remain beyond their reach. People need to learn, learn and learn, and build on that learning all the time so that, when change occurs, they have a surer foundation to build on. They also have old habits, and 'old habits die hard', so learning something new when the environment changes may not be straightforward. But if a portfolio of basic skills and knowledge is there, the potential for successful change is there too. Organizations need to invest in basic skills training and to establish a climate where learning is good. We shall return to these points in Chapter 14.

Gestalt psychology

A different way of describing learning, developed in parallel with the 'stimulus–response' school, is that of 'gestalt' psychology which states that learners see new patterns as a whole and impose meaning on them. In the area of perception, we tend to associate items that are similar or close to each other.

For instance, in Figure 5.1 the pattern is seen as a set of rows, even though the circles are equidistant, because the hollow circles form one similar set and the full circles a different one. There are other principles:

Closure – We tend to complete a pattern that is all but there. A circle with a small arc omitted is assumed to be complete. Some optical illusions rely on this, e.g. the Kanizsa triangle, as shown in Figure 5.2.

The eye sees a white triangle that isn't there. Where is the stimulus this time?

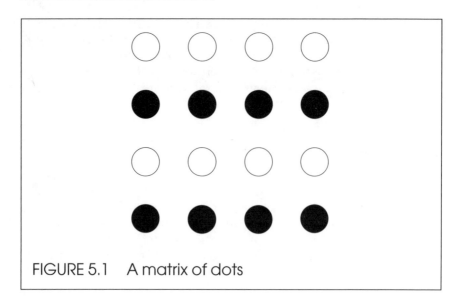

FIGURE 5.1   A matrix of dots

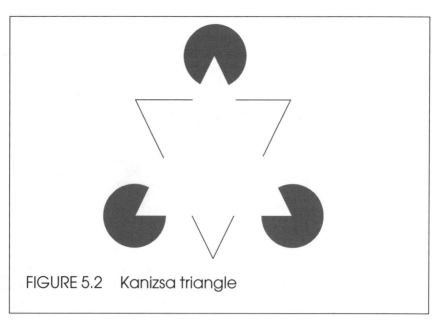

FIGURE 5.2   Kanizsa triangle

Good Continuation – Faced with crossing lines such as shown in Figure 5.3 we assume a–d is one 'item' and b–c is another. Yet it is equally possible that a–b and c–d are two pointed shapes which happen to meet at a point where they give the appearance of a letter 'X'.

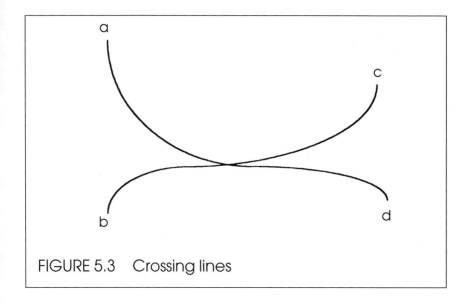

FIGURE 5.3   Crossing lines

There are some drawbacks to the gestalt approach, but the basic tenet that 'the whole is greater than the sum of its parts' rings true and lends support to the adult learning principle of 'whole-part-whole sequencing'. Adults generally like to see the big picture first. This will provide the motivation to break it down into parts and to acquire the necessary learning on each, prior to re-assembling it as a whole. See Chapter 7 for an example of how to design a learning event using this principle.

Gestalt, insight and crosswords: While gestalt psychology initially concentrated on perception, attempts were made to extend it to behaviour. Kohler's ape is a well-known example of the application of gestalt to insight. Suddenly the ape realizes that it can obtain food that is out of reach by joining two sticks together – the 'aha' experience. However, it may be that this type of learning can arise from trial and error, via a hierarchical learning strategy. (See Gagné's theory in Chapter 6.) Nevertheless, all of us will recall meeting an intractable problem, setting it aside and suddenly finding the solution 'in a flash' while thinking about something else. Sometimes, the solution will come by walking away from the problem for a time and returning to it afresh.

The opposite effect can occur when two people solve a crossword puzzle together. One of them attempts to construe a difficult clue, but the assumptions are wrong and will never work. If this partner vocalizes this construction, the wrong patterns are immediately set in the other's mind and the clue remains unsolved. The wrong d-lines have been etched.

Trainers need to be aware of suppressing insight and creativity by allowing too much close attention to be paid to how the problem should be solved or by preconceived notions of the 'best' solution.

Pleasure, pain, nausea, fear and learning

When you experience insight, it is not uncommon to have a feeling of pleasure. When you make new connections between hitherto unrelated facts or experiences, there is satisfaction. This pleasure or satisfaction can help the new learning to remain and can even lead to a feeling of humour. Mathematicians feel these emotions when producing or understanding an elegant proof. Lewis Carroll, who could see the world in very novel ways, was a mathematician.

Not all learning is pleasurable though. Tom Morton, attempting to create a world record by memorizing the digits of the mathematical symbol 'pi' (3.14159...) is reported to have felt physical pain during his efforts. Have you ever been in a stationary train next to another train, when your train appears to move out of the station? But in fact it is the *other* train that is moving. When it finally leaves, the station is still there – you have not moved at all. You suddenly realize this and experience some temporary nausea, due to the sudden challenge to the accepted fact. If this emotional reaction can happen in such a simple situation, what might happen where an established fact is suddenly challenged due to change, in a more complex work situation?

We have tried to illustrate that the mind is not just a computer and that there is a link between the mind and emotion: the link is two-way. Emotions can govern how the mind performs. Incoming signals may be internal as well as external. We have found time and time again that the learning environment needs to be comfortable, safe and relaxed. On a long classroom course the first event on the first day was an 'entry test', a written test of prerequisite material. The vast majority of students passed. But regularly one or two failed and had to leave the course. Because of this practice, all but the most confident students were quivering wrecks for most of day one, even after passing the test.

Memory, automatic processing and schemata

A fundamental part of the learning process is the function of memory. There appear to be three levels of memory.

1. Sensory memory (SM), where information from stimuli arriving via the senses is briefly stored.
2. Short-term memory (STM), which can take information from sensory memory and exchange information with long-term memory.

STM has very small capacity (perhaps seven or so items) and information stored there decays rapidly.

3.   Long-term memory (LTM), the 'bulk' storage facility of our brain. It is believed by many psychologists that LTM has an apparent capacity of effectively infinite size and that information stored there may stay indefinitely. However, finding the right information when needed is notoriously difficult.

Because of the mismatch between the potential amount of information around us that we could take in and the capacity of STM, it is likely that a great deal of filtering, attenuation or other form of selection goes on between SM and STM. Even when we do our best to focus attention on a task or on learning new information, we may miss something. Trainers should not assume that whatever they say to a student reaches LTM and is indelibly painted there. It may not even reach SM if the student's mind is on other things.

How do we cope with *divided attention*, when we need to do two things at once? Without this ability, driving a car would be impossible. So how do we manage to divide our attention? Task difficulty is an important factor. Practice undoubtedly helps, so might task similarity. On the other hand, some theorists suggest that dissimilar tasks (e.g. driving a car and talking) use separate mechanisms and therefore will not interfere with each other. However, there is little doubt from common experience that practice is the answer. The result of practice is that certain processes can become 'automatic', in the sense that they are fast, do not require attention and there is no conscious awareness of them taking place. On the other hand, they are 'unavoidable'. Given stimulus A, then result X always happens. It is as though an automatic process is a complex set of de Bono's d-lines (or linked sets of d-lines), and entry at a certain point always produces the same outcome. This has advantages and disadvantages. Reaction to danger can be made swiftly, without conscious consideration of all potential stimuli. Information travels into SM and is compared via STM with selected parts of LTM at high speed and appropriate action is triggered based on prior experience or learning. On the other hand, the automatic nature of the process can sometimes mean that part of the incoming signal is distorted or even ignored.

Ask a typical audience to 'count the Fs' in the following sentence:

> FEATURE FILMS ARE THE RE-
> SULT OF YEARS OF SCIENTI-
> FIC STUDY COMBINED WITH
> THE EXPERIENCE OF YEARS

Usually, 70–80 per cent notice only three if shown this sentence for 10–15 seconds. The others may see four or six. Even armed with knowledge of this outcome, the majority still fail to detect more than three on a second or third showing. Reading is so automatic that we do not actually 'read' words like 'of'. Or if we do, perhaps we 'read it to ourselves' for speed and read 'ov' instead.

Automatic processing also causes difficulties of 'unlearning'. Eysenck[4] reports an experiment by Shiffrin and Schneider where subjects had committed to memory certain 'correct' consonants between the letters B–L and had to recognize them as quickly as possible when they were displayed visually. However, the visual display could also include 'distractor' consonants between the letters Q–Z. The subjects' reaction times improved dramatically with practice. Then the trial was reversed with the same subjects – that is, the 'correct' consonants were now between Q–Z and the 'distractors' between B–L. Performance was greatly impaired; it took almost 1 000 trials to recover the level of performance achieved at the very start of the experiment. This simple example reinforces the message that, at a time of change, there will be a great deal of 'unlearning' to do, and the nature of the human mind means that the very ability which allowed the initial learning to take place so efficiently is now the block to learning new ways and new knowledge. Sportspeople who have acquired bad habits of their sensory-motor system over the years will be well aware of the difficulties of rebuilding a golf swing, a tennis stroke and the like. Anyone who has locked the front door of an empty home, gone on holiday and then wondered if the door had indeed been locked will also understand what 'automatic processing' means.

How information is actually stored in and retrieved from LTM is unknown, yet its properties are vital to understanding the way we learn. Memory experiments hint at how LTM is organized. When people are given lists of random words to remember and then repeat back, they tend to recall them in logical groups (bird, dog, fish ... chair, table, stool ...). If the original list is grouped in such a logical way, the recall rate is higher. A common way to remember lists of unconnected items is the 'peg' method:

> one   = gun (associate item one with 'gun')
> two   = shoe (associate item two with 'shoe')
> three = tree (associate item three with 'tree')
> etc.

A set of mental images, connected in a highly improbable but vivid story, connects the items, which can then be recalled completely and in order.

Theories of hierarchical structure, semantic relatedness and observations about association attempt to explain how we store knowledge of words, of language and of facts about the world. But it is probable that LTM contains much larger blocks of organized knowledge which Sir Frederic Bartlett called 'schemata'. A 'schema' is a set of connected actions, events and facts, such as getting into a car and driving off. The totality of all our current schemata is our mind-set: our unique view of the world to date. Our mind-set and our schemata are unique to us. If we have similar mind-sets to others, we often share their ideals and empathize with them: family, friends and work colleagues. A set of schemata covering protocols of behaviour may form a 'culture' at a tribal or national level. In a work context, it may represent 'how we do things around here'. The importance for organizational change is obvious.

We use schemata to piece together new information. When a new fact is learned, we try to make sense of it by relating it to what we already know which is closely associated with it. Sometimes, if it does not fit, we will bend it to do so. The special memory-surface is at work channelling it into a more comfortable place. The trainer can use this to advantage. Students will usually try to fit new learning to existing knowledge – adult learning principle: association. Therefore the trainer can teach new knowledge and skills as an extension to the students' existing base. If, however, the existing base is 'wrong' and is to be re-learned, this could be a mistake.

BEHAVIOURIST PSYCHOLOGY

Ivan Pavlov's famous pioneering work, now called 'classical conditioning', associated a ringing bell with presentation of food to a dog. Soon the dog salivated on hearing the ringing bell alone. This type of 'learning' relates to a different type of behaviour from that discussed above – the response of the nervous system. Behaviourist psychology's emphasis on such responses – of pleasure, fear, pain, humour and other emotional states – distinguishes it from cognitive psychology. Yet both have something to tell us about how we learn and both have their place in training. Inappropriately timed negative reinforcement (punishment) or poor teaching conditions can alienate a child from learning a topic – or even from learning itself – for ever.

An allied but different form of conditioning is usually known as 'operant conditioning'. Its best-known proponent was B.F. Skinner. Its basis lies in the reinforcement of behaviour. 'Positive reinforcement is anything that, occurring in conjunction with an act, tends to increase the probability that the act will occur again' is a useful definition as stated by Karen Pryor,[5] a dolphin-trainer. The art of its use in training is to give something the subject wants, such as food or praise, *while the behaviour is occurring*. Negative reinforcement, something the subject dislikes or wants to avoid, can similarly be used to eradicate unwanted behaviour. However, it is generally better to use positive reinforcement to encourage desired behaviour and let undesired behaviour wither on the vine.

This application of behaviourism has been seen as somehow 'inhuman' or 'manipulative', even denying human free will. However, its principles are the basis of some animal training that can produce staggering results, including getting live clams to open to order. Computer-aided instruction (CAI, sometimes called computer-based training – CBT) relies heavily on the same principles. In a work context, the manager (or supervisor or team leader) can use these principles to obtain desired behaviour by simple words of praise (or less frequently, reprimand) delivered at the time. Most employees want to know how they are doing and a short word of prompt feedback is enough for routine contact, in tandem with regular appraisal reviews. In the learning context, this represents a further adult learning principle: feedback. Adults need to know how they are progressing when learning something new. They may work it out for themselves (or as noted be provided with it by a computer program), but usually, especially in the early stages, they will want direct feedback from their trainer or mentor.

The word 'operant' is used in the term operant conditioning because the subject can choose whether or not to perform the behaviour; the behaviour is under *operant control* as opposed to *experimental control* in the case of classical conditioning. This leads to another principle of adult learning: learner control.

There are a number of attributes to reinforcements that are relevant to trainers and supervisors:

- they must be desired by the subject
- they must have variety
- they should be positive rather than negative
- they should be as small as the trainer can get away with (otherwise the subject becomes satiated)
- they should happen almost at random (otherwise the prize becomes too automatic)
- they should be for extra-special performance as the subject matures (otherwise the subject learns to try less hard but still be rewarded)
- the reward may be associated with a signal (a conditional stimulus, or 'cue') so that the subject considers the signal to be equivalent to the reward (e.g. shouting 'good shot' to the tennis student just after the stroke, rather than awarding fulsome praise at the end of the game). In role plays, especially in the early stages of training communication skills, we would sometimes break out of role to emphasize the success or otherwise of the displayed behaviour – soon a mere nod, smile or frown (in role) would produce the desired effect
- subjects may learn to reinforce their own behaviour; fortunately we are not machines and do possess some element of free will
- subjects may prefer one type of reinforcement to another; this may depend on their personality type
- there is such a thing as 'latent' learning.

Latent learning

Latent learning is best explained by the North Country story concerning dumb John. John's parents were dismayed because for six years he had failed to talk, despite all their coaching. On his seventh birthday, he suddenly complained 'Ey, Mum, this tater pie's 'orrible'. 'John, yer've spokken. Why aster nivver spokken afore?' asked John's mother. 'Tater pie's bin awreet upter neow,' said John.* We should be very cautious of students who show few overt signs of learning, but we should find other ways of discovering whether or not learning is taking place. Quieter, less demonstrative students will often have learned as much without showing it.

*Translation: John: 'Mother, this potato pie is horrible.' Mother: 'John, you have spoken. Why have you never spoken before?' John: 'The potato pie has been all right until now.'

Self-reinforcement

Self-reinforcement is very powerful and even less detectable. In a sport such as tennis or golf, a good shot will 'feel right', and the subject will try again and again to experience the same feeling. Self-reinforcement can equally happen when a pleasant and desired response is given to a human encounter.

Shaping and self-shaping

Shaping is the term given to desired alteration of behaviour. Using the above guidelines, a good trainer can shape behaviour with ease. Self-shaping is inherently difficult because reinforcement is generally not a surprise. Some outside agency needs to be involved – a trainer or mentor to provide the surprise element, or a computer in the case of computer-aided instruction. Given sufficient will power, subjects can create self-shaping situations. For instance, they can give up smoking by placing in a vase every day money equal to the value of the cigarettes not smoked that day, and then at the end of the week exchanging the money for a bottle of whisky. The subject focuses *positively* on an attractive outcome (the bottle of whisky) rather than focusing on avoidance of the *negative status quo*. The image of a cigarette is displaced by the image of a vase full of money.

Imitation

People learn by imitation. The offspring of a violent parent, at first too young to retaliate, will first learn:

1.   violence gets you your way, provided you have inherent physical advantage, therefore

2.   in your peer group, to gain goods or self-respect, you should look for those who are physically inferior and threaten them or hit them
3.   when physically able to stand up to the violent parent, violence is the tactic of choice for settling family arguments.

In corporations, the violence is usually less physical, but the train of logic is similar. Leaders should be constantly alert to the examples they are setting, the behaviours they are reinforcing and the subtle ways in which they might be drawing power from position. Trainers and teachers should be just as humble. Their power exists only as long as the teacher–pupil relationship does. The best teachers and trainers will be sought for by their students long after the training encounter ends. Kung Futse (Confucius) is reported to have said:

> I HEAR AND I FORGET
> I SEE AND I REMEMBER
> I DO AND I UNDERSTAND

When teaching a new skill, a good trainer will first demonstrate it without words, then repeat it with explanation and, finally, ask the students to try it for themselves. The principle in use is 'active participation' – live involvement in the learning process as early as possible. Active involvement with no skills or knowledge can be grossly embarrassing and demotivating, so skilled trainers will look for signs of readiness and eagerness before issuing the challenge.

Immediate application, learner control, feedback and time on task

From the behaviourist school we can underline three adult learning principles already mentioned, and deduce one more. Because the learner needs reinforcement while learning, tests and exercises shortly after a learning experience provide this before use on the job: 'immediate application'. Tests are sometimes seen as threatening, yet if the quality of teaching is high, tests are welcomed.

A further principle – that of 'learner control' – is a consequence of what we have called self-shaping. This is the tendency of the normal subject to want to exert self-control over the learning process. The learner will not want to solve only easy tasks, but to move on to harder ones, as though the reward of an easy task completed is too easily come by. This odd behaviour is one of the more encouraging aspects of the human psyche.

Tests and exercises are a particular form of 'feedback'. Trainers should never forget the value of less formal feedback during all their contacts with students. However little they may seem to want it at the time, all trainees need feedback. Whether it is positive or negative, students look to each subtle glance, sigh or smile from their trainer, especially during the early days, for approval or otherwise. With no internal mechanism for knowing how well they are performing, students will tie themselves into knots when confronted by a stony-faced trainer. 'Feedback' is vital, as already mentioned.

A new and final principle that we may derive from behavioural studies is 'time on task'. It appears that, when learning, there is a limit to how much we can take in at once – in terms of the length of time spent on learning a single task, in terms of the time spent and material covered during a seminar about a single topic or during a course leading to a certain qualification. Learning seems to be episodic. We seem to learn in self-contained chunks. Every learning episode needs to have a finite set of objectives, each of which is manageable by the student. Karen Pryor reports that dolphins have a finite span of attention during training and that, no matter what the reward is, they switch off sooner or later. In the case of humans, concentration on a specific new learning task can wane after only a few minutes. Concentration on a topic, say during a lecture, may last less than an hour. During this period, a good lecturer will frequently alter tack, tell a relevant anecdote, make a surprising statement or introduce a new slant to hold or recover students' attention.

ADULT LEARNING PRINCIPLES

Starting from the human brain and a simple model of how the mind might work, we have reviewed the cognitive, gestalt and behaviourist schools of psychology. We have examined what these tell us about how humans learn. We have related these to adult learners because these are the people who are involved in organizational change.

So far we have derived eight principles of adult learning. In summary these are:

○   Association
○   Building on previous experience
○   Immediate application
○   Active participation
○   Whole-part-whole sequencing
○   Feedback
○   Learner control
○   Time on task

In the next chapter we will look at other psychological theories and models of behaviour and we shall discover yet further principles.

FOOD FOR THOUGHT

A honey-bee has fewer than 10 000 neurons. A human being probably has more than 100 000 000 000 neurons, as many as ten million bees have or more. Bees can build a hive, navigate, collect pollen and perform a special dance to tell other bees where the flowers are. What is the human being ultimately capable of?

In order to function properly, our 100 billion neurons need to become organized in response to experience. This process of organization then creates blocks that prevent us seeing the world as it actually is. This is the fundamental problem of 'learning to change'.

6

... AND HOW DO
THEY LEARN?

A theory should be as simple as possible, but no simpler.

A. Einstein

BACKWARD LINKS

○   Theories of psychology and behaviour
○   Who are the learners . . . ? (Chapter 5)

FORWARD LINKS

○   Putting adult learning characteristics to work (Chapter 7)
○   Designing and delivering learning (Chapter 8)
○   Organizing learning (Chapter 9)
○   Measurement and evaluation (Chapter 10)
○   Organizational trends (Chapter 13)

AIMS

This chapter aims to help the reader:

○   Be aware of certain features of the human mind which affect learning
○   Understand how various theories of psychology can be used to derive some principles of how adults learn
○   Be aware of the key elements governing a practical move from an organization's education needs and adult learning principles to curriculum and event design

97

O   Understand how learning events can be designed to make effective
       and synergistic use of learners, instructors and time.

GAGNÉ'S HIERARCHY OF LEARNING

In Chapter 5 we briefly related findings from various schools of psychology:
cognitive, gestalt and behaviourist. Is learning a set of 'stimulus–response'-
trained behaviours, or a gradual build-up of a more and more complex set
of experiences against which we interpret new information, or a sudden
flash of insight, or is it more than any of these? R. M. Gagné attempted to
relate simple forms of learning to complex forms in his well-known
proposal of a hierarchy of learning. See Lovell,[1] for instance, for further
reference.

   Gagné proposed a list of eight hierarchically related types of learning,
each building on the previous one in the following way.

1.   Signal learning: as described earlier as 'classical conditioning'
2.   Stimulus–response (S–R) learning: 'operant conditioning'
3.   Chaining: a sequence of two or more learned (S–R) connections
4.   Verbal association: the learning of verbal chains, as in a constructed
       sentence
5.   Discrimination learning: making appropriate different responses to
       slightly different stimuli – involves handling interference
6.   Concept learning: learning a common response to a set of different
       stimuli possessing common characteristics – involves abstraction
7.   Rule learning: chaining two or more concepts
8.   Problem-solving: involves re-combining old rules into new ones –
       often inhibited by 'preconceived ideas'

Gagné's hierarchy is related to two further adult learning principles:
'problem-centred vs subject-centred' and 'integrative holistic thinking'.

   Adults appear to find satisfaction in problem-solving. They learn new
material better and with greater motivation when it is presented in the form
of subject matter required to solve a problem *which is relevant to them*. Note
the last five words. Life is too short for the typical adult to want to know the
answers to all problems. To some, there is satisfaction in understanding in
its own right; but for most people, problems relevant to their life, their work
and their relationships with others are those which command greatest attention. Given that problem-solving is at the highest rung of Gagné's ladder, the
previous rungs give the trainer significant clues as to how to structure learning episodes (see Chapter 7, 'Putting adult learning characteristics to work').

   By integrative holistic thinking we mean the type of learning where adults
(and children) explore whole pictures by analytic thinking to see how the

parts relate to each other. This is related to what Peter Senge in *The Fifth Discipline*[2] calls 'systems thinking'. Unfortunately too many of us fail to think this way. Where we need to see the broad picture by piecing together its component parts, we too often fail to recognize how the parts relate. We prefer to deal with each part in turn and rely on past experience for sub-optimal solutions. Because we have not learned how the parts dynamically interact with each other, we often produce 'solutions' which make matters worse rather than better. A hallmark of a truly great teacher is the ability to draw on students' past experience and knowledge and to teach them to understand what is going on in 'the bigger picture'. A great leader sees the bigger picture, yet can relate it to others in the context of 'their part' in it.

KOLB'S LEARNING STYLES

David Kolb in 1975 drew attention to individual learning styles. Each of us tends to have a preferred style of learning, by engaging in four different types of activity:

O concrete experience
O reflective observation
O abstract conceptualization
O active experimentation.

This has fundamental implications for how we train or teach others. Faced with the challenge of using a new tool, some may first just try it, some may read the manual to understand how it works, some may wish to watch someone else use it first.

Those who learn from concrete experience tend to be people-oriented and feeling-oriented. They learn best from new experiences and role plays, and respond well to personalized counselling. They perceive their trainer as a coach or helper.

People who learn by reflective observation tend towards introversion, preferring to assess risk before experimenting. They look at things from many angles before judging. They respond best to lectures and tests, and see a trainer as a teacher or taskmaster.

Abstract conceptualized learning is learning by thinking, analysis and planning: deductive thinking following on an understanding of the situation. Such learners prefer to study alone, to read a lot and benefit from clear, structured presentation of ideas, seeing their trainer as a communicator of information.

Active experimenters learn by doing. They tend to be extrovert and do not mind taking risks. They enjoy practice, small group discussions and feedback. They appreciate projects, case studies and self-paced instruction. They see their trainer primarily as a role model.

The principles of adult learning which we have so far set out apply to a different extent to each of these learning styles. This points to a further principle: individual learning rates and styles. Everyone learns in different ways and at different rates. Age matters too. Trainers need to structure learning events to provide the maximum variety of learning opportunities via different styles and to expect learning events to have different appeal to different students. The best learning comes from varying the learning style as appropriate. People tend to have their own preferred style, but it is a mistake for anyone to persist with a single style. Thus, someone who naturally learns best by 'lecture', by soaking up information and examining it from many angles (reflective observation), needs to spend time alone to structure that information, to analyse it as a whole and to form a conclusion, a plan of action (abstract conceptualization). Then that person needs to try it out, take a risk that the analysis and thought might be faulty (active experimentation) and to move on to learn from the experience of testing the knowledge out (concrete experience). A mismatch between actual and predicted experience will then feed back to the starting point of reflective observation, and the cycle is recommenced. Thus Kolb's theory is often referred to as a 'cycle', which can be entered at any preferred point. Good trainers will not only provide learning opportunities matching the different styles, but will carefully monitor their students' attempts to move round the cycle. A student who sticks to one particular style, say reflective observation, without ever putting theory into practice, is likely to end up with a distant and unreal view of the world. One who forever 'experiences life' without ever thinking through the meaning of the experiences and how they relate to each other may appear fickle and insubstantial.

PSYCHOANALYTIC SCHOOLS

Of the five approaches to psychology identified in Chapter 5, what have the psychoanalysts to tell us? One name stands out as one of the great contributors to civilization: Sigmund Freud. His seminal ideas of the id (the instinctive, pleasure-seeking primal force), the ego (the rational mediator between the id and reality) and the superego (the moral side of the personality, our conscience) provide a balance to behaviouristic ideas and portray the human as a much more complex object. They also mark the start of recent theories of personality.

We shall extract from Freud's theory the effect of age on learning. The id demands of the child are countered by the ego and superego influences from its parents with, in many cases, neurotic outcomes dating back to childhood. Freud, who as a clinical neurologist treated the emotionally disturbed, developed psychoanalytical theories stressing the effect of childhood experience, of the parent–child interaction. Freud's approach is depressing. We are formed, he says, by age five or a little later. 'Give me the child until he is seven and I will give you the man.' Recent writers have set more store by mankind's ability for self-improvement. Yet the effect of age on learning is not to be ignored.

Freud's daughter, Anna, conducted the psychoanalysis of Eric Erikson and transferred to him her interest in the psychoanalysis of children. Settling in New England, Erikson became interested in phenomena which Freudian theories could not readily explain. He studied native Indian tribes and isolated the phenomenon of identity confusion. Erikson ventures eight stages of human psychological development. The earlier stages mirror Freud, with the pre-pubertal years resolving one way or the other the crises of:

trust	vs	mistrust
autonomy	vs	doubt and shame
initiative	vs	guilt
industry	vs	inferiority

Post-puberty resolves in time order the crises of:

identity	vs	role confusion
intimacy	vs	isolation
generativity	vs	stagnation
ego integrity	vs	despair

The ages at which these crises occur vary considerably between individuals. The importance of age for learning and for trainers is twofold:

1. By adulthood, attitudes of trust, autonomy, initiative and industry (and their opposites) have already been set and may be difficult to influence

2. The remaining crises points concerning identity, intimacy, generativity and ego integrity may have yet to be experienced; thus the motivation of the subjects who are undergoing learning may be highly influenced by their psychic age. Motivatory exhortations welcomed by the mid-30-year-olds such as 'If you get through these management exercises, you'll be able to double your span of control' may be complete anathema to the 50-year-old ready to settle for a quiet, yet responsible, life containing opportunity to influence quietly the next generation.

As well as the effect of age on motivation, there is the effect of age on learning, of which motivation is part. Personal lifespan objectives are part of the rest of the story – are they just paying the bills (in their twenties), gaining in status and earnings (thirties and forties) or in earning the respect of age in comfort (fifties and sixties)? Do not forget other effects of age – how entrenched we have become, how quickly we jump to conclusions, how hard we find it to look at things another way. These are all the challenges of age which the trainer must allow for in the audience. Because older learners may find learning more difficult, they may react badly to situations which threaten their self-esteem. They may not like tests. Younger learners, better able to cope and welcoming the challenge, may thrive on these. Older learners may prefer to have more time to explore things in their own time, like Canadian Army physical training exercises, where students set their own benchmark and aim to improve on it over time. What other students achieve is immaterial to them. This supports the adult learning principle stated previously of individual learning rates and styles. As we shall see later when discussing measurement and evaluation, it is important in situations of retraining that emphasis on technical 'marks' is balanced by equal emphasis on personal qualities (which should benefit from the ageing process), and on demeanour and effort.

HUMANIST SCHOOL OF PSYCHOLOGY

The humanist school of psychology is exemplified by Abraham Maslow's 'Hierarchy of Needs'. Maslow's theory postulates that we are motivated by a set of needs at escalating levels such that, as each need is satisfied, motivation moves on to search for fulfilment of the next higher need. Thus, after fulfilment of the basic physiological needs for food and drink, motivation moves on to satisfying the need for safety, then belonging/love, then esteem, until finally self-actualization – the highest need, the fulfilment of a person's potential as a human being. Maslow further postulated parallel needs of curiosity and the need to know and understand. He came to his conclusions partly by studying the best and healthiest people he could find. In this respect, he took completely the opposite approach from Freud. However, as a result, Maslow's experimental evidence is limited and narrow, and some psychologists have therefore remained unpersuaded. Nevertheless, there is something that strikes a chord with most of us, and there is no doubt that literature relating to the humanist school, concerning positive mental attitudes and personal excellence, is increasing and commanding attention among many trainers.

Maslow's thinking, and that of other humanists, help to support our previously stated adult learning principle of learner control, as well as a further principle we may call meaningful instructional cues. The learner not only needs frequent feedback at the time of learning something new, but needs to understand the broader picture of what change the learning is intended to produce and the benefit to the learner. Furthermore, during the learning episode, the learner will seek to check up by wanting answers to questions like 'How am I doing?', 'Did I do that right?', 'If not, how can I do better next time?' The trainer needs to allow for these questions to be raised by providing excellent pre-course literature to set expectations, together with frequent mid-course checkpoints with a mentor. We shall discuss this further in Chapter 9, 'Organizing learning'.

A related principle is checking for understanding. Besides more formal checkpoints with their mentor, students need to be able to check for understanding as they learn. They need to know that they are 'growing'. Learners hate feeling lost. However, they may also hate showing themselves up by asking an apparently stupid question. Good trainers will encourage a 'safe' learning environment where it is okay to acknowledge ignorance. They can even act as a role model by admitting their own ignorance (as long as this does not lose them their credibility) and asking the class for its views. As we shall see when discussing non-classroom learning, one attraction of computer-based learning is the relative psychological safety of its environment.

Stephen R. Covey's book, *The Seven Habits of Highly Effective People*,[3] offers a wealth of ideas based on what he calls the 'character ethic'. Like Maslow, Covey examined the factors common to effective people. Covey's seven habits are divided into what he calls:

Private victories:
O   Be proactive
O   Begin with the end in mind
O   Put first things first
Public victories:
O   Think win–win
O   Seek first to understand, then to be understood
O   Synergize,
with a final exhortation to:
O   Sharpen the saw – to keep fit, alert and ready.

Covey's ideas have commanded wide attention among trainers, business people and others. They can be applied to leadership, time management and improving personal relationships at work and at home. A fundamental plank of Covey's arguments is that the human being is capable of self-driven change. We wholly support this.

NEURO-LINGUISTIC PROGRAMMING (NLP)

NLP cannot be ignored by any modern trainer. As with Maslow, Covey and others, its primary originators in the early 1970s, Richard Bandler and John

Grinder, looked at excellence. They studied the work of excellent communicators, especially in the world of therapy. They examined how we take information in, how it is filtered and processed, what external signals are emitted during this process and the key role of language in all of this. Hence the name:

Neuro   – the brain and the senses
Linguistic   – language
Programming – internal thought processes

Although NLP studies and applications began in the areas of therapy and counselling, it has had a significant impact on education and in business, where it is gaining in popularity in understanding, for instance, what goes on between two people in a sales situation. There are in NLP many concepts and techniques which are not necessarily new. We have used some of them over the years, known by other names. However, NLP puts a structure and models in place which allow us to understand them better.

To give just one illustration: in a sales call (a one-to-one meeting where A has a need and B hopes to satisfy that need by selling A a product or service), it is possible to break the sequence of events into four basic processes:

OPEN → FIND NEEDS → PROPOSE → CLOSE

Each part can be further sub-divided, but for now, let us just look at the opening. This consists of two parts:

GAINING RAPPORT
ESTABLISHING INTEREST AND ATTENTION

Many of our students found great difficulty in 'gaining rapport', while to others it came naturally to fall into relaxed conversation and to move on to business. We would therefore coach students in techniques of 'mirroring' body language (if A leans back, then so should B) and of discussing a topic of interest to A. Sometimes this resulted in hilarious role plays where whatever A did, B tried to copy, and the conversation never went any further than golf.

NLP contains the fundamental concept of 'pacing' where B can gain rapport by 'pacing' many aspects of A's behaviour and surroundings. 'Mirroring' body language can be called 'posture' pacing. Matching the other person's emotions (if A is energetic and excitable, then B behaves likewise, without overdoing it) is 'emotional' pacing. Matching the other's voice is 'tone and tempo' pacing. Dressing appropriately into the other's surroundings is 'cultural' pacing, and so on. Such actions tend to help the initial rapport that is necessary for most successful selling.

NLP can be used in the other steps of a sales call and more widely in management – in fact in any contact with other people. It is especially useful in training. For instance, NLP places great emphasis on sensory acuity – of using senses to the full to extract information from our surroundings. This can be applied successfully to learning situations. Can events and activities be structured so that the student receives input through many senses? Many children learn the alphabet by grouping the letters and singing them to a tune. The use of all our senses to learn is very powerful, supporting the adult learning principle of active participation.

NLP also accentuates the *positive*. To stop smoking, don't think of 'not smoking'. You are still thinking about 'smoking'. Think of being richer, breathing clean air, feeling better, having a fresh-smelling house and clothes, and living longer to enjoy all these. Enter your de Bono d-line set from a different point!

ACCELERATED LEARNING

The expression 'accelerated learning' has come into currency as a result of the application of some of the foregoing. Starting from how the brain works, it advocates:

○ multi-sensory techniques applied to learning preferences
○ mnemonic models
○ a good 'state of mind' for learning
○ a gestalt understanding of a subject
○ memorizing key facts
○ demonstrating what has been learned
○ reflecting on learning outcome and style.

There is a close overlap between these recommendations and the adult learning principles that we have extracted from psychological theory. Let us next summarize these.

THE THIRTEEN ADULT LEARNING PRINCIPLES

The principles are as follows:

1. Problem-centred vs subject-centred
2. Immediate application
3. Building on previous experience
4. Association
5. Individual learning rates and styles
6. Learner control
7. Whole-part-whole sequencing

8.   Integrative holistic thinking
9.   Active participation
10.   Time on task
11.   Meaningful instructional cues
12.   Checking for understanding
13.   Feedback.

IMPLICATIONS FOR THE TRAINING ORGANIZATION

1. PROBLEM-CENTRED VS SUBJECT-CENTRED

As adults age, they tend to move away from learning a subject for its own sake as it is at school. They focus on what has to be learned to satisfy present needs. This often appears as a problem-solving approach, during which learning occurs almost as a by-product. It can even be noticed in displacement activity form like crossword-solving, although there may be some benefit for brain function in such activity. Effective course design will therefore emphasize 'need-to-know' rather than 'nice-to-know'.

2. IMMEDIATE APPLICATION

Learning will be enhanced if immediately reinforced in a relevant situation. So training should (1) provide knowledge and skills which can be used immediately on frequently met real-world problems, and (2) provide exercises to test knowledge and skills before using them on the job.

3. BUILDING ON PREVIOUS EXPERIENCE

A group of adults in a training situation will bring with them a vast array of previous experience – usually more so than the instructors. Training should harness this experience to widen the scope of learning for all – including the training staff itself.

4. ASSOCIATION

Learners associate past experiences with new learning content. Learning events should therefore bridge the old to the new; they should build on known information and skills.

5. INDIVIDUAL LEARNING RATES AND STYLES

Everyone learns in different ways and at different speeds. This is especially pronounced as we age. We suggest that each person has an 'entitlement' –

the maximum they can achieve with their current learning patterns. Training should provide a variety of instructional methods to accommodate this, and to enable each person to reach their entitlement. Furthermore, training should try to help each person to improve their learning patterns and increase their entitlement.

6. LEARNER CONTROL

Adult learners usually wish to exert their own control over the learning process. This is influenced by how they were taught at school or in higher education, and by how recent this experience was. New graduates can sometimes be very happy with a teacher-centred style of training like formal lectures, but learners who left formal education some time ago would not. Therefore instructors should generally be facilitators, not lecturers. Optional events should be provided to meet individual needs and interests. Space should be provided in the curriculum for some learners to repeat exercises which they found difficult the first time. Training should use a wide variety of teaching methods including self-paced learning. These methods include the use of multi-media technology as discussed in Chapter 8.

7. WHOLE-PART-WHOLE SEQUENCING

Most adults prefer to see the 'whole picture' first, then break it down into its elements, understand each element in turn and then reassemble the picture with a better understanding. Course design should reflect this. Training could design events which begin by presenting a picture of a familiar scenario to do with the organization, perhaps a current problem area or a future plan. Then the students can be asked to examine and explore different aspects in turn before going back to the original picture, now with better understanding.

8. INTEGRATIVE HOLISTIC THINKING

Many adults learn by exploring whole pictures and using analytic thinking to form conclusions about how parts relate to each other. Trainers should create learning events to allow this to happen.

9. ACTIVE PARTICIPATION

Seeing, hearing, talking and doing facilitate learning on an increasing scale of effectiveness. Trainers should therefore involve adults in the learning process as actively as possible. This does not mean total experiential learning. There will be times when the subject matter is so new to the students that they can contribute little. It will be most effective to provide initially a teacher-centred approach, followed by active student involvement as soon as possible, as shown by the following principle.

10. TIME ON TASK

Concentration in a stand-up lecture rarely lasts for more than 10–15 minutes before the learner's mind wanders unless checked. In a one-hour lecture, students will tend to concentrate for the first ten minutes or so, and also for the last five minutes or so, as they note the minute hand reaching a vertical position, or an instructional cue (see below) from the lecturer such as '...and finally'. Therefore tutorials need to be broken up at frequent intervals. This can take the form of the trainer asking the audience questions, setting an exercise to practise what has been taught, and so on. Visiting speakers, often the bane of the lives of the training department, need especially to be carefully controlled. Dave Peoples[4] advises that the speaker should intersperse the presentation every six to eight minutes with 'spice' to combat this concentration lapse. This 'spice' may be a relevant anecdote, a joke, a total change of direction with a striking visual or aural aid, and so on.

Even with such meticulous planning of a lecture or presentation, the elapsed concentration time can rarely extend beyond 45 minutes, or at most an hour, before some sort of physical or mental break for the students. We would severely question any course which contained single lecture-type events longer than this, especially if there were no breaks in between. This is an example of a 'process standard' which the training department should define (see Chapter 9).

11. MEANINGFUL INSTRUCTIONAL CUES

Learners come to a course with expectations. These may have come from reading the pre-course literature, from what their manager told them (if anything), from colleagues who have experienced the course previously or from their own preconceptions. Much of this will be a distorted view of the course.

The first implication for training is the need to provide excellent pre-course literature. In the mind of the students, the course actually starts well before they arrive on day one. On day one, the trainer must check very early on the students' expectations of: what is to be learned, how it will be learned, expected outcomes, and evaluation criteria. If there are any conflicts, the trainer must resolve these immediately. This will generally be by re-setting the learners' expectations in line with the course. In extreme cases, it may be that the course objectives are not totally relevant to the class which was present on the day. Training should be flexible enough to react to this, for instance by allowing 'optional time' in the course and by using available resources, including the students themselves, imaginatively.

Further cues should be provided during the course to enable students to check their progress against the agreed objectives. These can take the form of frequent exercises, tests or off-line discussions with trainers or mentors.

12. CHECKING FOR UNDERSTANDING

All learners hate feeling lost. With adults especially, this feeling can quickly erode confidence and lead to them switching off. Thus training needs to provide, in addition to tests, regular opportunities to check understanding and progress, together with reinforcement exercises to ensure comprehension and retention. The approach of trainers in the classroom should be empathetic and reassuring. Students should never be afraid to ask a question. There are no stupid questions – only stupid answers. The Learner's Charter states 'It is your right to ask for an explanation. Do not put your hand down until you have understood it.'

13. FEEDBACK

Adult learners need to know how well, or how badly, they are progressing. Trainers must give consistent feedback, with explanations of why the learner is right or wrong. Training should give recognition for success and remediation for errors.

ADULT LEARNING CHARACTERISTICS: SYNERGY OF THE THIRTEEN PRINCIPLES

We have used the above principles over many years to design learning events, courses and whole curricula. They have proved to be a solid foundation. We will now discuss how they can be used in a systematic way consistent with the SATE model.

The reader will have noticed that there is overlap and connection between many of the thirteen principles. We have hinted at this already. For instance, principles 1, 3 and 6 (problem-centred vs subject-centred, build on experience and learner control) combine to reveal an adult learning characteristic of 'problem-solving'. In a similar way, seven such characteristics emerge as described below. Before moving to these characteristics, a word of caution. We suggested that for any given individual, some of the principles listed above are true to a greater or to a lesser extent. If they were uniformly and exactly true, the trainer could be replaced by a computer. The challenge to trainers is to respond to the infinite variety of their students and to the way in which they display learning characteristics.

For some students, some of the adult learning principles may not actually apply. Take just one example: principle 1, 'problem-centred vs subject-centred'. Some adults will successfully complete a further education course out of sheer intellectual interest, without any apparent use for the knowledge or skills acquired. This may be due to a deeper need to enhance self-esteem or to fill in time. But for most adults, the wonderful days of childhood learning, when the whole world was there to be discovered, are over. Learning is, by and large, directed to meet a fairly immediate need, such as doing one's job.

THE KEY MESSAGES: THE SEVEN CHARACTERISTICS OF ADULT LEARNING AND THEIR EFFECT ON LEARNING DESIGN

The thirteen principles of adult learning can be condensed into seven key characteristics, with their effect on learning design.

1. CONVINCED OF NEED

Arises from principles 4, 5 and 6: association, individual learning rates and styles, and learner control.

Characteristic

Adult learners must be convinced that the course content is needed for them to do their jobs. How often has the reader sat through a lecture or presentation wondering 'Why am I here?' or 'What has this to do with my job?'

Design requirements

- Allow learners to see how the new information is linked to their job.
- Allow learners to assess their personal needs.
- Provide wherever possible options of content and learning style to meet individual needs.

2. ACTIVE PARTICIPATION

Arises from principles 5, 6, 9, 11 and 12: individual learning rates and styles, learner control, active participation, meaningful instructional cues and checking for understanding.

Characteristic

Adult learners must actively participate in the learning process, in their own way and their own time, yet must know where they have reached at any stage of the process.

Design requirements

- Allow learners to 'own' their learning and to take responsibility for it.
- Allow where possible learning by doing, by discovery, rather than by being told.
- Maximize the use of all the senses in learning activities.
- Provide cues to enable learners to gauge progress.

3. USE PRIOR EXPERIENCE

Arises from principles 3 and 4: building on previous experience and association.

Characteristic

Adult learners need to relate the new information to what they already know or have done.

Design requirements

- Make use of the learner's experience as a valuable source of learning.
- Allow learners to share experiences.
- Relate new information to prior experience.
- New information may conflict with previous experience, so present it carefully and thoroughly. This is specially important where significant change through training is sought.

4. PROBLEM-SOLVING

Arises from principles 1, 3 and 6: problem-centred vs subject-centred, build on previous experience and learner control.

Characteristic

Adult learners need to know how the new information will solve their problems. They need to be given the opportunity to work on the problem in their own way, making use of other resources such as other students, instructors, resources in the training department and elsewhere.

Design requirements

- Relate content and problems to real life.
- Present new information in the context of solutions to learners' problems.
- Focus on existing or potential problems rather than abstract ones.
- Provide opportunities for learners to exploit a wide range of resources.

5. IMMEDIATE APPLICATION

Arises from principles 2, 5, 10 and 13: immediate application, individual learning rates and styles, time on task and feedback.

Characteristic

Adults must immediately apply the new information or skills in order to start climbing their learning curve and to feel the ascent.

Design requirements

- Allow learners to practise skills within the course.
- Limit information presentation time before moving on to practice and application.
- Allow learners to practise problems or situations on their own or in small groups.

6. FEEDBACK

Arises from principle 13: feedback.

Characteristic

Adult learners need feedback soon after they use or try to understand the new information.

Design requirements

- Provide frequent feedback within the context of the course, by means of tests, by role plays or simulations, by peer assessment, or by instructor coaching and counselling.
- Give recognition for success and remediation for errors, with explanation.

7. HOLISTIC THINKING

Arises from principles 5, 7 and 8: individual learning rates and styles, whole-part-whole sequencing and integrative holistic thinking.

Characteristic

Adults have well-developed learning patterns in terms of attempting to understand a total situation.

Design requirements

- Introduce whole concept, break into parts, then reconstruct with improved understanding.
- Involve both analytic and intuitive thinking to cover different types of learning patterns.
- Offer a choice of pace and sequence of instruction.
- Use group work and brainstorming.

FOOD FOR THOUGHT: PROCESS OBJECTIVES

However clearly learning objectives are defined and translated into content, the way a course or curriculum is experienced by the students will have a major impact on its success. Therefore, in planning the course objectives, management should understand the way these objectives are intended to be achieved. We call these the *process objectives* of the course.

If we follow this to a logical outcome, the *process* of a course could change the *content*, in real time during the running of the course. Let us take a real-life example. One of our courses contained considerable material on mainframe computing. The company had just strengthened its personal computer (PC) marketing arm substantially, and many of these trainees arrived en bloc on this course. Much of the material, to do with inter-personal and financial skills, was still relevant. Also, many of the class members were headed for mainframe jobs and needed the mainframe content. We reacted by allowing the PC trainees to skip some of the mainframe material and to spend time with an experienced PC marketeer to obtain some additional information on what concerned them most. The process overruled the content.

Stephen R. Covey relates an even more extreme example.[5] Discussing habit number 6 'Synergy', he recalls when, after a comment from a member of his university class, built upon by the rest of the class, he abandoned his teaching plan for the course and the class wrote a book about principles of leadership. Assignments were changed, new projects undertaken, new teams formed. People worked much harder than before. Even years after that class, its members would meet and re-live the experience. Deep learning indeed.

7

PUTTING ADULT LEARNING CHARACTERISTICS TO WORK

If you're not continuously improving or continuously innovating, you can't stay competitive. If we stop learning, we stop growing.

Peter Neff, CEO, Rhone-Poulenc Inc.
Industry Week, 4 March, 1996

BACKWARD LINKS

O   Who are the learners . . . ? (Chapter 5)
O   . . . And how do they learn? (Chapter 6)

FORWARD LINKS

O   Organizing learning (Chapter 9)
O   Measurement and evaluation (Chapter 10)
O   SATE at work – I (Chapter 11)
O   Organizational trends (Chapter 13)

AIMS

The aim of this chapter is to show the reader, by reference to real-life examples, how adult learning characteristics can be used to design rich learning experiences.

INTRODUCTION

Chapters 5 and 6 showed how different theories of human psychology come together to point to seven key characteristics of how adults learn:

1.   They must be convinced of the need to learn
2.   They must actively participate
3.   They bring prior experience to the learning episode
4.   They like to solve problems
5.   They need to apply their learning immediately
6.   They need feedback on this application
7.   They learn by holistic thinking

In this chapter we will show how these characteristics can be used in practice to design effective learning experiences. We will reference many of our experiences in marketing education in IBM UK. We will explain why role play is particularly effective and give some examples.

CONTENT OF A LEARNING EPISODE

The content of a course, an event or any other form of learning episode has four key properties. Each one is a prerequisite to the next.

○   Validity
○   Significance
○   Interest
○   Learnability

Any stand-up lecture ought to satisfy the first point. To be valid, the content should be correct and up to date, but it will only be significant if it matches the needs of the audience. It will provide interest if the lecturer delivers it with a certain amount of sparkle, verve or humour. Unfortunately many otherwise excellent lectures fall down on the final criterion of learnability: they lack student involvement and so fail to maximize learnability.

'OPTIONS' TIME

The Entry Marketing Education (EME) curriculum in IBM UK spanned twelve months and consisted of about eight weeks' classroom courses, eight weeks' distance learning and eight months' supervised practical activity.

The classroom curriculum consisted of four courses, each lasting from three days to three weeks. It was common to all types of entrant, whether a new university graduate or a 40-year-old production manager from one of the manufacturing plants, and whether the student was headed for mainframe technical support or minicomputer sales. Some of the content inevitably failed to pass the 'significance' or 'interest' tests. In consultation with our user manager 'group of seven' (see Chapter 1), we amended the curriculum so that the earlier courses contained content and skills relevant to all our students, but when the final major course arrived, the students were allowed more choice over content.

We introduced 'options' time into the timetable. The students could choose to use this time, for instance, to increase presentation skills competency by further practice; attend 'Birds of a Feather' sessions on topics they nominated; drink coffee and chat; or sleep. This gave the class manager some interesting organizational and resourcing problems, but the initiative was hugely successful.

In 'Birds of a Feather' sessions, for instance, we (instructors and students) would choose a leader, which could be an instructor, a student or an outsider called in by anyone on the course. One such session might be 'negotiating'. The mix of attendees might vary from newly qualified graduates, via experienced salesmen from other industries, to purchasing managers from one of the plants. The sessions were highly participative. The content was developed by the participants and kept broadly on track by the leader. With a wide spread of parties, bringing experience from both sides of the bargaining table, plus interested onlookers asking 'stupid' questions, it is easy to imagine how such sessions bore fruit.

These sessions exploited every adult learning characteristic. In the above example of 'negotiating', we noticed:

○   'Convinced of need' – they chose the topic and they chose to come
○   'Active participation' – everyone had something to say or to learn
○   'Use prior experience' – this session centred around comparing experiences
○   'Problem-solving' – new insights into how 'the other side' operates, for the next time a negotiating problem is met
○   'Immediate application' – new learning could be applied in the next role play situation in the class
○   'Feedback' – via self-assessment of the points made by others from different perspectives
○   'Holistic thinking' – this was an excellent example of the synergistic effects of bringing together people from widely different backgrounds, with common goals, to build a fuller picture by sharing knowledge, skills and experiences.

Before we introduced optional time on this course, there were complaints from technically minded people that there was too little technical content, and from marketing-minded people that there was too much. We cut back a little on the technical content and introduced 'options'. The marketeers could go to 'negotiating' and the technicians to 'the internal functions of the latest release of the operating system'. Or so we expected. Oddly, this did not always happen. They often attended each other's classes. We mentioned earlier the 'negotiating' type of session and its benefits to a wide variety of students. It is also salutary for technicians when a salesperson attends one of 'their' sessions and asks 'But why is that function there at all – what does it mean to the user?' and they have to reply without using jargon.

EXAMPLES OF THE USE OF ADULT LEARNING CHARACTERISTICS

Some further examples of our use of adult learning characteristics were these:

1. CONVINCED OF NEED

We allowed optional attendance at certain events, as noted above. We showed the students the detailed results of their pre-course 'readiness test', a test taken before arrival on the course to ensure that the student met the entry conditions. By examining their results, they could identify gaps in their knowledge. Our process standards (see Chapter 9) demanded that every session should have an introduction containing 'expectations', usually in the form of event objectives and forward links. We asked every instructor, including visiting speakers, to explain *why* their input was relevant to the students.

2. ACTIVE PARTICIPATION

There was a strong emphasis throughout the curriculum on workshops, laboratory work (using personal computers linked to a minicomputer in the training department), role plays and presentations by the students. By concentrating on the relevance and style of several stand-up lectures, we were able to cut dramatically the time spent in lecture mode and replace it by active involvement sessions and 'options' time.

3. USE PRIOR EXPERIENCE

We noted above how 'options' time encouraged this. In addition, we trained instructors to encourage classroom interaction, to draw on the varied experience of the rich mix of students. At almost every event, there was a student who could add significantly to the knowledge of the instructor. In some cases, we asked a student who was specially qualified actually to take over a presentation or to lead a working session. For each event, the instructor was required to explain its backward links.

4. PROBLEM-SOLVING

We made extensive use of group sessions with clear objectives in discussion or laboratory mode. We provided students with the same information system tools as they would have when working and we designed events around significant problems that all the students might expect to experience at work.

5. IMMEDIATE APPLICATION

We used the output from one event as input to the next. We avoided unfinished exercises or pointless calculations. If we asked the students to perform a new task that they might consider boring or irrelevant, we took pains to explain why and how the skill or knowledge would shortly be used.

6. FEEDBACK

There were regular, brief, multi-choice tests of knowledge throughout. Instructors fed the results back immediately, with an explanation of right and wrong answers. Every role play or presentation, which might test knowledge or communication skills, was scheduled so as to give ample time for a debriefing by the instructor. For consistency, there were standard sheets to provide written feedback, which the student could also peruse and learn from after the event (see Chapter 10).

An 'adviser' system operated in parallel with the course lectures and exercises (see Chapter 9). The student's adviser provided continuity through the course and more personal contact than individual event instructors might provide. The adviser, normally a member of the instructor team, could supply additional feedback, especially about personal traits, and act as a sounding board or give extra coaching.

7. HOLISTIC THINKING

Events were grouped to provide different facets of a problem, so as to simulate a real-life problem which at first sight seemed complex and challenging. We helped the students to break down the problem into parts, to understand each part in turn, then to put the parts back together. The result was that they not only solved the problem given but grew in confidence to attack other apparently insoluble problems.

The whole curriculum was based on a case study of an IBM client company, which, although fictitious, was drawn from real-life experiences. The client company lived, breathed, contained friends and enemies, and by the end of the series of courses almost became part of our lives.

ROLE PLAY

Throughout the EME curriculum, there was a great emphasis on role play, a traditional method in training for interpersonal skills, especially sales training, with good reason.

A study by Hair, Erffmeyer and Russ[1] compared traditional and high-tech training methods in this area. Using a questionnaire sent to members of the American Society of Training and Development whose primary interest was in sales training, they analysed the perceived effectiveness of eight traditional training methods:

> Conference/discussion
> Lecture (with questions)
> Case study
> TV lecture
> Film, videotape or videodisk
> Role playing with feedback
> Business games
> Sensitivity training (T-groups)

and four high-tech training methods:

> Computer-aided instruction (CAI)
> Computer-managed instruction (CMI), where the computer system tests understanding and prescribes further training as necessary
> Teletraining – electronic meetings between physically separate students and instructors
> Interactive video – video segments followed by multiple-choice questioning and follow-up 'branches' to consequent situations.

Respondents were questioned on the effectiveness of each method in relation to learning objectives of:

> Acquisition and retention of knowledge
> Attitude change
> Development of interpersonal and problem-solving skills
> Acceptance of method.

The key findings were as follows:

UTILIZATION OF METHODS

The most frequently used were: conference/discussion, lecture and role playing.

The least frequently used were: computer-managed instruction, sensitivity training and teletraining.

In the future an increase in use was expected for: role playing, films/videotapes, computer-aided instruction, computer-managed instruction and teletraining; whereas a decrease was expected for: lecture, business games and TV lecture.

EFFECTIVENESS OF METHODS

In general, the most effective methods were perceived to be, in ranking order: role playing, interactive video, case study and conference/discussion.

The least effective were perceived to be, in reverse ranking order: TV lecture, sensitivity training, lecture and films/videotapes.

SPECIFIC EFFECTIVENESS

There was very little variation in the effectiveness of meeting the learning objectives listed above. Role playing and interactive video were consistently the top two methods across the board. Case study dropped to fifth on 'knowledge acquisition' and 'development of interpersonal skills'. CAI was low on 'attitude change'. The four least effective methods consistently occupied the bottom four positions – except sensitivity training which reached number six for 'attitude change'. A balanced curriculum will include a variety of methods, but role playing and interactive video are consistently effective.

INVOLVEMENT, TOUCH AND COST

The two key characteristics of the most effective methods are high involvement and high touch (student–trainer interaction). These, however, are directly linked to relatively high cost. The exact opposite is true of the least effective methods. Yet which do we see most often in practice?

EXAMPLE OF A ROLE PLAY

It need not cost a fortune to develop a good role play. Figures 7.1, 7.2 and 7.3 show a sample of a role play written in half a day. The key elements are:

O   the student brief
O   the 'calltaker' brief
O   the feedback sheet.

Match these with the seven adult learning characteristics. The target student was a junior salesperson with a PC dealership. The role play:

O matched the 'need-to-learn' since the fictional situation was typical of real life
O involved the student directly
O allowed the student to use prior experience
O presented a problem for solution
O provided an holistic situation
O provided feedback via the tailored feedback sheet
O encouraged immediate application via the debriefing of the role play.

Debriefing is as important as the role play itself. Too often we have seen a negative, blow by blow debrief by a calltaker that leaves the student deflated, thinking of everything that went wrong. We have two tips for the debrief:

1. Ask the student to reconstruct what happened during the role play and use this as a base for the debriefing – students can be surprisingly frank with themselves.
2. The student will remember one, or at most two, key messages from the role play; so home in on these and make sure the student can use them right away.

PRACTICE CALL
COMPUTERS FOR MBIS
STUDENT BRIEF

You are Jean Howard, Salesperson for PCco. You have just received the following telephone call from Ken Griffiths.

Ken is Head of Maths at Manchester Boys' Independent School. It is grant-aided and has 700 pupils. Although not as strong educationally nor as well-known as some of its nearby competitors, the school has ambitions.

He called you after a referral from his friend Tricia Rose at TBV. Ken said that the school needed more computing equipment and that he would like to see if PCco could help. He said they wanted a fair amount and obviously price was an important factor.

You asked to see him to get more information and he agreed.

FIGURE 7.1   Practice call – Student brief

PRACTICE CALL
COMPUTERS FOR MBIS
CALLTAKER BRIEF

You are Ken Griffiths, Head of Maths at Manchester Boys' Independent School. It is grant-aided and has 700 pupils. Although not as strong educationally nor as well-known as some of their nearby competitors, the school has ambitions.

You called PCco on the recommendation of a friend, Tricia Rose, who works at TBV. Jean Howard took the call and you told her that the school needed more computing equipment and you would like to know if PCco could help. You told her that the school needed a fair amount and obviously price was an important factor.

Jean asked to see you to find out more details and you agreed.

Background

You are new to the job and are keen to reflect the Head's ambitions for the school. You appear academic but are also at home with innovating and achieving results. You have two key needs which PCco should be able to address:

1. Good technical advice, because the existing equipment is a mixture of old Apples and outdated IBM clones all operating stand-alone.
2. Although price is indeed important, the eventual outcome is more important. You will press for keen prices but if presented with good arguments as to why the cheapest is not necessarily the best, you will accept them.

The budget is £40 000 and you would like about 50 machines with a wide range of software suitable for educational use and preparing pupils for the world of work. You would like them networked.

While the Head is supportive, the final decision is with the governing body who are unsophisticated and likely to pick the cheapest solution. They do not understand the importance of software.

FIGURE 7.2 Practice call – Calltaker brief

PRACTICE CALL FEEDBACK SHEET

	O	AS	S	NI
OPENING	O	AS	S	NI
RAPPORT				
ATTENTION				
NEEDS IDENTIFICATION	O	AS	S	NI
ADVICE				
KEEN PRICE				
INFORMATION	O	AS	S	NI
HISTORY				
BUDGET				
DECISION PROCESS				
INFLUENCES				
SELLING	O	AS	S	NI
QUESTIONING				
LISTENING				
PROPOSING				
OBJECTION HANDLING				
CLOSING				

'O'   OUTSTANDING
'AS'   ABOVE SATISFACTORY
'S'   SATISFACTORY
'NI'   NEEDS IMPROVEMENT

FIGURE 7.3   Practice call feedback sheet

COST OF ROLE PLAYS

The cost of writing a role play need not be excessive. Remember – the student will only learn one or two important points, so do not over-elaborate. The cost of delivery may be high if highly experienced trainers are used. But there are ways round this:

○   Use more advanced students as calltakers. The experience will add to their own learning.
○   Organize the students so that they take the role of caller and call-taker in turn.
○   Use line managers. They may learn something too and they will also understand better what training is trying to achieve.
○   Use retirees. Almost all organizations have access to a pool of experienced staff who will enjoy contributing and earn some pocket money.

In IBM we did all of these. Good briefing and good moderation of feedback are important, but with these, all these ways can work well.

ROLE REVERSAL

One benefit of students playing the role of the calltaker is that they begin to see things from a different point of view. In a sales or other form of customer service role play, it is usually that of the customer. Janis and King[2] reported on experiments where subjects played the role of the advocate of a new attitude to be learned. The very act of arguing for another product or service, even as an exercise, makes the subject aware of some of its virtues. The same technique can be used within organizations experiencing inter-group conflict, by swapping staff between groups to see how things are 'on the other side'.

WIN-WIN AND COMPETITION

A key skill in life is the ability to put oneself in the other person's shoes. In family life, in clubs and associations, in charitable organizations and in com-mercial businesses, we deal with other people. We transact with them, we do our best to get what we want out of that transaction and sometimes we think of what they might want out of that transaction too. Covey[3] highlights as a key habit that of entering such transactions with a 'win-win' aim in mind. But how do we know what constitutes victory for the other person? How do we know their wants and needs? By asking them? Does this work? Replies are often muted, evasive and sometimes even misleading. There are many books on psychology, interpersonal relationships and counselling which give advice on how to handle this, by 'active listening'. Recent developments in neuro-linguistic programming (NLP) offer some useful modern ideas; see, for example, Bagley and Reese.[4] An understanding of personality types is also helpful (see Chapter 14).

Based on these ideas, we constructed several events aimed at increasing the student's ability to think and feel like a customer. When we say 'customer', we do not restrict this to the narrow sense of a commercial client. Some role plays were based on 'internal customer' situations, like satisfying a manager that a client proposal was sound. In organizations, it is very helpful if employees feel that their co-workers next in line in the delivery chain are their customers. In the contexts of family, friendships and clubs, the concept that we are all each other's customer is just as valid. It leads us to place greater emphasis on understanding, trust, keeping promises and delivering on time, just as we would hope to do in a business context.

An acid test of a customer relationship is what happens when competition appears on the scene. If the reader has been with us so far it will be easy to picture competition in the form not of commercial competition, but in a wider sense. Within the family, there may be rivalry for the spouse's affections, disagreement over what the growing daughter should do with her free time at the weekend or different ideas for what the son should do after finishing secondary education. In some of our events we would encourage the students to project the approach on to their social life. Some did not need encouragement. They saw the lessons for themselves without prompting.

Let us look at two events: the finance day and Red Dog.

THE FINANCE DAY

Before we designed this event, there were several good lectures in the syllabus, covering: finance (discounted cash flow, financial ratios, lease vs purchase and so on), hardware (printers, tape units, disk drives) and competition's offerings with respect to the above.

The lectures were given by subject matter experts, all very competent in their field and all good presenters, but with the normal subject matter expert's tendency to cover too much. The evaluation at SATE level 1 (student reactions) tended to be acceptable, but not outstanding unless the presenter was an entertaining performer. The SATE level 2 results (student test scores during the course) were generally good since our students were usually diligent, the presenters clear, and their material well documented if at times a little heavy – often literally so. However, at SATE level 3 (applicability on the job) the results were patchy. If students used the information between courses and kept it up to date in the face of new product announcements and new competitive offerings, they would retain it for the next course, but in most cases this did not happen. Why not?

Turning back to the adult learning principles and characteristics set out earlier, a stand-up lecture, however well presented, had the following draw-backs:

- it had few forward links, since
- most of the information was not immediately relevant, therefore
- the learning could not be immediately applied; furthermore
- there was no feedback other than a test score
- most of the sample calculations had little point
- there was little active participation beyond audience questions
- there was no relationship with the students' job problems
- and there was no holistic approach – just setting out of facts.

Redesign of a day's lectures

We redesigned the content as a single day's event in the following way. Immediately after the morning class administration was over, instructor A, in the role of the client's computer manager, called the IBM client manager, instructor B. Instructor A had some good news and some bad news. The good news was that the new pilot application suggested by IBM had been so successful that several more data storage devices were needed. The bad news was that these were unbudgeted. A competitive manufacturer had by coincidence made a speculative phone call the previous day. It could offer the identical capacity at half IBM's price.

Since relationships between the client and IBM had been good so far, the computer manager wished to give IBM the opportunity to respond. Instructor B, in his role as the IBM client manager, then asked the class, who in role were part of his marketing team, what he should do. Replies varied from 'Forget it – go play golf' to 'Take her for a nice lunch'. When order was restored, the class began to ask questions, such as 'Are the competitive devices really identical?' and 'What does she mean – half the price?' Instructor B replied that their guess was as good as his and that they needed to handle the problem for him as he already had a game of golf fixed for that day. The computer manager had offered them an appointment at 3 p.m. that day (it was now 10 a.m.), when she would decide. Not wishing to leave them completely in the lurch, he had managed to obtain the services of a financial specialist and of a data storage device specialist, who were avail-able except for the lunch period.

By this stage, the class demanded to see them. Each specialist presented a few basic relevant concepts and facts, followed by intensive interrogation by the students. At noon, the class broke up into teams of three to prepare the meeting with the client. A skeleton 'help desk' was available until 2 p.m., run sometimes by the two specialists, sometimes by instructor stand-ins who knew little of the financial and product details. This caused frustration to some teams who 'missed' the experts. Other teams were 'luckier' – perhaps by delegating one team member to search for the specialist in the canteen. Yet others discovered that much of the key information was held on internal IBM databases, so the specialists weren't indispensable.

At 3 p.m., each team called on the computer manager, role played in parallel by members of the instructor team. After the role play, a general classroom session pulled together the lessons from the exercise. It was a highly exhausting day for all concerned. One of the more memorable student quotes was 'The learning curve resembled the north face of the Eiger'. Levels 1 and 2 measurements were far better than before, and although levels 3 and 4 cannot be measured easily for a single event, we often met students post-course in their workplace who remembered the day's events vividly and spoke of the understanding it had given them of how generically to approach a competitive problem, and how and where to find help in IBM. We taught them not just finance, but how to learn, by using all seven adult learning characteristics.

Further benefits of the new design

Some of the more perceptive students asked two important questions about the role play.

1.   'It was fortunate that you were on good terms with the computer manager – it was good of her to tell you. Do they all do that?'
2.   'If IBM was so close to the client, why did the need for more storage devices come as such a surprise?'

These questions show how a well-designed learning event can be open-ended. There was no limit to the lessons that could be learned. The better students will make their own forward links, relating it to existing work problems and using their brains and imaginations to pursue their own lines of thought. The instructors then become sounding boards, with the advantage of greater experience but not always with ready answers.

Since between courses our students worked on real-life business situations alongside experienced staff, they could often directly use their learning. It had high transferability because the event centred not around learning facts, but on understanding how to approach a competitive situation. They learned to challenge the apparent reality, to know how and where to get help, and to realize that knowledge of the specialist's lunching habits could be a vital piece of information.

Organizational learning

The training department, and through them the whole organization, can also learn from such events. We had 16 such role plays (48 students in teams of three) on each course, and patterns emerged. The students who did worst were those who assimilated the product differences and used them to be critical of competition. Even students who were more sensitive, yet still paraded facts and financial cases before the computer manager, did not generally come out best. *The ones who did best were those who went in to understand better the client's problem.* These were the students who genuinely tried to put themselves into their client's shoes. These students would keep to relevant differences – those important to the achievement of the client's objectives. They would then, using their new-found financial skills, work with the client to come to a conclusion favourable to both parties.

We fed back such observations not just to the class during the debriefing session, but to the wider body of IBM. It is interesting to note that IBM is now more client-centred in its approach than when our courses started. Many factors have led to this, so the role of training was only partial. Nevertheless, it was there. Wise general managers will maintain a dialogue with their training departments to gain feedback that they can use more widely, even to lead change in corporate behaviour. The role of training as a flight simulator, as a test-bed for new ideas, is little understood or exploited.

RED DOG

Another 'competitive' event – again a day, complete in itself yet leading to further learning – was 'Red Dog'. This event also aimed to have the students realize how the customer might think and feel. Using role reversal, we asked the students to put themselves, as a class, completely in another person's shoes. In this case, the shoes were those of their client, to whom for some three weeks they had been proposing a significant investment in technology that would have a very big positive impact on the client's business, and most likely on their own personal bank balance. The course had two days to run and the final presentation and client decision was due on the next day. So far in the course the existence of competition had not even been hinted at. And by now the students were comfortable with the client's business, its needs and their proposed solution. They were also practised in presentation skills, building rapport, listening, questioning and articulating, and were ready for the final day. It was conscious course design to leave the extra dimension of competition to the penultimate day.

The day started with a solemn announcement by the instructor that today we had special permission from our legal department to have a guest address us from a real-live competitor. We could of course not reveal the name, which for the role play we would refer to as the 'Red Dog Leasing Company'. Just as our guest was role playing, so we asked the class to role play the client's senior management.

The set-up was that the Red Dog salesperson was related to a senior manager in the client's organization, a manager who was not directly involved with the IBM proposal, but who nevertheless would be affected by it. The Red Dog salesperson claimed that, by leasing 'equivalent' equipment to the client, they could substantially reduce the hardware costs of the proposed solution. Therefore, the day before the final proposal, the board had brought together its management to hear the Red Dog case. The students were asked to put out of their minds any detailed knowledge of IBM products. They should pretend that they were responsible, polite managers from the client's organization who were interested in the Red Dog proposal because of large potential savings, but yet were ready to ask searching questions from a business viewpoint.

Red Dog's presentation

The typical pattern of the Red Dog presentation was as follows. For ten minutes or so (the 'initial attention span' period and also perhaps the politeness span), the audience was silent as they took in the fact that Red Dog understood their needs well enough to make a proposal saving over half the hardware costs, which translated into some 20 per cent of the total costs of the solution, whilst apparently doing everything the IBM solution did. Then one brave soul, usually a technician, would challenge the speaker somewhat aggressively on the basis of a fairly minor product difference. This was against the rules, but it was usually enough to light the blue touch paper. The audience was so committed to the IBM case – understandably so after working on it for three weeks – that they could not relate to anything else. Their mind-set was a total IBM one. Soon after the first interruption, pandemonium set in.

We never had to stop the event though. The 'guest' was a well-chosen IBM salesman, skilled in handling objections and fire extinguishing, with a keen desire to help train the students into skills he had acquired over the years. When the initial fury died down, the students started to ask some key questions. Is this equipment new? Does it have a warranty? Who will maintain it? Will it work with the latest software that we need? The Red Dog man answered most of these with confidence, fluency and truth. When receiving a valid objection, he turned the question round by asking the client audience, 'Although my equipment will not handle that feature, why do you need it anyway, what does it add to your business?' Only if they could make a genuine defence of that point did he concede it – and even then he placed it in the context of the massive savings he promised. The students quickly understood the technical strengths and weaknesses of the two competing proposals, in a way that stand-up lectures would not achieve so economically or effectively. And indeed this was the original design objective of the event. Yet the more we ran it, the more we realized something deeper was going on.

Students' reactions to Red Dog

We noted early on that some students engaged themselves quickly into the simulation, accepted the role of the client and asked polite but relevant questions at the right business level. Others could not cast off their mantle and persisted in somewhat trivial lines of attack, usually based on minor differences that a non-computer man in the client's organization could not be expected to know. Most of them started by showing their IBM background, but then listened to the arguments, warmed to the Red Dog man and by the end of the presentation were broadly neutral. The event closed with the Red Dog man asking for the audience's commitment to his case and the show of hands vote was always very close. But why did some of the students change their persona easily, some took longer and some never let their IBM mask slip at all? The proportions were typically 20 per cent:60 per cent:20 per cent. There was some correlation with the students' background. People with previous marketing experience tended to switch role readily, so did new graduates. The typical die-hard was an older student with either a technical IBM background or a strong loyalty to the company due to many years in plant or administrative employment. The reader may reflect on the effect of age and previous experience on adult learning behaviour; or on the effect of possible recruitment patterns prevailing at the time these employees joined the company in jobs that demanded adherence to standards and procedures, rather than flexibility and imagination. Were we asking too much in some cases for them to undergo a personality change? De Bono's d-lines can be etched very deep.

The exercise then continued 'back at the IBM office'. We asked the students to imagine now that they were the IBM team once again. It was the day before the decision. What were they going to do about Red Dog? Did they even know that Red Dog had called? Should they make a quick call on the client to make sure all was well? Would the client tell them anyway, especially if Red Dog had won? Oscar Wilde[5] would have enjoyed the many perceived facets of reality that emerged.

We concluded the day by telling them that in fact the client had rejected the Red Dog offer, so now all they had to do was to return to preparing their case. However, now that they had some experience of putting themselves in the client's shoes, what was likely to be happening over at the client's office?

Tomorrow would be a big day for the client too. Was it likely that they were also preparing for it? Might not the senior manager recommending the IBM solution be in a meeting right now with the chief executive officer, to brief the CEO for the IBM presentation tomorrow? What were they saying? What would they want to hear tomorrow? What questions were they likely to ask? We left the students to ponder and prepare. The following day they performed out of their skins.

THE KEY MESSAGES

O   Well-designed courses can often create opportunities for open-ended learning. Many students will make their own learning.

O   The use of optional time within a classroom course can create valuable learning opportunities.

O   By creative event design, students can learn how to handle competition better, to understand their clients more deeply, and to create win-win outcomes.

FOOD FOR THOUGHT

The training function can give general management valuable information about the organization's way of doing business. It can act as a test-bed for new initiatives. This is in addition to training's normal function of adding to the skills balance sheet (see Chapter 16). So:

1.   Why do companies 'send' students on courses without asking the training department for anything in return, and

2.   Why do companies regard training as non-core, outsource it and lose valuable feedback?

PART III

DELIVERY, FEEDBACK AND BENEFITS

❖

8

DESIGNING AND DELIVERING LEARNING

People are the common denominator of progress. No improvement is possible with unimproved people, and advance is certain when people are liberated and educated.

John Kenneth Galbraith

BACKWARD LINKS

○ The framework for change (Chapter 1)
○ Managing change (Chapter 2)
○ Analysing learning needs (Chapter 3)
○ Who are the learners . . . ? (Chapter 5)
○ . . . And how do they learn? (Chapter 6)
○ Putting adult learning characteristics to work (Chapter 7)

FORWARD LINKS

○ Organizing learning (Chapter 9)
○ Measurement and evaluation (Chapter 10)
○ SATE at work – I (Chapter 11)

AIMS

The aims of this chapter are to help the reader:

○ Understand the iterative nature of curriculum design
○ Appreciate how the principles of adult learning are applied to curriculum and course design

135

○   Understand the categories of available delivery systems
○   Gain an insight into each type of system
○   Compare and contrast them as an aid to choosing the appropriate one.

INTRODUCTION

We now come to those parts of the SATE model (see Figure 1.1) that should be very familiar to educationalists, trainers and human resource developers alike – curriculum planning and development, and delivery systems. Numerous books have been written on these subjects and it is not our intention to repeat what is already well documented. Consequently, we shall restrict ourselves to a brief discussion of what we consider to be the essential factors, highlighting those aspects where the SATE model offers guidelines and checkpoints, and the advances in delivery systems using modern technology.

CURRICULUM PLANNING

At its simplest curriculum planning is the process of designing learning events that group together to meet common objectives. This provides a logical path that develops an organization's skills to a required level. It also provides a roadmap that line management can use to plan their employees' development. That is why line management should be invited to suggest and comment on any changes to the curriculum (see the comments about the G7 group in the IBM UK example in Chapter 1).

The main objective of education in this phase is to produce a curriculum that complies with the specification drawn up by the project sponsor. At the very least the specification should include the following, taken from the summary report to the sponsor (see Chapter 3):

○   The business, performance and education requirements
○   The core skills and levels that need to be attained
○   Who the learners are, and their existing core skills and levels
○   The timescales for attaining the new skills
○   A career plan based on incremental skills levels
○   An initial return on investment (ROI) case.

It is education's role to take this specification and produce a training programme as described below.

1. HAS CLEARLY DEFINED OBJECTIVES

The objectives indicate the scope and content: what is to be achieved, by when, how well and so on. They also indicate where assessments can be made to monitor the learners' progress. Achieving course objectives consistently is one factor in this.

2. BRIDGES THE IDENTIFIED SKILLS GAPS

These are the differences between the core knowledge, skills and levels needed to accomplish the business objectives and the current ones. This is a prime design parameter of the curriculum as it directly affects its content. Any errors or omissions here can have serious repercussions that could prove expensive to rectify later. Ideally, current skills profiles will be recorded in some form of skills management system. If not then line, human resource and education management have to find out what they are.

Learning also occurs outside the classroom; an example of this is on-the-job training. A curriculum should contain descriptions of the entry skills as well as the exit skills of all of its courses. The exit skills of one course are not necessarily the entry skills for the following one. The difference is due to completing the prerequisites for the following course, including on-the-job training. Line management are responsible for arranging this, and even providing some of it themselves, as well as acting as coaches and mentors.

3. FACILITATES THE LEARNING PROCESS

If you have responsibility for the acquisition of training or advising management on training, the following should help you to assess the kind of training on offer. A well-designed curriculum or course will contain activities that encourage students to learn new skills in one event, then practise them, with feedback, soon afterwards. This learn-practice-feedback sequence reinforces the learning points. Learning is cumulative and associative. Where the curriculum relates learning events via forward and backward links, students can see how the progression builds upon previous knowledge and experiences. In this way complex skills can be mastered when the learning process is carefully sequenced and timed.

This cumulative learning of a skill follows a four-stage progression.

1. Stage one is the unconscious incompetent: there is an awareness of the particular subject, but no knowledge or understanding. As a consequence, when tested, the learner's performance is understandably weak.
2. Stage two is the conscious incompetent: the learner has been

exposed to the subject and may have copious material about it. Their performance is slightly better but still inadequate.

3. Stage three is the conscious competent: this is the 'painting by numbers' stage. The skill is now memorized at the front of the brain, but is getting in the way of the natural persona. As a result the performance is adequate but stilted.

4. The final stage is the unconscious competent: all of the 'rules' are now at the back of the brain and fully integrated into the learner's repertoire. The performance is good to excellent and very natural.

Most people go through these stages when learning to drive a car and, in our experience, students go through them when learning new skills. They also learn a great deal from observing each other and freely give and take constructive feedback. Of the delivery systems available (see later in this chapter), the classroom course is really the only one where this peer-to-peer interaction really happens.

4. ACCOMMODATES THE NUMBER AND CALIBRE OF LEARNERS

Knowing how many people there are for a particular course, together with the recommended class size, determines how often the course has to be repeated. (If you are considering buying training from outside, ask about the class size and the ratio of trainers to students. If personal skills training is involved, the number of students a trainer can comfortably work with on an individual basis is about six, although we have worked with as many as 12.)

5. MEETS THE SPECIFIED TIMESCALE

The timescale laid down by the sponsor determines how quickly the curriculum needs to be repeated to get all of the learners through it. Providing the human resources are available – trainers, instructors, administration support, etc. – it is feasible to run courses back-to-back or even overlapping. However, if they aren't available back-to-back courses are the best solution. If this is insufficient to meet the timetable slippage will occur. In our experience hints of slippage usually work wonders in prising trainers and instructors out of line functions.

6. CONTAINS INBUILT REFERENCE POINTS

These are places in the curriculum where evaluations can be made of how well the learners are learning. These are the four evaluation levels in SATE referred to in Chapter 1 and discussed in Chapter 3. We introduce them briefly again and add some information in context.

1.   Level 1 evaluation solicits the students' reactions to a learning event, usually immediately after that event has finished.

2.   Level 2 evaluation tests how well new knowledge and skills have been absorbed and understood. This also is usually measured soon after the event, such as the end of a course, and in the majority of cases measures the learners' exit skills. Levels 1 and 2 measurements are the responsibility of education management and are usually the subject of any end-of-course report.

3.   Level 3 evaluates how the new knowledge and skills are contributing to an improved job performance. This can be measured one to six months after a course. Line management, HRM and education management are involved in measuring this.

4.   Level 4 evaluates the impact of the training on the business results. This can be assessed some twelve months after the course and is of vital interest to the sponsor. Should this stretch beyond, say, 15 to 18 months the chances are that the circumstances will have changed and the situation should be reappraised.

7. COMPLIES WITH THE SPECIFICATION FOR THE CAREER PLAN

A well-defined training curriculum provides an excellent vehicle for management and employees to agree a training plan to support both the organization's and the individual's development. The training paths should reflect the employees' gain in core competencies, and their acquisition and gradual mastery of central skills. If your organization has a skills management system in which skills profiles indicate job or competency levels, the curriculum and course objectives should relate the exit skills to these skills levels.

8. IS COST-EFFECTIVE

The benefits from training are measured at the level 4 stage of evaluation – the effect on business results – and there will be clear views expressed about which factors should be measured to evaluate the progress being made. Benefits are one part of the ROI equation; the other part is the costs involved. This represents the organization's investment in the training programme.

COURSE DESIGN

SATE is clear that there should be a definite structure to a course in the form of a hierarchy of subject matter. At the highest level there is the course, which comprises one or more modules, where a module is a group of associated events having a common topic. Within each event there is one or more learning units. Generally, a module corresponds to a particular skill, knowledge or behaviour, with its events subscribing to the attainment of it. Each of the units within an event relates to a specific aspect of the skill, knowledge or behaviour being learnt. Whilst some modules apply only to certain courses, there may well be other modules which apply throughout the entire curriculum. For example, a training programme for salespeople will have a module on communication skills, which will reinforce, develop and test those skills on most if not every course. In contrast, a module on product knowledge may be appropriate to only one of the courses.

This stage of course development is concerned with producing a framework for the course. In doing this, sufficient information will have been gathered and decisions made to produce a course description, which is the major output from this phase. The steps involved are described below.

CREATE THE OBJECTIVES

Every course should have well-defined and measurable learning objectives which address specific job-related needs and which are arrived at in consultation with line management. Objectives are a statement of what the learners will be able to do, know or believe at the end of the course, at a given level of proficiency. As the course is made up of various modules, it is vital that their objectives are aligned with the course objectives and contribute to their achievement.

DESIGN THE EVALUATION STRATEGY

In the broadest sense evaluation is a quality control measure designed to answer two specific questions: (1) Did the course meet its objectives? and (2) How can the course be improved?

Obtaining level 1 (students' reactions) and level 2 (knowledge and skills gained) evaluations are directly under the control of the education function and are the simplest ones to measure. The decisions that have to be made about them are:

○   what information to collect?
○   when to collect it?
○   how to collect it?

A well-designed course evaluation sheet (level 1 feedback) can obtain students' views about:

○   whether the course met its objectives

O   the value of the course to the student's job
O   the course's strengths and weaknesses
O   the quality of the instruction, materials, etc.
O   certain hygiene factors: cafeteria, coffee machines, hotel standards,
         etc.
O   whether they would recommend it to others.

Level 2 evaluations are conducted within the course. Pre-tests, interim tests
and post-tests measure the learning achieved during the course, especially
with regard to knowledge. Skills and attitudes are best assessed by role
plays or real-life simulations. Levels 1 and 2 feedback are a rich source of
information for the education function. Chapters 11 and 12 discuss these in
greater detail. Level 3 evaluation (application to the job) can best be
obtained through observation and by talking to the students' manager. It
may be possible to see an immediate change in performance the day after
the course ends, but the real test is what has been *permanently* absorbed.
Measuring this some three to six months after the course will give a more
reliable indication of what has been truly learnt. The same argument applies
to level 4 evaluation. A reasonable period of time should be allowed to pass,
say 12 months, before an assessment is made about 'Did the course meet its
objectives?'

DEVELOP LEARNING PROCESS STANDARDS

Course objectives describe 'what' learning should be achieved; learning
process standards guide 'how' it will be achieved. They are based on the
unique characteristics of adult learners, which in turn are based on the adult
learning principles discussed in Chapters 5, 6 and 7. For example, we know
that adults learn most effectively when actively involved in learning. Therefore, an applicable learning standard might be to provide more activity
events than standard 'talk-and-chalk' sessions. Learning process standards
can be any or all of the following:

Applicable to all courses

We believe that learning should be enjoyable and this should be a guiding
standard. Additionally, we might decide that there must be a break of at least
five minutes every hour in any classroom lecture event (this may be
undiplomatic to enforce in the case of a visiting dignitary: the students' feedback for this session will indicate whether discretion was the better part of
valour).

Unique to a delivery system

We may decide, for example, that in computer-based training there will always be a pre-test, perhaps as a self-assessment, and that all tests will be based on multi-choice answers.

Unique to a specific audience

The profile of a class might show that a particular group of students is special and that a special set of standards would increase the learning rate. For example, a particular group may be experienced hires whose skills and knowledge exceed some exit skills. A learning process standard may well allow this group to nominate optional events where they could learn skills that are not part of the course.

Variety

One of the standards we would advocate is that of variety. People welcome variety; it keeps their interest. Vary the pace; vary the style; vary the people up front (the instructors) and the students should remain alert and attentive.

VERIFY THE DELIVERY SYSTEM

Some thought may have already been given to the delivery system for a course. There are several kinds of delivery systems available and selection should be based on effectiveness and cost. The various kinds of delivery systems currently available, their pros and cons, and their cost-effectiveness are discussed later in this chapter.

SEQUENCE THE LESSONS

Within the boundaries of a course there are several ways that the lessons can be sequenced. Some are more obvious than others, and we will comment on them appropriately.

○   Easy to difficult: this gradually builds up the students' knowledge and follows the adult learning principle of building on previous experience. The students feel increasingly confident as they master each successive stage.
○   Familiar to the unfamiliar: move from what the students know to the new, asking them to draw on their existing knowledge and experience to build bridges to the new areas.
○   Job performance order: this sequence teaches the skills in the order they are performed on the job. Examples of this include training a bomb disposal officer or a diamond cutter: one step omitted or out of sequence can spell disaster.

O   Whole-part-whole: this is another adult learning principle; present the total picture first, break it down into its constituent parts, master those, then build the parts back into the 'big picture'.

THE COURSE DESCRIPTION

At this point all of the foregoing is pulled together to enable the course description to be produced. To make sure that all of the information is available, and the appropriate decisions made, use the following checklist:

O   The course and module objectives are measurable or observable and they support the business and performance requirements

O   There is an evaluation strategy in place for each level

O   The learning process standards are based on the adult learning principles, the audience profile and they support the course objectives

O   The lesson sequence is a logical one to achieve the course objectives

O   The delivery system is appropriate to the course content and audience, and balances effectiveness and cost.

The course description is a summary of the course design and includes the following information:

1. Course title: stated in an unambiguous way so that managers and employees will have a clear understanding of what the course is about.
2. Audience: needs to be unambiguous to ensure that the right employees are enrolled on the course.
3. Course duration: used for planning purposes by line management and their employees.
4. Purpose of course: states what the course aims to achieve in terms of the target audience and the key skills to be acquired.
5. Course objectives: tells management and employees the outcome of the course stated as the expected performance.
6. Learning process standards: lists the quality standards for running the course.
7. Delivery system: should be appropriate to the course content.
8. Lesson sequence: lists the main sections of the course in the sequence best suited to its objectives.
9. Evaluation strategy: gives the timing and methods to be used to obtain appropriate feedback.

The course description provides a specification that other trainers and instructors can use in developing their individual events and units. The course description also serves as review material with management and is therefore a key document.

DELIVERY SYSTEMS

Delivery systems fall into one or other of two broad categories: (1) those aimed at group learning; they are trainer-led; and (2) those aimed at individual learning; they are learner-driven.

In the following reviews we comment on how each one relates to specific criteria – those factors that should be considered when choosing the appropriate solution for a particular course. These are:

○   *Job simulation*: the ability to simulate the actual job environment.
○   *Adaptability*: the flexibility to cater for a range of learner capabilities and expertise.
○   *Interaction*: the degree of interaction possible between the system and the learners.
○   *Measurement, evaluation and feedback*: the ability to test and give feedback on the learners' progress through the course material.
○   *Preparation time*: the average amount of time needed to prepare one hour of new instructional material. The figures given below are those that were used within IBM for planning purposes. Where there is a second set of figures please refer to note 1, Chapter 8 in the Notes section at the end of this book.
○   *Effectiveness*: this number is the relative amount of time needed to absorb a given unit of learning compared with the conventional classroom, taken as the base (1.0). Thus, a figure of 2.0 means that it would take twice as long to absorb information compared to the conventional classroom, whilst a figure of 0.5 means that it would take only half the time. The figures given are those that were used within IBM for planning purposes. Where there is a second set of figures please refer to note 2, Chapter 8 in the Notes section at the end of this book.

We finish each review with our views on the strengths and limitations of the system as we see them. (The delivery systems are also summarized in Table 8.1 on page 153.)

GROUP LEARNING SYSTEMS REVIEW

CONVENTIONAL CLASSROOM

Still the most popular delivery system in use today and probably for some years to come, it is especially suited to the learning of personal skills where practice and feedback from experienced trainers is essential.

O   *Job simulation*: an ideal vehicle for case studies and role plays, both
          of which emulate real-world situations.
O   *Adaptability*: an experienced trainer will observe, question, analyse
          and be able to respond to the varied needs of the audience.
O   *Interaction*: the highest degree of interaction of any of the systems.
          This occurs not only between the learners and the trainer, but also
          between learners.
O   *Measurement, evaluation and feedback*: a well-designed course
          will include points at which the learners' progress through the
          material can be assessed and commented on.
O   *Preparation time*: generally, there is broad agreement on this figure:
          40 hours per hour of instruction time or 30–40 hours per hour of
          instruction time.[1]
O   *Effectiveness*: we use this system as the base against which all the
          other systems are measured. Effectiveness = 1.0.

Strengths

O   consistency of material
O   it is a familiar environment for most learners
O   highly interactive and stimulating
O   encourages personal networking
O   learning by doing; if appropriate by using all senses – sight, sound,
          touch, etc.
O   courses have a relatively short development cycle
O   the content of the course is fairly easily modified.

Limitations

O   inconsistency of trainers
O   the learner cannot escape public triumphs or public disasters
O   can be expensive to run, if travel and hotel expenses are incurred
O   time has to be spent away from work – lost production
O   possible scheduling conflicts
O   not cost-effective for pure knowledge-based subjects.

REMOTE CLASSROOM

In this instance a trainer is connected via television network links to suitably
equipped remote classrooms, where the trainer and the material can be seen
on television monitors. In advanced systems the trainer can see the groups
in the individual classrooms as well as seeing any individual.

O   *Job simulation*: more suited to the kind of presentations given by
          subject matter experts.

○   *Adaptability*: the trainer has to be very experienced with this system in order to maximize the learning opportunity.

○   *Interaction*: although some interaction is possible, it is not as free flowing as in a conventional classroom.

○   *Measurement, evaluation and feedback*: quite suitable for monitoring the acquisition of knowledge and facts.

○   *Preparation time*: the time and effort required are greater than for a conventional classroom as the designer has to think a great deal about the process as well as the content: 100 hours per hour of instructional material or 80–240 hours per hour of instructional material.[1]

○   *Effectiveness*: it is considered to be as equally effective as the normal classroom for lectures by subject matter experts. Effectiveness = 1.0.

Strengths

○   consistency of material
○   changes to the material can be made quite easily
○   large class sizes are possible
○   can reach a national or international audience
○   can save travel and accommodation costs
○   suitable for events delivered by subject matter experts.

Limitations

○   inconsistency of trainers
○   requires a very skilled trainer
○   limited interaction possible
○   possible scheduling difficulties
○   capital costs are high, therefore high occupancy rates are needed to spread the costs.

TUTORED VIDEO INSTRUCTION (TVI)

TVI courses can be run in a normal meeting room, thus avoiding the need for the audience to travel long distances. The course uses videotapes, a video cassette player, a TV set and a facilitator.

○   *Job simulation*: the videotape is a good medium for demonstrating various situations such as customer care ones.

○   *Adaptability*: a good facilitator will be able to adapt to different learning styles to some extent.

○   *Interaction*: quite suited to interaction between learners, and learners with the facilitator.

○ *Measurement, evaluation and feedback*: role plays, demonstrations, teamwork, multi-choice tests and simple quizzes are all feasible.

○ *Preparation time*: the original material can be expensive and time-consuming to design and produce, but running costs are low compared to other group delivery systems: 80 hours per hour of instruction time or 80–240 hours per hour of instruction time.[1]

○ *Effectiveness*: TVI is not considered to be as effective a learning environment as a classroom course. Effectiveness = 1.5.

Strengths

○ consistency of material
○ well suited to subject matter expert presentations
○ can be distributed over many locations
○ provides an opportunity for personal networking
○ running costs are low, with reduced need to travel
○ tape can be viewed many times over for reinforcement
○ well suited to demonstrating role models, desirable attitudes and behaviours
○ well suited to 'Teach the teachers' sessions.

Limitations

○ inconsistency of facilitators
○ learners cannot interact directly with the presenter of the material
○ learners usually take longer to master the material
○ role play situations need to be believable, otherwise learners 'switch off'
○ source material can be costly to produce and modify
○ course needs to have a long life or a large audience to spread the costs.

INDIVIDUAL LEARNING SYSTEMS REVIEW

SELF-STUDY

For most of us the first experience of this form of learning was evening study during our school and college years. The characteristics of this kind of system are:

○ the material is usually a high-quality package, distributed to the learners

○ the material consists of books or manuals, possibly supplemented with audio or video material in the form of cassettes, or special radio and TV broadcasts

○   the material has a highly structured format
○   it is self-paced, learner-driven, with the learner choosing the pre-
     ferred path, time and setting for study.

The learner may have the support of a subject matter expert tutor con-
tactable by phone or mail, and to whom finished exercises are sent for
appraisal and comment.

○   *Job simulation*: not ideally suited to simulating work situations.
○   *Adaptability*: the material needs to be designed in a highly struc-
     tured form, with instructions given on how to proceed through it in
     a personalized way.
○   *Interaction*: best suited to the learning of knowledge subjects
     where interaction is not necessary.
○   *Measurement, evaluation and feedback*: it is quite easy to set tests,
     have the students mark them or send them to a tutor for marking
     and comment.
○   *Preparation time*: preparation takes longer than for a conventional
     classroom course: 60 hours per hour of instruction time.
○   *Effectiveness*: this is considered to be as effective as a normal class-
     room course in terms of acquiring knowledge and facts. Effective-
     ness = 1.0.

Strengths

○   consistency of material and process
○   well suited to knowledge subjects
○   a familiar form of study
○   learners study at a pace and time that is comfortable and convenient
○   learning is private
○   running costs are relatively low
○   reduces time away from the job
○   no scheduling issues
○   small changes can be made easily and cheaply.

Limitations

○   no opportunities for interaction with a trainer or other learners
○   no opportunity for personal networking
○   not suitable for the development of personal skills, attitudes and
     behaviours
○   learners need a high degree of motivation
○   the more sophisticated the media (cassettes, radio and TV broad-
     casts) the greater the development costs.

COMPUTER-ASSISTED INSTRUCTION – CAI

CAI spans the whole spectrum of learning whilst sitting in front of a computer terminal. This ranges in sophistication from a non-intelligent terminal connected to a host computer, sometimes known as computer-based training (CBT), to a personal computer (PC) using a wide range of capabilities such as text, graphics, sound and video motion – in short, multi-media.

COMPUTER-BASED TRAINING – CBT

Computer-based training uses a network of non-intelligent terminals connected via telecommunication links to a host computer. The education material resides on the computer and is available to all of the terminals; the learner controls the pace and path through the material.

The design of the course is very important to ensure that the material can accommodate a range of learner skills and is also user-friendly. Some interaction is possible, with feedback from the computer program presented in the form of text or simple graphics. Self-tests, pre- and post-tests, integrated measurement, evaluation and record-keeping functions are all possible. On-line printers can produce a hard copy of the learners' test results for discussion with their managers.

○ *Job simulation*: not suitable for simulating working conditions unless they involve working at a computer.

○ *Adaptability*: an experienced CBT designer can produce programs that accommodate a range of skills and expertise, and offer alternative paths through them.

○ *Interaction*: in the accepted sense of 'ask and respond', and 'test and measure' the system is limited to communicating in words and numbers.

○ *Measurement, evaluation and feedback*: as already discussed self-tests, pre and post-tests, measuring, grading and feedback are all possible.

○ *Preparation time*: special skills and expertise are needed to design and produce a CBT program so that it will accommodate a variety of skills and entry points. Consequently, preparation time is relatively high: 200 hours per hour of instruction time or 8–300 hours per hour of instruction time.[1]

○ *Effectiveness*: CBT instruction is considered to be more effective than conventional classroom courses in mastering knowledge-based material. Effectiveness = 0.7 or Effectiveness = 0.5.[2]

Strengths

○ consistency of material and process

- ○   reduced need to travel
- ○   learning is private
- ○   learning time is reduced
- ○   no scheduling issues
- ○   provides just-in-time training
- ○   CBT program libraries are available to all.

Limitations

- ○   there is no interaction
- ○   learners need to be self-motivated
- ○   they may not be comfortable with the system
- ○   design and development is lengthy and expensive, therefore not a suitable system for short-lived courses or a small number of learners
- ○   limited graphics and video facilities
- ○   if the host system fails, CBT is interrupted for all learners.

MULTI-MEDIA PERSONAL COMPUTER – MMPC

MMPC uses a suitably designed program on a personal computer (PC) to control a combination of text, sound, colour, animation and full motion video via a CD-ROM disk (compact disk-read only memory). Multi-media PC programs have caught the attention of parents, teachers and education experts alike. Parents are interested in anything that will help their children learn more or faster or better. Teachers are interested because of the extra dimensions that computer-based learning can bring to the curricula. Additionally, some governments are taking the whole issue of multi-media in education seriously, and are planning to link all education establishments to the information superhighway. They see it as an investment, as computer-literate people leave full-time education and take their knowledge and expertise into the workplace.

Professional trainers and education experts are interested because of the relatively low cost of the media and the degree of interaction that is possible. Companies are now marketing interactive training courses on CDs covering such topics as personal skills development, selling techniques, customer care and management development. We have tried programs like these with positive reactions. The simplest of the programs did little more than replace the equivalent manual, but at a fraction of the weight and volume. Other training programs we have tested have provided a record of a learner's test scores which could be written on a removable diskette and reviewed with the student's manager. This diskette could become the learner's performance log and be a suitable input to a PC-based skills management system.

O   *Job simulation*: the excellent audio and video capabilities enable the portrayal of believable work situations.

O   *Adaptability*: as with other forms of CAI, the design of the program is essential in providing options, branches and alternative paths through the material.

O   *Interaction*: the level of interaction can be quite high in an imaginatively designed CAI program.

O   *Measurement, evaluation and feedback*: well suited to this, provided the course has been produced by an experienced designer/programmer.

O   *Preparation time*: because this system requires subject matter experts, experienced designers and usually video recording facilities, it can be expensive and time-consuming to set up; its preparation time is the longest of them all: 250 hours per hour of instruction material or 40–1 000 hours per hour of instruction material.[1]

O   *Effectiveness*: whilst there are only a few years of data to study, the indications are that it is the most effective delivery system so far. Effectiveness = 0.6 or Effectiveness = 0.5.[2]

Strengths

O   consistency of material and presentation
O   learner is in charge of progress
O   learning is private
O   provides just-in-time training
O   audience size can range from local to international
O   is the subject of much development.

Limitations

O   learners may not be comfortable with the system
O   no opportunity for personal networking
O   learners need to be self-motivated
O   lengthy development time and cost requires a long-life course or a large number of learners to spread the costs
O   not suitable for material requiring frequent revisions.

SOME EXAMPLES OF TODAY'S DELIVERY SYSTEMS

REMOTE CLASSROOM

The Ford Motor Company in North America[3] is spending $100 million to set up a satellite network to conduct live training sessions. This network, called Fordstar, will broadcast to 6 000 Ford outlets. Mechanics from numerous sites will take part in the same teaching session, with each learner being able to talk back to the trainer through a microphone or to answer multi-choice questions via a keypad. The Ford dealers appear to benefit most here by avoiding much of the travelling and accommodation expenses associated with normal training. For example, a course that once took a mechanic away from the dealership for 33 days will be completed with just nine days' absence.

Via the Internet the University of Phoenix, Arizona, USA is offering an 'MBA from anywhere in the World, Online!'.[4] Students are expected to dial in using a suitably configured PC and participate five out of seven days per week during the 102 weeks' graduate programme. The students and tutors correspond via e-mail.

MULTI-MEDIA

Manufacturers of complex machinery are replacing their installation, operation and maintenance manuals with CD-ROM disks.[5] Troubleshooting by the customer becomes a case of answering a series of multi-choice questions to arrive at the likely problem, then moving through the repair process guided by a mixture of video, animation and voice instruction. The benefits from this are three-way:

1.   The manufacturers are able to reduce the time spent by specialist engineers' fixing simple problems, thereby reducing their costs.
2.   The customer saves extended down time on what may be key equipment, thus avoiding unnecessary costs.
3.   The machine operator acquires extra knowledge and skills as part of the job.

As part of its course material Britain's Open University uses television broadcasts for selected topics. In a programme about innovation in February 1996, BBC TV showed a film of a medical student removing a gall bladder using virtual reality rather than a real patient. Using special glasses and gloves connected to a computer, the student could 'see' the patient, grasp a scalpel, make the incision, call for suction and so on, all the way through the operation to the final stitch. It is easy to understand the benefits of this approach and of the tremendous possibilities that exist for other tasks requiring manual skills allied with precise and logical procedures.

TABLE 8.1   Summary of delivery systems

Delivery system	Audience type	Prepn time hrs per hr of instruction	Effectiveness	Strengths	Limitations
Classroom	Group	40 (IBM) 30–40[1]	1.0 (IBM)	Consistent material. Familiarity. Highly interactive. Experiential learning.	Inconsistent trainers. Expensive to run. Lost production.
Remote classroom	Group	100 (IBM) 80–240[1]	1.0 (IBM)	Consistent material. Save travel & hotel costs. Large class sizes possible.	Inconsistent trainers. Limited interaction. Scheduling difficulties.
Tutored video instruction	Group	80 (IBM) 80–240[1]	1.5 (IBM)	Consistent material. Low running costs. Suitable for expert presentations.	Inconsistent facilitator. Takes longer to master. Costly source material.
Self-study	Individual	60 (IBM)	1.0 (IBM)	Self-paced. Familiarity. Running costs low. No scheduling issues.	No interaction. Lot of self-motivation needed. No personal networking.
Computer-based training	Individual	200 (IBM) 8–300[1]	0.7 (IBM) 0.5[2]	Reduced travelling. Available to a dispersed audience. Just-in-time training.	No interaction. Lot of self-motivation needed. Expensive development.
Multi-media personal computer	Individual	250 (IBM) 40–1 000[1]	0.6 (IBM) 0.5[2]	Self-paced. No scheduling issues. Just-in-time training.	No personal networking. Lot of self-motivation needed. Expensive development.

THE KEY MESSAGES

O   Education management must produce a design that is acceptable to the sponsor, line management and the learners.
O   There must be an agreed specification.
O   Ideally the current skills profiles of the employees will be recorded in some form of skills management system.
O   A well-defined and thoughtful training curriculum provides an excellent vehicle for management and employees to agree a training plan to support both the organization's and the individual's development.

FOOD FOR THOUGHT

A 13 year old girl sits down in front of a PC, puts on a headset and adjusts the volume. Thirty minutes later she takes it off and walks out of the room with an expression and bearing that exhibits satisfaction at a job well done. She is one of 400 using adaptive self-paced tuition in the 3Rs at her particular school. She achieved a mark of 100 per cent for her 30-minute study, using a system that, after the first few sessions spent diagnosing her strengths and weaknesses, had tailored her work to address her specific needs. It has done this for the other 399 pupils and has also recorded their marks, performed detailed analyses and sent a report electronically to the master PC in the teachers' office. By the time she graduates, she will have benefited from hundreds of hours of 'personal tuition' and be computer literate.

Taken from an article in the
Sunday Times, 1 December 1996

This is an example of computer-managed instruction (CMI) referred to in Chapter 7.

9

ORGANIZING LEARNING

Training can be one of the most effective (and cost-effective) ways of passing on skills and a powerful force in organisational development.

J. O'Connor and J.Seymour,
Training With NLP,
HarperCollins, London, 1994

BACKWARD LINKS

○ Analysing learning needs (Chapter 3)
○ Putting adult learning characteristics to work (Chapter 7)
○ Designing and delivering learning (Chapter 8)

FORWARD LINKS

○ Measurement and evaluation (Chapter 10)

AIMS

The aims of this chapter are to help the reader:

○ Consider one possible structure of the training function
○ Appreciate the importance of process standards
○ Understand how the training function can operate successfully using a team approach
○ Gain an insight into how a few unusual techniques and procedures can add to the training function's effectiveness
○ Consider how the key points can be used as a template in assessing the viability of an external training provider.

INTRODUCTION

Not every organization is large enough to have its own training department. However, most of the organizations we have worked with had a person, or a group, responsible for the training function. If you are at all involved with training, we hope that this chapter will provide you with a template against which potential training providers can be assessed. It also points to pertinent questions you should ask of a third party provider, which are summarized for your convenience at the end of the chapter. We discuss the training function and its interface with the rest of the organization, its structure and responsibilities, and some of the not-so-obvious roles it is called upon to play. The 'model' that we describe is appropriate to 'mass production' training, that is, one that caters for large volumes of students over time, and it is one that we know works. It provides a quality approach to the structure and content of courses through a hierarchy of responsibilities, as well as providing a supportive environment in which the students can continuously learn.

TRAINING'S INTERFACE WITH THE 'OUTSIDE WORLD'

The prime interface of the training function is with line management as they are its major 'customers'. After all, they provide the training function's feedstock – the trainees, without whom no transformation or change project would be possible. Line management also define the desired performance requirements that the curriculum has to meet (see Chapter 3). Having defined them, line management also need to review them periodically in light of new products, changing marketplace, new intakes of recruits, and so on. We found it advantageous to work with a representative group of line managers (seven of them, so they were called 'the G7 group'), communicating with them on a regular basis for a two-way exchange of ideas. In this way we could learn about, and prepare for, new products and services (see the IBM case in Chapter 1), and we could feed back the lessons of new marketing exercises such as 'Red Dog' in Chapter 7.

Within these fairly formal relationships there is another one that is even closer: the manager–trainee–trainer axis. Certainly in our experience, and from what we have observed in other companies, this is the most steadfast and productive of relationships. If this relationship doesn't exist in your organization, find out what's preventing it happening and get rid of the obstacles. If you don't, the relationship between line management and training will be merely that of arm's-length customer and supplier – not a partnership – and the trainees' learning process will be impaired. Why is a good working relationship so important? Line management share the responsibility for their people's development with training. For example, line management have the responsibility for the on-the-job training aspects of a curriculum and for ensuring that their trainees' pre- and post-course work is completed satisfactorily. Thus, they carry on where the training function leaves off and also prepare their people in time for their next course.

In order to play a full role in this, and sustain the learning momentum, line management may also need to be trained – as coaches, tutors and mentors. This is a task where suitably qualified trainers can help line managers in, for example, reinforcing their role-playing and debriefing skills. It also presents a good opportunity to discuss standards of evaluation and grading *vis-à-vis* the trainees' level of experience. On the opposite side of the coin the trainers can work with trainees on a course for weeks at a time. Under these circumstances the trainers can find themselves acting as surrogate line managers and therefore need to understand, and be comfortable with, some of the fundamental responsibilities of line management. Because of the opportunity this presents some companies, IBM included, use an assignment in training as part of management development.

STRUCTURE AND RESPONSIBILITIES

The design, development and delivery of a new curriculum of any significance, such as that associated with a large-scale transformation, represents a project in its own right, and it should be approached accordingly (see Chapter 2). One aspect of this is the formation of a team of people having the right skills. It is also important that they have well-developed team skills, the right attitude and blend well together. For this group to operate effectively it must have a good manager, perhaps better called a 'leader'. Whether the title is 'manager' or 'leader' it needs to be a person who has the necessary managerial skills, that is:

O   is skilled at shaping 'round and square pegs' so that they fit into the right holes
O   has the authority to acquire the human and physical resources required
O   can motivate people to surpass already enviable quality standards
O   will act as the final arbiter in any unresolved conflicts
O   will manage the career paths of the individuals.

Additionally, if the team is to be self-directed and empowered to make fairly major decisions, the leader should know when to keep out of the way and let them get on with it. If the Systems Approach To Education (SATE) model is being followed the leader should understand its principles.

Everyone in the training function can be a team member of one or more teams. They may be the team leader in one team and a team member in others, but they are all team players. Whilst work on these teams can take up the majority of their time most teams are transient in nature, brought together to work on a particular project, then disbanded at its completion. In this respect the situation is just like any other project. On the other hand, using the following structure some people can have permanent roles to play within the training function. While there is no hierarchy of authority in the structure, there is a clearly defined hierarchy of ownership and responsibility. This pyramid represents the core structure of the training function as we see it and is shown diagrammatically in Figure 9.1.

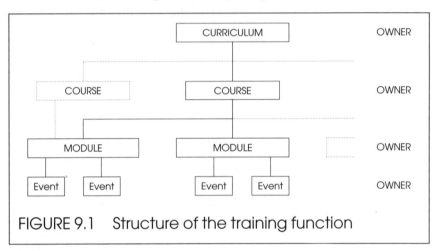

FIGURE 9.1　Structure of the training function

CURRICULUM OWNER

At the top of the pyramid is the curriculum owner who:

❍　is responsible for ensuring the curriculum meets the business objectives

❍　owns the content and sequence of the curriculum

❍　is a SATE practitioner

❍　is responsible for maintaining an ongoing dialogue at a broad topic level with line management about the objectives of the curriculum, its content and sequence, and how any new material should be introduced

❍　constantly reviews the quality and effectiveness of the curriculum in meeting line management's needs

❍　keeps abreast of the latest innovations in training and development

❍　determines with the training manager and line management how often the curriculum needs to be repeated in order to accommodate the number of trainees in the required timescale.

COURSE OWNER

Next comes the course owner who, as the name implies:

O   owns the content, sequence and *modus operandi* of a particular course, including any pre- and post-course work

O   agrees the course objectives with the curriculum owner

O   is a SATE practitioner

O   keeps abreast of the latest innovations in training and development

O   tracks enrolments for classes to ensure a viable class size. (Bearing in mind that there are fixed costs associated with running a course regardless of the number of trainees, the closer the class size gets to the maximum the lower the cost per trainee.)

O   arranges the staffing of a particular class with the relevant instructors and trainers

O   constantly reviews with the curriculum owner the quality and effectiveness of the course via the trainees' and trainers' feedback

O   produces and maintains a class procedure manual that details how a class should be managed.

MODULE OWNER

In the hierarchy the next level is the module owner. A module is a common topic running through one or more courses. For example, typical modules could be finance, marketing, procurement, design, negotiation and so on. If the subject is progressively developed through a series of events on one or more courses, it is a module and should have an owner. Likewise, if a case study is used as a vehicle for learning exercises in one or more courses it too should be treated as a module and have an owner. A module owner:

O   agrees the objectives and sequencing of the module with the curriculum owner

O   is responsible for ensuring there are no gaps or unplanned duplication between successive events within the module, including course and non-course work

O   constantly reviews with the course and curriculum owners the quality and effectiveness of the individual events

O   keeps abreast of the latest advances in training and development with a view to implementing the best practices

O   compiles a library of videoed events to use as coaching material for new instructors

O   is an acknowledged subject matter expert for the module topic

O   invokes the appropriate level of approval for changes suggested by the event owner; this could involve both the course and curriculum owners depending on the nature of the change.

EVENT OWNER

An event is the smallest learning unit within our hierarchy, and a collection of events makes up the schedule or timetable for a course. As explained in the previous section, events concerning the same subject belong to that subject's module. An event owner:

○   agrees the event objectives with the module and course owners
○   has responsibility for the content, structure and process of that event, including the instructor material and trainee handouts
○   has responsibility for developing suitable material to test the trainees' understanding of the subject matter (level 2 evaluation)
○   constantly reviews the quality and effectiveness of the event with the module and course owners
○   keeps abreast of advances in training and development with a view to implementing best practices
○   is an acknowledged expert in the subject matter
○   works closely with the module owner to ensure consistently high quality, effectiveness and relevancy.

The concept of module and event ownership means that the same people are involved and responsible across one or more courses, possibly even different curricula. In this respect it is very much like the structure within secondary and higher education where there is, for example, a mathematics department, an English department, and so on, covering one or more curricula. This is unlike other industrial and commercial training structures we know of where typically each member of the training staff is assigned to a particular course and works exclusively on that one. It is easy to appreciate that in these circumstances a topic common to more than one course could be treated totally differently from one course to the next with possible overlaps and, worse still, gaps. Imagine the confusion in the trainees' minds when, after having worked hard to master a basic skill on one course, very little of it is used on the following course and a totally different approach is introduced instead. The introduction of module and event owners eliminates this kind of problem.

Having described one possible structure of the training function let us now go on to consider how it works on a day-to-day basis. The various teams which can operate within this structure are guided in their design and implementation work by process standards developed by the training function. These are responsible for the consistently high standards of the courses offered.

PROCESS STANDARDS

Having defined the purpose of the course and the individual learning objectives, it is important to define the process standards. These reflect the quality requirements of the course and usually describe 'the way we do things around here'. Sadly, defining process standards is neglected by many training departments. They are therefore defined, *de facto*, by the individual class manager (if one exists), or even worse, by the individual instructor. Students like a certain consistency of approach. There is nothing wrong with the occasional 'wild goose' instructor to add variety and spice, but if all the events appear to have their own rules about handouts, setting expectations, use of practicals, testing and so on, the students will be confused and will not learn properly. Hence, a good question to ask of an outside training supplier is 'What process standards do you have on your courses?'

EXAMPLES OF PROCESS STANDARDS

1) Student feedback

At the end of each day or event, the students complete a feedback sheet, allocating scores and optionally offering comments. At the beginning of the following day, the class manager feeds the results back to the students and addresses their comments.

2) Explaining objectives

At the start of each course, module or event, the corresponding objectives are clearly stated in a consistent format.

3) Link to job performance

Early on in the course, the connection is made clear between the course content and objectives, and the students' job performance.

RELATIONSHIP OF PROCESS STANDARDS TO ADULT LEARNING CHARACTERISTICS

Each of the seven characteristics (see Chapter 6) points to the need for some specific process standards.

1) Convinced of need

Allow students to influence the course content, for instance through the use of 'options' time as explained in Chapter 7 or by sending out questionnaires when designing a new course or updating an existing one.

2) Active participation

Give students maximum control over their own learning, with plenty of practical examples relevant to their own situation.

3) Use prior experience

Relate new information in terms of the students' own experience. Allow them to use their prior experiences freely in discussion and to share these with other students.

4) Problem-solving

Present new information in the context of solutions to the students' existing problems. Focus on these rather than abstract concepts. Use case studies in settings familiar to the students and let these create 'real-life' problems for the students to solve.

5) Immediate application

Keep presentation time short and let the students use the new information immediately. We saw in Chapter 7 the effectiveness of reducing this presentation time to nil, by presenting a typical problem and letting the students ask for whatever information they needed.

6) Feedback

Create opportunities for the students to test their new knowledge or skills within the course and provide immediate positive feedback, whether praise or remediation, with an explanation of why the student is right or wrong.

7) Holistic thinking

Introduce a whole concept, break it into parts and rebuild. Once again, a case study is a good vehicle for this. Because students learn in different ways, offer a choice in pace and sequence of instruction.

There are many other examples of the use of process standards in a classroom setting, but the above should provide a basis for application in the reader's own environment or for a discussion with a potential outside supplier.

PROCESS STANDARDS FOR COMPUTER-AIDED INSTRUCTION (CAI)

As with classroom-based instruction, process standards also apply to CAI systems. For example, an overall standard might be: whenever the student answers a question, the computer responds not only with a 'yes' or 'no', but offers an encouraging explanation of why the answer was right or a supportive explanation if it was wrong.

The use of computers for instruction can be inferior to the classroom, due to lack of personal contact. On the other hand computers offer extra advantages because they do not tire, are consistent, and can objectively store and analyse data such as student responses. CAI, in its various forms, has the potential to add to the learning process in new ways. Many of the previous examples of process standards apply equally in principle to CAI-designed programs. In addition, further standards special to CAI might be developed to match the seven adult learning characteristics:

1) Convinced of need

Enable students to select a path through the program to match their own needs. When using multi-media, show video clips from familiar job situations.

2) Active participation

Use exercises, assessment tests and simulations frequently.

3) Use prior experience

Because CAI programs are pre-written when the student uses them, they do not lend themselves well to this characteristic. One suggestion is to set the students' assignments outside the program and to return with answers to use in exercises. Another is to set tests which specifically ask the students to answer questions from their own experience.

4) Problem-solving

Multi-media is particularly well suited to the application of this characteristic. A role play or simulation typical of the student's work situation can pose a problem for the student to solve. Depending on the student's reply, the consequences can take different paths, heightening the sense of reality, yet allowing the student to backtrack and try a different solution.

5) Immediate application

One great advantage of classroom-free techniques like CAI is that there is a wealth of software on the market, alternatively it can be tailor-made (at some expense, as noted earlier). But either way, it can be pulled off the shelf by the student for 'just-in-time' training. If the libraries of software are well chosen and well managed, the student will apply the learning on the job right away.

6) Feedback

Programs should provide frequent inbuilt tests, with remediation possibilities, backtracking and revision where necessary. It may be that the remediation comes from outside the program, from a mentor for instance. Therefore it follows that a well-managed CAI process will provide the student with access to such a person. This may be a more experienced colleague, the student's manager or a subject matter expert. Good software will have a pre-test and a post-test, so that the student can track progress.

7) Holistic thinking

Again, multi-media is a great aid for this characteristic. A program that mixes colour, pictures, motion, graphics and sound to augment the bare text is likely to be more effective than one showing text alone.

These then are the process standards. It is our view that they demonstrate the training function's commitment to total quality management (TQM). Their 'customers' (the students and their managers) would very soon notice a variation in standards and react accordingly. The definition and application of standards is even more important in the case of distance learning, when the 'instructor' may be hundreds of miles away and off-line. Under these circumstances it is imperative that the students and their managers can rely on a consistent approach and presentation of each and every learning event.

Having put in place a structure and standards, it is now time to review how the training function operates. We shall do this in the logical sequence of design, run and review, and in terms of their respective teams.

THE DESIGN TEAM

Before the design team starts work the broad content and duration of a new course will have been agreed between the curriculum owner and line management, and a course owner will have been chosen to lead the team, which will include the relevant module and event owners as the other members.

Our experience is that rarely is a new course totally new, where every event has to be designed from the beginning. For many proposed events there are usually existing ones that can be either used unchanged, adapted or bought in. It is the totally new events that will occupy most of the design time, and the figures given in Chapter 8 give a good guide to the amount of time to be allowed. Once the initial designs have been settled and the outline timetable agreed, it is beneficial to run a 'quarter-time walk through'.

The quarter-time walk through is so called because it takes approximately a quarter of the time to go through the full timetable. Thus a four-day course can be covered in a day. Each event is presented by its event owner to the rest of the team in timetable order and covers:

○ the objectives
○ the duration
○ the delivery system
○ the content in headline form
○ the proposed method of measurement and evaluation
○ any unresolved issues.

This is then discussed by the team and appropriate recommendations made for the final version. The benefits of a quarter-time walk through are:

○ checking the overall design of the course
○ checking that the objectives are relevant
○ checking the timing, flow and style to ensure a balanced course
○ assessing the logistics of running the course
○ assessing the overall plan for measurement and evaluation
○ checking for overlaps and gaps
○ checking that the design meets the training function's standards.

This is a key milestone in the project and marks the start of the expenditure of most of the production effort. It is therefore very important that this effort be channelled in the right direction.

One of the milestones agreed by everyone at the end of the quarter-time walk through is the date of the 'full-time walk through'. As the name implies the full-time walk through is a full rehearsal of all of the events in the course's timetable. It is not meant to take up all of the time allocated to that event, but to test all of the logistics associated with the course. The session is started by the course owner who:

○ presents the detailed timetable
○ presents and discusses the course objectives
○ explains the measurement and evaluation exercises and standards
○ discusses what information will be fed back to the trainees' managers.

In essence this is a run through of the opening session of the course, more or less as it would be presented to the trainees, using actual foils and handouts where appropriate. Then it is the turn of the event owners who:

○ present their event in detail
○ use actual foils and student handout material where appropriate
○ discuss any syndicate exercises, together with the desired outcomes

○   discuss the assessment material and criteria
○   discuss the desired qualifications of the event's instructors.

The benefits of the full-time walk through are:

○   checking that the objectives are relevant and can be met by the average trainee
○   checking there is no conflict between events in detailed content
○   checking that the course is a balanced one
○   checking that the logistics are manageable
○   checking that the standards are being met
○   checking that the course can go into final production and that class dates can be finalized and announced
○   assessing the staffing requirements for the course and feeding that information back to the training manager.

One further topic that concerns the course design team is that of grading and grading standards. If the trainees are to be assessed via tests, simulation exercises, interviews, etc., then there should be agreement on what constitutes a grade of 'pass', or 'satisfactory', or 'average' for each assessment. From this datum it is fairly straightforward to agree on the grades either side of it. If in addition the overall performance is to be assessed, either using grades or a pass/fail system, there should be agreement on standards and how these are to be applied. For a detailed discussion on grading and grading standards, see Chapter 10.

If there is to be a report for each trainee's manager the course owner should design a draft version for discussion with the curriculum owner and line management. Our experience is that managers' views vary widely in what they want to read in a report; some want a great amount of detail while others only want comments on out-of-line performances, either good or bad. As it is hardly practical to tailor reports for individual managers a composite design is invariably agreed upon.

For now let's assume the course design team's work is done; the instructor notes are ready, the trainee notes are ready, rooms are booked and everyone is keyed up for the first class. What we need now is a team to run the class – the class run team.

THE RUN TEAM

CLASS MANAGER

Class managers are scheduled on a per class basis, sufficiently far ahead so that they can 'shadow' the preceding class manager and act as an assistant. In this way valuable lessons can be learnt ahead of time, thus promoting a policy of 'no surprises'. It is also a valuable opportunity to understand the culture of the training function. In our view it is vital that anyone who is managing a class should understand the fundamental credo of that responsibility. The guidelines that our class managers operated under were:

> As a class manager, motivating students, building class morale and promoting a positive learning environment are your prime objectives. Be guided in your activities by the learning achieved by students rather than popularity. While student evaluations are input in evaluating class attitude and meeting curriculum objectives, it is not the intent to evaluate class managers based on student critiques. Performance evaluation is based on the overall quality of your class, which is a result of your organizational skills, managing your class schedule, motivating your students, anticipating problems and taking corrective action, and managing the talents of your advisers.

This ensured that the focus remained firmly on fostering the learning environment and on keeping the trainees' morale as high as possible, not on 'buying' inflated 'happiness sheets' (level 1 evaluations).

Well before the running of the course the course owner will have identified and committed advisers (see below) and instructors, and have the first draft of the proposed timetable for discussion with the class manager. This discussion is also an ideal opportunity to go through the class procedure manual, which describes in detail the logistics of the class and the responsibilities of each member of the run team. One of the most important sections of the procedure manual is the one describing the role of the adviser.

THE ADVISER

On courses lasting, say, more than a week, with a number of graded events, including role plays, presentations, demonstrations, as well as tests for understanding, the students will benefit from having their own personal tutor who would act as a guide, mentor, coach and adjudicator. We call this person an adviser who:

- ◯ should be a role model, preferably an experienced trainer
- ◯ would work with a small group of trainees, say six in total; a small enough number to get to know each of them individually during the course
- ◯ would provide feedback, counselling and advice to their students, monitor their performance on the course and have frequent meetings with each one to review their progress
- ◯ would be responsible for writing their trainees' end-of-course reports when applicable
- ◯ would work closely with the class manager to ensure an effective course.

There is a further function for the adviser that we touched on previously. Because of the nature of the role it is also a good breeding ground for potential line managers, as an adviser is in many respects a surrogate line manager. Some day-to-day issues can be handled fairly easily and swiftly by an adviser, without recourse to the student's immediate manager.

While the class manager and the advisers form the major part of the operational team charged with running an effective class, there are other people and groups who have important roles to play as well. One of these groups is administration.

ADMINISTRATION

First into action for any specific class is administration and their involvement is longer than anyone else's. For residential courses they need to reserve hotel rooms, possibly some six months before the class begins. Two or three weeks after the class is finished they will be updating the record-keeping system. As the class draws nearer administration will have:

○   checked the number and names of the attendees
○   confirmed hotel rooms if needed
○   sent out joining instructions, including reminders about any precourse work
○   booked classrooms, syndicate rooms, audio and video equipment, etc.
○   organized handouts, consumables, photographs and all of the many other things that are needed for an effective class.

MEASUREMENT AND EVALUATION (M&E) COORDINATOR

The M&E coordinator has the responsibility of running, correlating and feeding back the results of all graded events on the class. Graded events are level 2 evaluations and can include: exams, demonstrations, presentations, test pieces and simulations, such as one-to-one customer care situations.

As well as feeding back the results of these exercises to the class manager and, where applicable, to the advisers (for onward transmission to their students), the M&E coordinator also logs all results for subsequent analysis by the module and event owners. They can tell from the results if any exam questions were unfair or if topics were not covered adequately, or if there was subjective inconsistency among assessors, and so on. The results can also be compared with those from previous classes to detect any significant changes in performance. Advisers can analyse the results for each of their trainees and determine if there are individual areas of weakness that need to be addressed. These issues are covered in more detail in Chapter 11, but the success of the assessment regime depends in the first instance on the diligence, administrative and analytical capabilities of this coordinator.

At the end of the class levels 1 and 2 feedback results are summarized and commented on in a report by the class manager, which is sent to the advisers, the course owner, the curriculum owner and the training manager. The results of these summaries and the amount of variation, both from previous classes and the department's internal standards, are of interest to the review team, discussed next.

THE REVIEW TEAM

The composition of this team is typically the curriculum, course and relevant module owners. The main document for discussion is the class manager's report, which should highlight any significant divergences, unfavourable groundswell of trainees' comments, failures in logistics and so on, and also give an overall rating for 'customer satisfaction' based on the trainees' grading of the class – the level 1 feedback. Whilst this is of secondary importance to the level 2 results – the amount of learning achieved by the students – a large variation warrants further investigation to find an explanation. Important issues become the subjects of a review project aimed at deciding:

○   what changes need to be made
○   who is responsible for implementing them
○   when do they need to be completed
○   what new measurements are required to ensure that the changes are successful.

Relevant event owners are brought into the review project to work on the necessary changes and, if the scale of the changes warrant it, quarter-time and full-time walk throughs are completed. Once changes have been signed off by the relevant owners, procedure manuals modified where necessary and a change bulletin (internal memorandum) issued by the course owner, the changes can be implemented for the next class and the cycle repeated.

The suggested procedures for exercising and controlling change may seem to be very pedantic ones, but our experience is that a formalized approach is much preferable to an informal, uncoordinated one. Neither line management nor their trainees will have total confidence in a training function that appears to lack control standards.

THE LIAISON SYSTEM

If there is a significant change programme under way, supported by a new training curriculum, there is a benefit in having regular contact between line management and their trainees on the one hand, and the trainers on the other. This is especially true if the new curriculum introduces new pre- and post-course work, new techniques, and new measurement and evaluation criteria. The off-course work is the responsibility of line management, and it is very important that there should be consistency in the application of standards, especially of grading, by both line management and the training function. Thus one of the main objectives of the liaison system is to 'spread the gospel'. Each trainer can be assigned a department, function or group to liaise with and can have the following remit:

○   maintain regular contact with the trainees and their managers
○   physically visit the group every two months to:

 1.   brief management on the progress of their trainees
 2.   brief management on the key events within the training func-
       tion
 3.   answer, or note, any issues raised by management
 4.   help management to run a training session for their trainees
 5.   explain the implications of any new measurement and evalua-
       tion criteria
 6.   demonstrate, by osmosis if necessary, how the new criteria
       should be applied
 7.   solicit management's views about the ongoing curriculum, and
       how it could be improved

○   feedback to the curriculum, course, module and occasionally event
       owners line management's comments for consideration.

This system will also enable the training function to keep abreast of the key issues of the day affecting the primary business functions of the company. The training function can anticipate requests for changes or additions to courses, and have suitable event material ready to 'plug in' when the time comes. The liaison role can be a formal part of the job specification of all instructors and trainers within the training function.

We hope that this whistle-stop tour of our experiences and thoughts on the roles and responsibilities of the training function has at least provided you with food for thought and with a template to apply to potential suppliers. Their internal standards are every bit as important as their organization. Make sure they measure up to yours!

QUESTIONS TO ASK YOUR POTENTIAL SUPPLIER

1.   What process standards do you use?
2.   How can I influence the design of your course?
3.   Is your course graded by the students?
4.   What kind of grades does it get?
5.   What kind of report do I get?
6.   If I am dissatisfied what remedies do I have?
7.   Can you give me the names and telephone numbers of three recent clients?
8.   How do you measure the students' learning gain, and what results do you achieve?
9.   And so on.

THE KEY MESSAGES

○   If the manager–trainee–trainer relationship doesn't exist in your company, find out why and remove the obstacles.
○   To play a full role in on-the-job training, line management may need training as coaches, mentors and tutors.
○   The concept of module and event ownership ensures consistency of approach across different courses.
○   Process standards are the training function's commitment to total quality management.
○   In any training project where significant change is required, the use of advisers on courses is extremely beneficial.

FOOD FOR THOUGHT

Teamwork brings great advantages. It pools the collective intuitive knowledge of the team members and can produce brilliant solutions to the most intractable of problems. It also builds strong motivation – far stronger than can be given by mere cash incentives.

S. Joynson and A. Forrester, *Sid's Heroes*,
BBC Books, London, 1995

10

MEASUREMENT AND EVALUATION

What gets measured gets done.

Anon

BACKWARD LINKS

O   The framework for change (Chapter 1)
O   Managing change (Chapter 2)
O   Analysing learning needs (Chapter 3)
O   Organizing learning (Chapter 9)

FORWARD LINKS

O   SATE at work – I (Chapter 11)

AIMS

This chapter will clarify the levels at which testing of learning can take place. By the end of the chapter the reader will understand:

O   The business importance of measuring the effectiveness of training at all levels
O   The links between these measurements.

INTRODUCTION

Measuring the effectiveness of training is not easy, yet basically it is simple. As we saw in Chapter 1, IBM's Systems Approach To Education (SATE) defines four levels of measurement of a learning episode:

Level	Evaluation
1	Student reactions
2	Gain in knowledge or skill
3	Performance on the job
4	Effect on business results

The measurements should be defined top-down, starting from business results, following SATE methodology. Most organizations measure at level 1, some do so at level 2. Sadly, this is often as far as it goes. A survey by the UK Industrial Society[1] noted that out of 457 organizations who responded, only 25 per cent claimed a systematic training evaluation process. The rest either had none or could not identify it. In what other area of corporate activity would so little measurement and control take place? Encouragingly, similar surveys by the Society in 1996 and 1997 reported an increase in the positive responses from 25 per cent to 41 per cent in 1996 and to 44 per cent in 1997. This chapter helps yet further organizations to see the need for more systematic training evaluation.

A SIMPLE EXAMPLE: PCco – LEVEL 4 AND LEVEL 3

Let us illustrate how the SATE model can work with a hypothetical company, PCco, based on a real-life example. PCco sells and services personal computer hardware and software. Service calls and technical enquiries come via a support desk to individual engineers. These calls are sometimes routine, but can represent a sales opportunity. After fixing the fault or answering the immediate question, a good engineer will sometimes keep the client's attention and sell on other products or services. The best time to sell life-saving services is just after having saved someone's life. However, in this case, PCco's management suspect that their engineers are just fixing the immediate problem or answering the question put to them and are missing sales opportunities.

The starting point is: what business result does PCco want? Management feels that £1 000 per engineer per month of 'on-sold' business is a fair goal. This is the level 4 goal, which is easily measured. The next step is to decide what improvement in performance is needed on the job. PCco management know that an engineer averages 50 calls or enquiries per month and that a typical on-sell is worth £200. The engineers' target is to on-sell five of those 50 calls or enquiries, or 10 per cent. This is the level 3 goal. It is not quite so easily measured. To begin with, how do PCco's managers actually know what on-selling is taking place at the moment? The engineering call/enquiry records are kept separate from order records, so who is to know, except via anecdotal evidence? In our experience in the UK, clients tend to trust engineers more than salespeople, and engineers often associate with the client more readily. It would not be surprising therefore if on-selling were actually happening now. But how to measure it? Is it actually being measured now? If not, the on-line call enquiry system could be extended by two simple fields:

○   on-selling opportunity identified and offered to client _ _ _ _ _
○   client's decision and reason _ _ _ _ _

This would both capture the right information and remind staff of the opportunity to on-sell. PCco could also consider the following:

1.   Devise a bonus system for on-selling by engineers. This is an option. Some engineers might feel this to be against their culture.
2.   Explain to all affected staff the business reasons for this initiative and what is expected from them.
3.   Provide suitable training for the engineers who will be doing on-selling.
4.   Feed back to affected staff the results of this initiative, with details of successful on-sells. They will learn from each other.

Notice that training is only one part of the changes that PCco need to make. PCco are now in a position to define this training. To on-sell, an engineer will need the following knowledge, skills and attitudes:

1.   A wide enough knowledge of PCco's products and services and those it could buy in from third parties to make a technically valid and practical on-sell proposal to the client.
2.   A good enough grasp of the basics of finance to make this proposal sensible from a business viewpoint.
3.   Empathy with the client and good questioning and listening skills.
4.   Good articulation to summarize understanding and offer a clear, justified solution.
5.   The attitude that says, 'It's okay for an engineer to sell. It's the best thing for the client, PCco and the engineer.'

The training must be designed round existing skills and knowledge, and may be tailored (more expensive) or bought-in (less flexible).

LEVEL 2 AND LEVEL 1

Knowledge such as product and financial knowledge can be tested by pen and paper or computer methods whereas skills, such as interpersonal communication skills, are more difficult to assess. This is usually done by observation, interviews or role play. Attitudes are the most difficult to assess.

The best guide is often the overall impression of the student's own comments, verbal and written. To measure the effectiveness of training, measurements of all these desired learning gains should be made before and after the training session. This is the level 2 measurement: what was the gain in learning?

This leaves the level 1 measurement. What did the students think of the training? This is the measurement that almost all organizations carry out and it can be the least important. For high level 1 evaluations, get amusing speakers, show a succession of entertaining cartoons during breaks and provide lavish lunches. Provided level 1 feedback is obtained in an unbiased fashion, it is of immense value. It can highlight strengths and deficiencies in content, structure, instructor skill and learning environment. It can offer positive suggestions on all of these for the future, but it is not a key measure. Often a course is needed which challenges the students, which questions their preconceptions. Some will react negatively. The average ratings will then be lower than for more comfortable courses. For this reason, level 1 feedback must include space for students' comments so that its evaluation is not merely a spreadsheet exercise. Watch out for comments like 'It hurt, but it was worth it', especially if the event is aimed at changing attitudes or behaviour.

THE AUTHORS' EXPERIENCES

Levels 3 and 4 will be special to the organization. For instance, each of the four cases outlined in Chapter 1 would have had their own unique levels 3 and 4 goals. Levels 1 and 2 can be illustrated generically. Our experiences over several years in IBM's training function and elsewhere have provided us with a sound basis for some suggestions on factors governing levels 1 and 2 measurement.

LEVEL 1 FEEDBACK – STUDENT REACTIONS

Figure 10.1 shows a typical level 1 evaluation sheet. It is not ideal; for instance, its layout encourages students to tick boxes in a vertical line in an undiscriminating fashion, and the comments areas duplicate each other. However, it is good that the students can supply qualitative feedback as well as quantitative, and the more opportunities they get the better. A good point about this sheet is the lack of 'marks' from 1–5. The tick boxes are clearly headed by adjectives, ranging from 'awful' to 'very good'. Too often, such feedback sheets contain the option to allocate marks without making it clear whether '1' means 'awful' or 'very good'. In such cases, some students will misinterpret the system, making any analysis useless. An improvement on

EVALUATION SHEET

Please help us evaluate and improve the quality of the seminars by rating and commenting on the following items:

Title of seminar	
Name of presenter	
Venue:	Date:

SEMINAR	Awful	Poor	OK	Good	V.Good	Comments
Presentation style						
Presenter's knowledge						
Maintaining interests						
Seminar content						
Usefulness to you						

Seminar likes:	Seminar dislikes:

ADMINISTRATION	Awful	Poor	OK	Good	V.Good	Comments
Booking procedure						
Organization of event						
Venue						
Refreshments						

Administration likes:	Administration dislikes:

What were the best aspects of the seminar?	What, if anything, irritated you?	How will you use what you have learned?

FIGURE 10.1 A typical level 1 evaluation sheet

EVALUATION SHEET SUMMARY

Prog. Title: BGP Session 1   *Instructor:* Jack/Ken   *Venue:* TP   *Date:* 1.6.95

	Average score
Style	4.1
Knowledge	4.6
Maintain interest	4.3
Content	4.3
Usefulness	4.3
Booking process	4.2
Organization of event	4.3
Venue	4.3
Refreshments	4.1

Comments

Seminar likes/best aspects

Hearing other people's problems in dealing with business
Practical examples, discussion
All the above contents and organization
Being introduced to different ideas from other people
Very entertaining, stylish
Flowing style, personal involvement
Finishing on time
Generally very interactive
Generates ideas and thought-provoking

Seminar dislikes

When trying to link each person to what they were 'trying to get out'
Now-Then . . . more practical examples given
Constant changing of slides

Use of learning

Analysis of the way I approach decisions
Take a closer look at ourselves as a company

FIGURE 10.2   Level 1 summary sheet

EVALUATION SHEET SUMMARY

Prog. Title: BGP Session 2   *Instructor:* Jack/Ken   *Venue:* TP   *Date:* 8.6.95

	Average score
Style	4.4
Knowledge	4.5
Maintain interest	4.6
Content	4.3
Usefulness	4.6

Comments

Seminar likes/best aspects

Feedback – good
The nice people
Brainstorming
Informative
More practical examples given this week
Enjoyed all aspects of today's seminar
Interaction
A very good atmosphere to talk and relate in
Some early drifting but second half maintained interest
Very thought-provoking towards own situation
Setting objectives

Participants in group good
Helpful information
Very good
Group work
Practical points
ZX case study
Interaction and group sessions

Seminar dislikes

Too fast – feel slightly rushed
No chicken tikka butties!

None – don't like egg sarnies
Not long enough

Use of learning

To my advantage – the company's
In my business
I will hopefully be able to spot my weaknesses earlier
To be able to implement SWOT, PEST objectives
Focus on objectives
Implement own objectives

FIGURE 10.3   Another level 1 summary sheet

the feedback sheet would be to add spaces inviting the student to suggest what topics might be left out or added at future events.

After collecting feedback sheets from the class, the class manager can then analyse the marks, in this case allocating 1 to awful and 5 to very good, and collate the comments. Figures 10.2 and 10.3 show typical results; Figure 10.2 includes administration marks, being the first of a series of classes. With a small informal class, as in this case, student marks tend to be generous. An average score of less than 4.0 ('good') should be looked at. A score of less than 3.5 indicates cause for concern. If it is less than 3.0 something has gone badly wrong.

What matters as much is the set of comments from the students. Figure 10.3 shows in this case that there was a good, relaxed learning environment and that the class valued the interaction, group work and the practical aspects including the case study. This is evidence of the value of design meeting adult learning characteristics. Less encouraging are the comments concerning use of learning in both figures. They are much less numerous and less specific.

At the end of a course of events, it is useful to get an overall assessment (see Figure 10.4). Note the repetition of high/low against the marks 5/1 to minimize confusion. Averaging feedback on a typical course produced the following:

Student's Overall Course Evaluations (5 = very good, 1 = awful)

Met course objectives	4.3	Met student's objectives	3.9
Quality of instruction	4.6	Quality of organization	4.5
Quality of materials	4.3	Quality of exercises	4.4
Quality of refreshments	3.6	Overall level	3.3 *
Use of knowledge	4.0	Overall assessment	4.3

The class manager would, apart from changing the catering supplier, be generally happy with these marks. However, in this particular case, he would have noted that despite an overall acceptable assessment of 4.3, scores of 3.9 for 'met student's objectives' and 4.0 for 'use of knowledge' indicate potential concern that the course did not quite meet the students' on-the-job needs. This was a multi-company course provided by a training supplier and in such conditions it is difficult to meet the needs of all the students. Nevertheless, the class manager would want to investigate further to improve the course next time if at all possible. At IBM, our advisers had copies of their students' course feedback sheets so that they could 'flesh out' any adverse comments in the personal end-of-course reviews. This proved a good way of clarifying any critical or obscure remarks. Figure 10.5 shows an

* The ideal score for this is 3.0 (just right)

BGP OVERALL ASSESSMENT

Please indicate your assessment of the course in the following respects, where 5 = high to 1 = low. Please circle your response.

		HIGH				**LOW**

Q1 To what extent did the course meet its stated objectives?   5   4   3   2   1
Comments _____

Q2 To what extent did the course meet your own objectives?   5   4   3   2   1
Comments _____

Q3 Please indicate your assessment of the quality of:

a)   INSTRUCTION   5   4   3   2   1
Comments _____

b)   ORGANIZATION   5   4   3   2   1
Comments _____

c)   MATERIALS   5   4   3   2   1
Comments _____

d)   PRACTICAL EXERCISES   5   4   3   2   1
Comments _____

e)   REFRESHMENTS   5   4   3   2   1
Comments _____

Q4 Please indicate your assessment of the level of the
course (where 5=far too high, 3=just right, 1=far too low)   5   4   3   2   1
Comments _____

Q5 To what extent will you use the knowledge and   5   4   3   2   1
experience gained during the course?
Comments _____

Q6 What is your overall assessment of the course?   5   4   3   2   1
Comments _____
_____
_____
_____

NAME_____ COMPANY _____

FIGURE 10.4   An overall level 1 assessment sheet

BGP SESSION EVALUATION

Please indicate the level of interest (high, medium, low) for you personally for each of the topics below.

SESSION	TOPIC	H/M/L
1	WHAT IS GROWTH?	
	5 STAGES OF ENTERPRISE	
	CASE STUDY EXERCISE	
	CHARACTERISTICS OF SUCCESSFUL GROWTH	
	COMMENTS _____	
2	OBJECTIVES AND PLANNING	
	SWOT, PEST & CSFs	
	CASE STUDY EXERCISE	
	COMMENTS _____	
3	WHAT IS MARKETING?	
	ADVERTISING & PROMOTION	
	THE MARKETING PLAN	
	CASE STUDY EXERCISE	
	COMMENTS _____	
4	WHAT ARE THE MAJOR FINANCIAL STATEMENTS?	
	HOW ARE MONEY TRANSACTIONS RECORDED?	
	INTERPRETATION OF FINANCIAL STATEMENTS	
	COMMENTS _____	
5	UNDERSTANDING RATIOS	
	IDENTIFY BORROWING REQUIREMENTS FOR GROWTH	
	IDENTIFY BANK CRITERIA FOR LENDING	
	CASE STUDY EXERCISE	
	COMMENTS _____	
6	THE EFFECTIVE MANAGER	
	MANAGING YOUR TEAM	
	PROFILES	
	PEOPLE AND TEAMS	
	COMMENTS _____	
7	INTERPERSONAL STYLES	
	SELECTING STAFF, MOTIVATING & APPRAISING	
	EMPLOYMENT LEGISLATION	
	LOANS, GRANTS AND SUBSIDIES	
	COMMENTS _____	

NAME_____ COMPANY_____

FIGURE 10.5   A session evaluation sheet

example of an evaluation form aimed at finding out the relevance of the course content. For each topic within each of the seven sessions of the course, the students mark their level of interest, with a simple high/ medium/low mark. By averaging these marks and monitoring over several runnings of the course, irrelevant material disappears and the more useful material is increased. To improve the feedback further, the questions 'What other topics would interest you?' or 'What topics could be left out next time?' might be added.

IMPROVING COURSE QUALITY VIA QUESTIONNAIRES AND FEEDBACK

At the end of a long course it is important to obtain qualitative, face-to-face feedback as well as analysing questionnaires. On two successive runnings of the same course, we got the following results. In this case, 1 = very good, 5 = awful. (The lack of a convention whether 1 means best or worst is why evaluation sheets need to make their own convention absolutely clear.)

EMA END OF COURSE QUESTIONNAIRES		
	EMA40	EMA45
Met stated objectives	1.9	2.3
Met own objectives	2.1	2.8
Help in my job	2.0	2.9
Standards of instruction	1.8	2.0
Materials	1.9	2.3
Level (3.0 = ideal)	3.0	3.1
Practical exercises	1.5	1.7
Overall evaluation	1.6	2.5

FIGURE 10.6   Two successive level 1 comparisons

Scores of less than 2.0 were fine, above 2.0 a possible cause for concern. Clearly, something was amiss between EMA40 (week 40) and the next course EMA45 (week 45). The overall student satisfaction went from 1.6 (very good to good) to 2.5 (good to average). The marks for 'meeting stated objectives', 'standards of instruction', 'materials' and 'practical exercises' slipped a little, but the marks for 'met own objectives' and 'help in job' shifted almost a full point, like the overall evaluation. We researched the profile of the EMA45 student intake and compared it with the end-of-class interviews, one-on-one with the students' advisers. Two things had happened. First, we had introduced 'options' (see Chapter 7). Second, the intake on this particular course was biased towards new graduates, strong in technological knowledge, but lacking practical experience. We had introduced too much freedom too soon and had not in their view provided enough 'meat'. Students came to the course expecting to be taught and went away commenting on a 'lack of direction', 'not enough practical knowledge provided', 'no clear roadmap of the course', 'a lack of pressure due to no examinations', and so on.

Clearly, there was room for improvement on both sides. We provided a roadmap; we added exams; we offered a selection of options to all students before arrival; we spent more time on setting expectations; we constructed exercises where all the students – new graduates, ex-secretaries or qualified accountants – could show their worth. The ratings returned to normal.

LEVEL 2 FEEDBACK: GAIN IN KNOWLEDGE/SKILLS AND CHANGE IN ATTITUDE

Measuring knowledge gain seems, on the surface, quite easy: you teach some facts and theories, set a test, preferably multi-choice to make marking easy and supposedly objective, and rank the students. But what are you measuring? The ability to retain facts and theories until the test is over? Some experts, for instance, will advance the argument that an examination set after two years' learning is superior to a 'modular' examination system where tests are set regularly. By this token, a marathon runner is superior to a sprinter. The argument is sterile; it confuses learning with memory retention.

These reservations aside, level 2 measurements are a vital link in the SATE measurement chain. Without them, how shall we know if the instructors have got their message across? There are four areas that we can attempt to measure:

○ knowledge
○ skills
○ personal qualities
○ attitudes.

To test knowledge, multi-choice tests are an excellent vehicle; they can be completed quickly, are easily marked and, if well designed and comprehensive, they provide a fair test of students' ability. Some tips:

○ keep the choices clear, unambiguous, avoiding negatives and double negatives
○ keep the choices of similar length
○ make all responses plausible
○ keep track of correct responses over time and watch for trends that might indicate leakage of correct responses

○   the right choice should be selected 70–80 per cent of the time; a higher percentage means the question is too easy and a much lower percentage means it is too hard.

Some further tips: give the multi-choice tests more depth by grading the responses for 'correctness'. For example:

○   award 2 marks for the very best answer
○   award 1 mark for a good answer
○   award 0 marks for a neutral answer
○   award –1 mark for a damaging answer (a foul)
○   award –2 marks for a dismissal offence answer (the 'sin bin')
○   tell the students about the marking scheme.

Tests can check on knowledge fairly effectively and can to an extent test for skill. Yet, (a) knowing something is not the same as applying that knowledge, and (b) demonstrating a skill needs a combination of knowledge and execution.

We need to move therefore from pen and paper tests to practical tests and observation. An experienced craftsman will readily observe how an apprentice approaches a task requiring skill. Is the apprentice gauche, clumsy and ignorant or is the apprentice slick, deft and in command? Such tests are the basis of many skills assessment techniques. We will illustrate this in the context of the marketing role play referred to in Chapter 7.

MEASUREMENT OF ROLE PLAYS

Learning interpersonal skills very much follows the same pattern as learning any other skill:

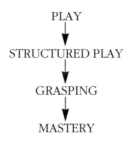

A child learning football (soccer) will kick the ball around aimlessly at first (PLAY), then join in simple games with friends, with as many in the teams as want to play and using coats as goalposts (STRUCTURED PLAY). The child will pass through the GRASPING stage to show enough confidence and fluency to play for the school team and, if able and dedicated enough, will reach MASTERY to become a professional. This model maps closely to the 'unconscious incompetent' model described in Chapter 8.

We found that a similar pattern holds true in teaching interpersonal skills, in our case one-to-one marketing skills. Our curriculum therefore started with a stress-free, ungraded, simple marketing skills course. In this, we introduced the students, via friendly role plays, to typical marketing situations. This was the 'PLAY' stage. The feedback would be supportive and positive. The next course introduced grading. This moved into 'STRUCTURED PLAY'.

To illustrate how this worked take the role play from Chapter 7.

PRACTICE CALL

COMPUTERS FOR MBIS

CALLTAKER BRIEF

You are Ken Griffiths, Head of Maths at Manchester Boys' Independent School. It is grant-aided and has 700 pupils. Although not as strong educationally nor as well-known as some of their nearby competitors, the school has ambitions.

You called PCco on the recommendation of a friend, Tricia Rose, who works at TBV. Jean Howard took the call and you told her that the school needed more computing equipment and you would like to know if PCco could help. You told her that the school needed a fair amount and obviously price was an important factor.

Jean asked to see you to find out more details and you agreed.

Background

You are new to the job and are keen to reflect the Head's ambitions for the school. You appear academic but are also at home with innovating and achieving results. You have two key needs which PCco should be able to address:

1.   Good technical advice, because the existing equipment is a mixture of old Apples and outdated IBM clones all operating stand-alone.
2.   Although price is indeed important, the eventual outcome is more important. You will press for keen prices but if presented with good arguments as to why the cheapest is not necessarily the best, you will accept them.

The budget is £40 000 and you would like about 50 machines with a wide range of software suitable for educational use and preparing pupils for the world of work. You would like them networked.

Whilst the Head is supportive, the final decision is with the governing body who are unsophisticated and likely to pick the cheapest solution. They do not understand the importance of software.

FIGURE 10.7   Calltaker brief

PRACTICE CALL FEEDBACK SHEET

OPENING	RAPPORT ATTENTION	O	AS	S	NI
NEEDS IDENTIFICATION	ADVICE KEEN PRICE	O	AS	S	NI
INFORMATION	HISTORY BUDGET DECISION PROCESS INFLUENCES	O	AS	S	NI
SELLING	QUESTIONING LISTENING PROPOSING OBJECTION HANDLING CLOSING	O	AS	S	NI

`O`   OUTSTANDING
`AS` ABOVE SATISFACTORY
`S`   SATISFACTORY
`NI` NEEDS IMPROVEMENT

FIGURE 10.8   A simple feedback sheet

Following the role play (or practice call as it is often termed), the calltaker debriefs the student, preferably by reconstructing the events and getting the student to lead the debrief. At the close, any student growing in maturity will want to know 'How did I do?' The student is asking for graded feedback, not anodyne words which do not mean much and point to no direction for improvement. Comments such as 'That was great!' or 'Well, OK, but you could have sold me better' tell the student nothing. We found a breakdown of the call into components, into skills displayed, with concrete evidence, a much more useful form of feedback.

In the role play above (Figure 10.7), a tailored feedback sheet (Figure 10.8) is a useful point of discussion from which the student will carry away some learning.

The student can see what needs or information were missed, or what parts of the selling process were well or badly done, and can improve next time. Grading schemes such as the above give rise to two vital questions:

1.   What, in this case, do 'O', 'AS', 'S' and 'NI' actually mean? What are the standards of performance?
2.   How can we be sure that different calltakers apply such standards evenly? That is to say, what is the moderation process?

We shall return to question 2 in Chapter 11. Let us first address question 1. The first statement is that any practice call must be a fair and reasonable test at the stage of the student's development when it is carried out. The bar should be raised as the student gains experience and knowledge. Given that the practice call is fair for the student's current stage of development, then the grades centre around what 'S' means – what is 'satisfactory'? We suggest the simple test that the student moved the business forward rather than backward. Perhaps not significantly forward, but enough 'S' points were scored overall to earn a second visit. A majority of 'NI' scores means that the business opportunity moved into reverse or disappeared completely. 'AS' scores, on the other hand, might mean that the calltaker was very positively influenced by the call and was moved to favour the student's solution above other present alternatives. 'O' scores, given in perhaps 10–15 per cent of situations, indicate that, subject at most to proof of assurances, the calltaker was ready to sign the contract or make a decision to do business.

To address question 2, how to ensure good moderation among different calltakers, we used three complementary techniques:

1.   each call had a prior calltaker briefing, where the call was presented and discussed with marking guidelines
2.   each call had a tailored evaluation sheet, completed and given to students, such as shown in Figure 10.9

EVALUATION FORM – MARKETING OPPORTUNITY CALL

Student:	Date:	Class #:
Role: Carla Colby	Team #:	Time:
Adviser:	Calltaker:	Room:

LSP/CTSC   O AS S NI

Comments _____

_Rapport_General interest _Earn the right
_Needs_Public_Hidden   _Need to know
_Summarize_Qualify   _Info/Doc gather
_Present appropriate soln.
_Close on_Plan of action
_Handle objections

IDENTIFY NEEDS   O AS S NI

Comments _____

_Solution design strategy   _Other issues?
_Viable hardware?   _Personal needs?
_Viable software?   _Hot buttons?
_MVS situation?
_What needs?   _Plan of action
_Franchise project
_Opportunity?
_Size?_Risk?_Needs?
_Info?_Docs?_Sources?
_Decision factors?
_Support?

WHY IBM?   O AS S NI

Comments _____

_IBM support
_Credibility
_Capacity plan
_Consultant

SELLING SKILLS (+) Strength (=) Satisfactory (-) Weakness

_Interaction _____
_Questioning techniques _____
_Listening _____
_Respond to customer _____
_Professionalism _____
_Able to articulate ideas _____
_Maintain control of call _____
_Enthusiasm _____
_Tenacity _____

OVERALL EFFECTIVENESS OF CALL   O AS S NI

Comments:

STRENGTHS   AREAS FOR IMPROVEMENT

FIGURE 10.9   A tailored evaluation sheet

3.   each call was logged on a database and statistics were produced of calltaker grades over a period, providing feedback to calltakers themselves.

CALL EVALUATION

There are four key points to make regarding the call evaluation sheet:

(a) Each call measured certain different skills – in this case:

> Logical selling process (LSP),
> Customer-tailored sales call (CTSC)
> Identify needs
> Why IBM?

All calls measured the first two skills. Other calls might measure different skills such as demonstrating product knowledge, presenting solutions, and so on. A simple grading system with one overall grade for the call is at best a compromise, and at worst tells the student nothing about the good and bad parts of the call. Our calltakers still assessed the overall effectiveness of the call, but the students saw how this judgement came about.

(b) There are one-line 'aide-mémoires' against each skill which the calltaker could tick or cross or query according to taste. The calltakers were briefed to regard these as guidelines. A single point made well may be as effective as several points made weakly.

(c) As well as recording grades against each skill and for the whole call, using the 'aide-mémoires' flexibly to reflect what happened during the call, the calltaker also completed the 'selling skills' section. These reflect in a very simple way the calltaker's impression of the student's interpersonal skills in nine dimensions. The calltaker had guidance against each dimension to aid judgement, for example: 'Questioning techniques' ... Award a '+' if most of the following occurred:

○   The student demonstrated knowledge of how to use a variety of questioning techniques
○   The quality of the questions had a positive impact
○   The number of questions used to gain information was appropriate
○   Each question was asked once only, unless clarification was necessary
○   Questions were used creatively.

Over a course a student might perform up to ten such calls with different calltakers; consistent patterns emerged and the student learned from this

EVALUATION FORM – MARKETING OPPORTUNITY CALL

Student: D DUCK   Date: 30 February 2010   Class #: TCLB/08
Role: Carla Colby   Team #: 4   Time: 15:30–16:10
Adviser: P. Scott   Calltaker: A critic   Room: 509

LSP/CTSC   O **AS** S NI

_Rapport_General interest
_Needs_Public_Hidden
X Summarize **X** Qualify
_Present appropriate soln.
_Close on_Plan of action
_Handle objections

_Earn the right
_Need to know
_Info/Doc gather

Comments *Tendency to tell me goals, etc. at the start – get me involved by asking questions – even if you know the answers.*

IDENTIFY NEEDS   O **AS** S NI

_Solution design strategy
_Viable hardware?
_Viable software?
_MVS situation?
_What needs?
_Franchise project
_Opportunity?
_Size?_Risk?_Needs?
X Info? **X** Docs?_Sources?
? Decision factors?
_Support?

_Other issues?
_Personal needs?
_Hot buttons?

_Plan of action

Comments *Don't assume I want only two days' training – ASK me what I think I need and want. Needed a bit more probing of the franchise project and its issues. Be careful of the technical points you raise, and be certain of your facts – don't waffle; if you don't know, say so and get back to me asap with the facts.*

WHY IBM?   **O** AS S NI

_IBM support
_Credibility
_Capacity plan
_Consultant

Comments *Good – even got in FSL. You'll need to be more specific about migration plans and the help you can give me. Consultancy issue handled particularly sensitively.*

SELLING SKILLS (+) Strength (=) Satisfactory (-) Weakness

+ Interaction ____
+ Questioning techniques ____
+ Listening ____
+ Respond to customer ____
+ Professionalism ____ *Calm, sympathetic and professional* ____
+ Able to articulate ideas ____
= Maintain control of call ____
+ Enthusiasm ____
+ Tenacity ____

OVERALL EFFECTIVENESS OF CALL   O **AS** S NI

Comments: *Made good progress for IBM; need to probe more for size and risk of the franchise project. (It won't take much to turn the ASs into Os!)*

STRENGTHS   AREAS FOR IMPROVEMENT
Sympathetic, professional manner   *Bit more questioning.   Check your technical facts!*

FIGURE 10.10   A completed evaluation sheet

vital feedback. This 'push-down' learning, from feedback and simulations such as 'Red Dog' (see Chapter 7), is a powerful agent of individual change.

(d) The most important section is at the bottom. These are the key learning points about strengths and areas of improvement. Students will not learn, really learn, more than one or two significant points from a call. A good call-taker will feed these back here. These points underline the 'push-down' learning which can bring about change. Figure 10.10 shows a completed evaluation sheet.

END-OF-COURSE REPORT

By the end of, say, a three-week course, the student had experienced some ten such calls, four pen and paper examinations, worked in teams with people of quite different backgrounds and had three or four one-on-one adviser meetings. The student's adviser summarized all this in an end-of-course report such as Figure 10.11. This went to the student's manager and contained overall grades by skill, comparison with the individual class and all classes to date, and written comments and recommendations. The adviser's job was over. The manager and the student took over.

LEVEL 3 AND LEVEL 4 EVALUATION

In the case of Entry Marketing Education (EME) in IBM UK, our clear performance (level 3) objective was to increase, course by course, the students' product knowledge and marketing skills during the training period. Accordingly, each course had a 'readiness test' that a student had to pass before entering the course and, during that course, further tests were made and calls were performed and evaluated to check on every student's progress. At the end of the EME process, every student staying through the programme attended one or other of two 'schools', depending on whether they were going into marketing or technical support. These two schools had absolute standards of performance that were unchanged, except for technical up-dating, over the years. The level 3 objective of EME was to prepare students well enough to complete these schools as qualified professionals. These schools were delivered by a totally different group within IBM that made extensive use of field managers to validate the current intake according to the current needs as perceived by managers in the front line. Our level 4 objective was to satisfy the company's staffing requirement of 1 000 newly qualified marketeers in just over two years, approximately two-thirds of whom were redeployed staff from other parts of the company, and to do so with a curriculum lasting 12 months instead of the previous 18. This objective was achieved.

Basic Marketing Skills – Student Report

Confidential – Personal

Name:	D. DUCK		Class No:	BMS/47
Branch:	Picture Development		Date:	10–31 Nov
Location:	Hollywood		Students:	36
Manager:	W. Disney			

Exit Skill	Grade	Class Profile				Classes to date			
		%O	%AS	%S	%NI	%O	%AS	%S	%NI
LSP/CTSC	AS	6	50	42	3	3	55	41	1
Needs identification	AS	14	55	28	3	12	53	34	1
Application solution	O	6	55	39	0	8	61	30	1
Product knowledge	AS	31	47	19	3	17	60	22	1
Marketing solutions	AS	8	69	19	3	9	61	29	1
Finance/applications	AS	3	78	16	3	9	69	21	1
Marketing support	AS	3	25	69	3	1	37	61	1
Selling skills	AS	3	50	44	3	5	42	52	1

O	Outstanding	**AS**	Above Satisfactory
S	Satisfactory	**NI**	Needs Improvement

Adviser's comments

Donald put an enormous amount of effort into the class, setting himself high standards, and was rewarded by good grades and instructor feedback. He rose to the challenge of being in a strong team, and contributed well to both the team and the class. It was particularly rewarding to see Donald overcome his nerves in calls so well that he (and his team) achieved perfect grades on one call and to watch the corresponding growth in his self-confidence.

Adviser's recommendations

Donald should keep the momentum going by doing more practice calls. Now he knows he can do the calls well, he should try to relax and not be so hard on himself when things don't go perfectly! To prepare for his next course, with its focus on account management, Donald would benefit from some exposure to branch work, for example account planning sessions, going on calls with sales and SEs.

I enjoyed working with Donald and wish him well in his career.

Signed Class Manager   Signed Adviser

FIGURE 10.11   A typical end-of-course report

THE KEY MESSAGES

○ Provided level 1 feedback is unbiased, it is of immense value to the training function.

○ Level 2 measurements indicate the impact of training on the individual employee.

○ Levels 3 and 4 measurements indicate how effectively the training has been absorbed at the individual and organizational level.

○ It is vital to the business that the effectiveness of training is measured at all of these levels.

FOOD FOR THOUGHT

When most UK companies do not systematically measure the benefits of training, is it surprising that it is often held in low regard? If companies knew what they were getting, they might invest more. Measurement is imperative.

11

SATE AT WORK – I

The scientists had another idea which was totally at odds with the benefits to be derived from the standardization of weights and measures; they adapted to them the decimal system, on the basis of the metre as a unit; they suppressed all complicated numbers. Nothing is more contrary to the organisation of the mind, of the memory, and of the imagination ... The new system of weights and measures will be a stumbling block and a source of difficulties for several generations.

Napoleon I, on the introduction of the metric system

BACKWARD LINKS

O   The framework for change (Chapter 1)
O   Measurement and evaluation (Chapter 10)

FORWARD LINKS

O   Organizational trends (Chapter 13)
O   Implications for management and workers (Chapter 14)
O   Implications for educators (Chapter 15)

AIMS

The aims of this chapter are to help the reader:

O   Understand how a good measurement and evaluation system can assist the evaluation of assessors
O   Understand how such a system can prove the benefit of multi-media aids to the acquisition of soft skills

○   Be aware of the extent of use of formal measurement and evalua-
      tion techniques for training in UK companies
○   Be aware of the relationship between SATE, Kirkpatrick and the
      Carousel techniques
○   Be aware of how the SATE/Kirkpatrick measurement level
      approach has been used in three UK organizations and understand
      how this links to the rest of the business.

INTRODUCTION

Measurement drives quality and improvement: quality of assessment, quality
of training methods, improvements in management, improvements in results
at all levels. In this chapter, we shall illustrate how the SATE measurement
model can address all of these. We give examples in each area.

The first example concerns quality and consistency of assessment, in this
case in the very difficult area of assessing interpersonal skills. We shall use
the illustration of 'call grading' as explained in Chapter 10.

QUIS CUSTODIET IPSOS CUSTODES – WHO WILL GRADE THE GRADERS?

Carefully scripted calls, call briefings, tricks of the trade like desk 'tent cards'
with the calltaker's name facing the student and a potted script facing the
calltaker, together with detailed evaluation forms, all help to create a level
playing field for the students. Yet in spite of all this students everywhere
recognize some calltakers as 'tough' and some as 'easy'. Moderation of subjective marking is a universal problem. We established a final moderation
technique.

Figure 11.1 shows how we related an individual student's grades to those
of the current class and all such classes to date. This was possible because
we kept to a consistent grading system over some 20 runnings of the class
over two years and every grade given by every calltaker for every skill in
every call by every student over this period was recorded on a computer
database. This meant that as well as accumulating grades for each student
over many calls by many calltakers, we could turn the database round to
focus on the calltakers. We could check what grades they had given to all
the students on all the calls they had taken. This was the most effective
moderation technique of all. It was of enormous value in (a) obtaining
consistency between calltakers – vital to create a level playing field and a
sense of fairness towards the students – and (b) avoiding 'grade creep', a

Basic Marketing Skills – Student Report

Confidential – Personal

Name:	D. DUCK	Class No:	BMS/47
Branch:	Picture Development	Date:	10–31 Nov
Location:	Hollywood	Students:	36
Manager:	W. Disney		

	Class Profile					Classes to date			
Exit Skill	Grade	%O	%AS	%S	%NI	%O	%AS	%S	%NI
LSP/CTSC	AS	6	50	42	3	3	55	41	1
Needs identification	AS	14	55	28	3	12	53	34	1
Application solution	O	6	55	39	0	8	61	30	1
Product knowledge	AS	31	47	19	3	17	60	22	1
Marketing solutions	AS	8	69	19	3	9	61	29	1
Finance/applications	AS	3	78	16	3	9	69	21	1
Marketing support	AS	3	25	69	3	1	37	61	1
Selling skills	AS	3	50	44	3	5	42	52	1

O	Outstanding	**AS**	Above Satisfactory
S	Satisfactory	**NI**	Needs Improvement

Adviser's comments

Adviser's recommendations

Signed Class Manager   Signed Adviser

FIGURE 11.1   A student's grades – A comparative report

phenomenon observed in subjective examination marking where marks increase even though standards have not changed.

This last issue is of particular concern to UK educators in the 1990s. Bear in mind that our calltakers were also our instructors. They were therefore testing their own abilities as trainers and the temptation to self-flattery was potentially overwhelming.

SAMPLE CALLTAKER STATISTICS

Figure 11.2 shows grades given by 19 different calltakers on a certain call over seven runnings of the same course, ranked in order from the most generous to the least generous marker. The column headed 'AVG' shows the average mark, where 3=Outstanding, 2=Above Satisfactory, 1=Satisfactory and 0=Needs Improvement. The average 'AVG' mark (or global average) over all these events was 1.55, that is, midway between 'AS' and 'S'. The column headed 'STD' means standard deviation. This is an indication of the 'spread' of marks given by an individual marker. Two different calltakers could average a mark of 1.5, with one giving 100 'AS' and 100 'S' marks, and the other 50 each of 'O', 'AS', 'S', and 'NI'. The latter marker would have a wider 'spread', and, one could argue, would provide more discriminating feedback as a result. Instructor N, with easily the widest spread (STD=1.00), was widely thought by the students to be a 'tough' calltaker. The reality was that instructor N's average grade of 1.43 was only marginally below the average of 1.55. It was the spread that gave instructor N the macho image. Presumably, students who received 'NI' marks expressed their disappointment freely whereas those who received 'O' marks kept quiet. Maybe that was connected with why they received 'O' marks in the first place.

We fed these statistics back to the calltakers. Although the global average grade of 1.55 was reasonable, the spread between calltakers' marks of 1.89 (implying that most students were 'above satisfactory') and 1.19 (implying that most students were barely more than 'satisfactory') was too large. Providing this feedback had the desired effect of reducing the range of average grades given subsequently. We also compared the global average grade of 1.55 with those for the last two runnings of the same class. These were 1.60 and 1.41. This gave us confidence that there was no 'grade creep'.

SUMMARY OF LEVEL 2 MEASUREMENT FOR ROLE PLAYS AND 'SOFT' TOPICS

When making subjective evaluations of interpersonal skills in role plays, it is important to:

O   analyse the skills you are looking for
O   brief the calltakers consistently in some detail

CALLTAKER	O	AS	S	NI	AVG	STD
A	24	32	28	3	1.89	0.85
B	3	19	11	0	1.76	0.60
C	7	40	25	3	1.68	0.70
D	1	4	4	0	1.67	0.67
E	8	15	21	1	1.67	0.79
F	8	32	30	2	1.64	0.71
G	2	7	9	0	1.61	0.68
H	7	40	33	4	1.60	0.71
I	1	27	13	4	1.56	0.68
J	0	19	17	0	1.53	0.50
K	0	11	5	2	1.50	0.69
L	1	13	11	2	1.48	0.69
M	3	32	33	4	1.47	0.67
N	9	14	18	10	1.43	1.00
O	1	19	29	2	1.37	0.59
P	0	3	6	0	1.33	0.47
Q	1	7	7	3	1.33	0.82
R	0	9	25	2	1.19	0.52
S	3	11	33	7	1.19	0.72
TOTAL	79	354	358	49	1.55	0.72

O (Outstanding) = 3 points, AS (Above Satisfactory) = 2 points
S (Satisfactory) = 1 point, NI (Needs Improvement) = 0 points

FIGURE 11.2   Calltaker analysis of graded calls

○ provide documentation which aids calltaker consistency yet avoids time-consuming bureaucracy
○ allow calltakers to express their reaction simply to students' personal characteristics
○ allow calltakers to comment briefly on one or two positive characteristics of the student and one or two areas of improvement.

By collecting the quantified data consistently in a suitable database, it is easy to invert this data to assess the assessors. The same technique could be used in principle and, with modern computers, in practice too, to alleviate concerns about inequitable school examination marking. If GMAT (the Graduate Management Aptitude Test used by business schools worldwide) can be moderated properly, so can a national school examination system.

PERFORMAX

Once a robust level 2 grading system is established, it can be used to test the effectiveness of different learning methods. To illustrate this, we will use the example of Performax. Performax is a multi-media learning system installed in IBM US Education in the early 1990s. It uses a personal computer with a library of video clips and a video camera trained on the student.

As applied to a sales call, a typical sequence might open with a role player representing a client, saying 'Welcome, what can I do for you?' The video clip halts and invites the student to make a choice out of four possible types of reply. If the choice is correct, the system will confirm this and give the reason. If it is wrong, the system will supportively explain why, inviting the student to choose again. When the right choice is made, the system invites the student to *perform* the selected action. The video camera rolls under student control. When the action is complete, control returns to the personal computer which moves on to another video clip. At the end of this, another choice of action faces the student, and so on until the call is complete. There is no 'correct path' through the set of clips, so the library can generate many different calls. The more correct the student's reply, the more information is supplied and the more effective the call. At the end of any call, the student can play it back as an entity, because Performax will store the video of the student's replies and mix them with the selected route of library clips. The effect is startlingly realistic. The final built-up video looks like a real-life call. From personal experience of Performax we conclude that:

○   because it is self-paced and re-usable, it increases learner control, motivation and confidence

○   it never gets tired or irritable like a real calltaker; it is consistent and provides objective feedback

○   because of the above, it is non-threatening; it can even be fun and exciting

○   in contrast, real-life role plays are often dreaded by students, especially early in their training

○   students we interviewed rated Performax highly, some using the system voluntarily after hours. One said, 'You observe yourself, your traits and your faults, therefore you learn'.

Students commented that the right time for Performax was after they had been made aware of the *structure* of a sales call but before real-life practice calls. Like practice machines at tennis, whether springs and metal, or a human. The correspondence follows the stages of learning described in Chapter 10. The analogy is:

EXPLANATION OF CALL STRUCTURE		'RULES OF THE GAME'
ELEMENTARY UNGRADED PRACTICE	PLAY	A FRIENDLY KNOCK-UP
	↓	
PERFORMAX	STRUCTURED PLAY	A TENNIS PRACTICE MACHINE (METAL OR HUMAN)
	↓	
GRADED PRACTICE CALLS	GRASPING	'PARK' GAMES; FRIENDLY BUT SCORED
	↓	
REAL-LIFE CALLS	MASTERY	COMPETITION TENNIS

Not only do students feel better and learn better with a 'practice machine', but the results are better. Figure 11.3 shows the result of a controlled study of students who had used Performax and of a control group who hadn't. Two 'raters' (graders) took practice calls and awarded marks on a scale of 0 = very poor to 4 = very good. One rater averaged a mark of 1.0 for the control group and 2.6 for the Performax students. The other rater (slightly kinder) averaged 1.3 for the control group and 2.8 for the Performax students. This difference of about 1.5 points is much greater than could happen by chance between raters. This leads us to believe that multi-media systems such as Performax not only save on instructor time, but can be effective at training students in interpersonal skills, especially early on in the process.

MANAGEMENT RESULT IMPROVEMENTS BY MEASURING LEARNING

Back at PCco (see Chapter 10) something interesting happened when management announced a sales training course for engineers and told them

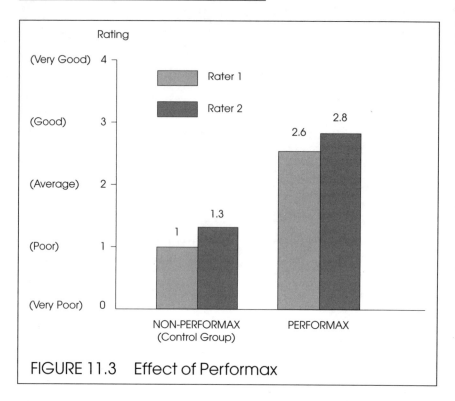

FIGURE 11.3   Effect of Performax

why. The engineers started to call their clients proactively. The most junior engineer struck lucky and obtained an order within two days. The culture was already changing and the training course had yet to start. By linking training to business results, companies not only get better value from training, but focus attention on those results and not on just performing the job. SATE measuring can enhance business performance.

SATE/KIRKPATRICK/CAROUSEL

SATE is not the only training model that links business results to training. At the turn of the 1950s Dr Donald Kirkpatrick, now Professor Emeritus at the University of Wisconsin, presented his four-level model.

1.   Reaction
2.   Learning
3.   Behaviour
4.   Results

In a recent interview[1] Dr Kirkpatrick was reported to make several points:

1.   Evaluation becomes more complicated and expensive as it progresses from level 1 to level 4.
2.   It is almost impossible to obtain reliable results at level 4, because results such as profit, sales, productivity and other business measures derive from factors other than training.
3.   Nevertheless, the better you measure results at levels 1, 2 and 3, the more likely you are to find evidence of level 4 success.
4.   For training programmes aimed at improvement in skills such as leadership, it is hard to measure direct financial benefit.
5.   Factors other than the quality of the training course determine level 3 and level 4 improvement. These include:
  ○ the trainees' desire to change
  ○ the right climate in their work environment
  ○ prior and follow-on encouragement and reward.

We have seen how in the case of PCco, management provoked learning *prior* to the course. In many cases the opposite is true. Students are *sent* on courses. On their return, any desire on their part to change is soon extinguished by disinterest in their new ideas.

  For this and other reasons, the UK Industrial Society's 'Carousel' model (originally called the 'Endless Belt') – shown in Figure 11.4 – starts with business needs, like SATE. This model is based on an approach originating

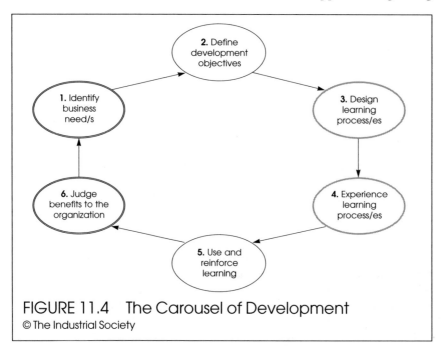

FIGURE 11.4   The Carousel of Development
© The Industrial Society

in the UK Department of Employment in connection with the UK National Training Award scheme. It was extended by the Industrial Society in the UK and is summarized in their report *Managing Best Practice – Training Evaluation*, July/August 1994.[2] The Carousel is a six-stage approach. The key difference from Kirkpatrick is that it applies evaluation earlier, before training happens, by analysing the need for training and its objectives, as with SATE. The six stages of the Carousel are:

> **Stage 1** (identify the business need/s) links with **Stage 6** (judge benefits to the organization). It is the link which is of most interest to senior managers, because it deals with the pay-off from their investment.
> **Stage 2** (define development objectives) links with **Stage 5** (use and reinforce learning). The line manager defines the destination at stage 2 and makes sure that the learning is applied at stage 5.
> **Stage 3** (design learning process/es) links with **Stage 4** (experience learning process/es). These stages heavily involve the trainer. The connection between these two stages produces validation: a necessary but narrow judgement, less far-reaching than the overall process of evaluation which requires all six stages.

The three main advantages of the Carousel are:

1.   It starts with business needs, some of which may not require any training solution: thus cost-effectiveness is built in.
2.   It encourages use of a wide range of learning processes, not just training courses, and enables all of them to be evaluated on a similar basis.
3.   It brings about a dialogue between trainers and line managers and clarifies their respective roles:
      - Senior managers need only be concerned with stages one and six
      - The learner's line manager must contribute both at stages two and five (briefing and debriefing) and must clarify the 'destination' which is sought, leaving it to the trainer to select the route or routes.[3]

After stage 6, the lessons learned can be fed back into the business plan (see *kaizen* references in Chapter 12) and the development plans reworked. This process allows for broader learning experiences than a training course, such as a secondment, and it is strongly linked to employee development. This is in tune with current trends to empowerment and 'push-down' learning, but as yet very few organizations in the UK appear to follow this model.

SATE has the same four-level evaluation structure as Kirkpatrick, but is strongly driven by business and performance needs like the Carousel. The Industrial Society report[4] offers several case studies with supporting documentation, to which the reader is referred for further detail. However, some key conclusions follow.

TRENDS IN TRAINING EVALUATION IN THE UK

The Industrial Society's report,[5] based on a survey of 457 training and personnel professionals, made the following observations:

O   The commitment to training evaluation in 1995 increased compared with 1994. Eighty-three per cent of the surveyed organizations reported an increase in commitment over the next two years. The chief reason for this pressure was business efficiency, reported by 75 per cent of respondents. In a close group, in the range 35–45 per cent, respondents stated as reasons the Investors In People initiative (see Chapter 12), influence of senior management, and pressure from trainers themselves. This conclusion alone gives us heart that we are not preaching in the wilderness. When business needs, senior management, trainers and a government initiative come together, something must be going on. The Industrial Society's surveys of 1996[6] and 1997[7] confirmed this commitment and the pressures behind it. The most significant change was the effect of Investors In People. The percentage of respondents reporting it as a pressure for more systematic evaluation rose from 45 per cent in 1994 to 56 per cent in 1997.

O   Methods of evaluation are becoming sharper and more results-oriented. Although 'happiness sheets' (trainee reaction questionnaires: Kirkpatrick/SATE level 1) are still by far the most common tool at over 80 per cent response, there is a gentle but significant increase in other tools, which could be described as forms of levels 2/3 measurement. For example:

	1994	1997
Level 2		
Pre-course brief (trainee/manager)	51%	56%
Post-course debrief (trainee/manager)	46%	54%
Level 3		
Follow-up questionnaire to trainee (2–6 months post-course)	22%	27%
Follow-up questionnaire to manager (2–6 months post-course)	14%	15%

These figures could be improved much further. The 1994 survey asked how many respondents *planned* to use manager follow-up questionnaires, compared with the 14 per cent who actually *used* them in 1994; 41 per cent of respondents replied positively. Yet by 1997, the *actual* figure was still only 15 per cent. The spirit may be willing, but the flesh is weak. In 1997 39 per cent are planning to use manager's follow-up questionnaires – but will they do so in reality? The 1997 survey noted that difficulty of establishing measurable results and lack of time (the most rapidly increasing factor) were the two main inhibitors to successful training evaluation. It may be that level 3 measurements, like follow-up questionnaires, are seen to be desirable, but managers lack both the methods and the time to implement them. This is essentially an issue of priorities. Some organizations, as noted later in this chapter, have achieved such measurements. Perhaps their examples, and some of our own experiences detailed elsewhere in this book, will motivate others to measure the higher-level benefits of training.

The Carousel training model allows for learning gained from experiences outside the classroom. The Industrial Society's 1994 report examined which areas were subject to current evaluation of any sort. Training courses, unsurprisingly, came out top with 86 per cent. The next – distance learning, project experience, secondments, coaching/mentoring, work shadowing and so on – all came out at 27 per cent or less. As we shall see in Chapter 13, organizational trends towards empowerment, teamwork and multi-skilling are extending training's role far beyond the classroom confines. Yet the conclusions in the UK appear to be that the only significant evaluation of training is that carried out in the conventional chalk-and-talk environment.

TYPES OF EVALUATION APPROACH

Even classroom evaluation is sadly lacking. When asked in 1994 which model their organization's evaluation method most closely approached, the results were astonishing:

> 25 per cent: Kirkpatrick/Carousel/other
> 75 per cent: No systematic evaluation/Don't know

The later surveys showed some improvement in the positive 25 per cent figure to 44 per cent in 1997, but there is clearly some way to go.

As a crumb of encouragement, organizations reported as the top six benefits of evaluation:

> – link between training and business strategy
> – improvement in training methods
> – better guidance on future training needs
> – more credibility for the training function

– more senior management commitment to training
– better prioritization of training activities.

Finally, the top three business areas where quantifiable results could be found were in:

– quality measures
– customer satisfaction
– improved productivity.

CASE STUDIES

The 1994 report describes case studies with examples of measurement and evaluation documentation. These and the wealth of associated statistics in this and later reports are well worth the study by organizations whose methods are unsystematic or non-existent. We summarize the main conclusions from three case studies which support our arguments for SATE/Kirkpatrick/Carousel or any other model which links training to business. The examples are those of Barclays Bank, UK Customs and Excise, and Scottish & Newcastle. We add comments relating to our own experiences with SATE.

BARCLAYS BANK (DOMESTIC BANKING)

In 1988, the bank undertook a major review of its training, with four key recommendations.

O   Training should be aligned to the business
O   It should be designed in relation to workplace competencies (knowledge and skills)
O   There should be a focus on delivery systems, especially distance learning
O   Evaluation of cost-effectiveness of training is important

In 1990, the central training team devised an evaluation method based on Kirkpatrick, with the focus on overall cost-effectiveness, since this was the business need. Training occurs only after a sponsor and a training need are identified and a training needs analysis is carried out. Line managers should brief and debrief students attending a training event. Evaluations occur as follows.

Level 1: Student reactions questionnaires used on a sampling basis
Level 2: A statistical analysis of tests on samples of students before and after the event

Level 3: As level 2, but measuring job performance
Level 4: Based on individual training events and the desire of the
sponsor to prove cost-effectiveness

Especially in a large organization, we have already noted the difficulty of
relating the effect of individual training events to overall business performance. Therefore some intermediate result needs to be chosen – in this case
operational cost-effectiveness. This is entirely reasonable. In IBM we chose
the target of the number of qualified marketeers trained to a set standard
over an agreed period.

UK CUSTOMS AND EXCISE

Once again, the process starts with a sponsoring department and a training
needs analysis (TNA). There is a strong emphasis on the importance of a
high-quality TNA, on the need for clear prior agreement on performance
indicators, success criteria and the evaluation process.

The TNA establishes at the outset *exactly* what the training is meant
to achieve, as with PCco. There is strong involvement of line managers,
especially during level 3 evaluation. The evaluation methods are as
follows:

Level 1: Built into all programmes routinely via questionnaires
including reactions to training staff and methods, and use-
fulness for job
Level 2: Pre- and post-tests, plus checks versus an 'ideal' skills list,
together with trainers' observations.

So far, these two levels seem to follow the pattern described earlier in detail
using our experience in IBM Education. The next levels offer a good example of how some organizations follow up training.

Level 3: This depends on the specifics of the sponsor's need.
Measurable factors of success or performance criteria are
agreed at the start and the training department designs a
post-course programme of interviews and questionnaires
to evaluate the effect of training. Other data can be used
such as appraisal data, observations of changes in behaviour and monitoring of action plans drawn up during training
Level 4: This is the responsibility of the sponsoring department. It
will sometimes be a project in its own right

SCOTTISH & NEWCASTLE RETAIL

This organization went through significant change between 1990 and 1993, moving from six independent retail businesses to a single unit and acquiring the Chef and Brewer Group along the way. To weld these different cultures into one, training and development was regarded as critical. Evaluation was an integral part of the training cycle. When a new 'pub' concept is launched, it is vital to develop staff skills to communicate it in a congruent way to customers. Training plays a vital part in this.

Employees have an annual review when training and development needs are identified, relating to the current and future job. Training events are designed to meet both individual learning objectives and business needs. During these events, there is a strong emphasis on up-to-date, realistic case studies, echoing our own practices in IBM's EME based on adult learning characteristics. A further parallel with our practices is Scottish & Newcastle's use of line managers. They are involved before and after the course, as with Barclays and Customs and Excise. But in addition, line managers take part in training events and play a full part. They provide material for case studies and role plays, make informal presentations and take part in exercises. In IBM we found that this link of line managers with training was a highly effective way of:

O   keeping material current
O   keeping material realistic
O   ensuring that line managers valued training
O   allowing line managers to see first-hand the current calibre of trainees and instructors
O   encouraging teamwork.

All this helped to cement the relationship between training and the rest of the company.

Scottish & Newcastle's evaluation system contains the following features:

Level 1: Daily 'happiness sheets', analysed and fed back into a changed agenda if necessary. Each trainee has an action plan journal which records learning points versus personal objectives

Level 2: This journal provides trainees with material for an action plan at the end of the course. Trainees also complete an end-of-course feedback sheet with feedback on several points including *relevance*

Level 3: The above action plans are linked to the employee's personal objectives. There are quarterly progress reviews. Several programmes have formal follow-up reviews after 12 weeks, attended by senior managers. Participants explain how they have followed up the course outcomes. The result is often a valuable sharing of ideas and, in some cases, a corporate commitment to taking up some of the trainees' solutions. This is another excellent example of how training can be a positive contributor to company development

Level 4: Training is not evaluated separately at this level since it is inseparable from other contributors to business goals. It is seen rather as an integral part of the entire business approach

THE KEY MESSAGES

From these case studies, together with our own experiences in IBM and smaller companies typified by PCco, we can draw some conclusions. We offer the following observations and advice.

1.   Training must be planned in line with business needs, via individual performance needs.
2.   This is especially true at a time of significant change.
3.   Before starting on training design, identify a sponsor.
4.   Carry out an appropriate training needs analysis. The larger the project, the wider its scope or the more people affected, then the more thorough the TNA should be.
5.   Involve line managers:
    ○   with definition of the course content (for example via a 'G7' group – see Chapter 1)
    ○   in pre- and post-briefings of learners
    ○   in following up action plans for the learners
    ○   during the course itself, as active participants.
6.   Build a clear and agreed evaluation method up to level 4 and design it as an integral part of the entire training design.
7.   Communicate the evaluation method, monitor it and publish the results.
8.   The database of evaluation scores at all levels is of immense value, in addition to its basic purpose of measurement. Guard it carefully. Use it imaginatively, as we did for assessing the assessors.

FOOD FOR THOUGHT

If you think your organization needs training ask yourself why and what it will achieve. Then ask your training department to supply the necessary events; if they do not ask you about the purpose or the desired result, sack them. Ask an outside provider for the training; if they do not ask about the outcome either, reject them until you find one who does. You will then have found the right trainer.

12

SATE AT WORK – II

The future will belong to companies and economies which compete on the basis of superior skills, responsiveness and innovative capability... What cannot readily be bought are teams of skilled, committed and experienced people.

Sir John Banham, *The Anatomy of Change*,
Weidenfeld & Nicolson, London, 1994

BACKWARD LINKS

- O   The framework for change (Chapter 1)
- O   Analysing learning needs (Chapter 3)
- O   Who are the learners . . . ? (Chapter 5)
- O   . . . And how do they learn? (Chapter 6)
- O   Putting adult learning characteristics to work (Chapter 7)
- O   Designing and delivering learning (Chapter 8)
- O   Measurement and evaluation (Chapter 10)

FORWARD LINKS

- O   Organizational trends (Chapter 13)
- O   Consider the value for your own organization of the initiatives described

AIMS

The aims of this chapter are to assist the reader to:

- O   Appreciate that training and learning are common threads in the criteria for some important quality awards and accreditation

○   Compare how these criteria map some of the fundamentals of the
       Systems Approach To Education – SATE
○   Review how enterprises have benefited by meeting the relevant
       qualifying criteria
○   Understand the role of vocational training in the development of
       employees.

INTRODUCTION

In this chapter we review some of the national and international initiatives
that encourage organizations to change. While some of these initiatives are
aimed at improving quality there are others aimed at encouraging the growth
of people or increasing the calibre of management systems. In the qualifying
criteria for the respective awards or accreditations published by various institutions, there is a strong emphasis on the roles of training and learning. In
many cases these criteria reflect some of the fundamental principles of the
Systems Approach To Education. Where this is the case we draw the point
out. Many organizations have achieved excellent results by following these
criteria and we have chosen some of them as illustrations. In many respects
these results are equivalent to SATE's levels 3 and 4. We cannot claim that
these benefits are due solely to training, but we do suggest that without the
element of training the results would have been less spectacular.

QUALITY AWARDS

Change has always been a factor in commerce and industry, usually as a
result of new technology, markets or legislation. Occasionally the change
has been massive, as in the introduction of the steam engine. As a rule,
though, the changes to organizations have been modest in nature, with the
largest of them being either to centralize or decentralize, necessitating the
revamping of the organization chart. Before the 1970s the pace of change
was sufficiently slow so that only the most lethargic of organizations
suffered any lasting competitive damage. But this cosy scenario was
changed by a variety of factors, one of them being Japan.

After years of being ridiculed for producing shoddy goods, Japan has
shown the world the fundamental importance of quality and timeliness in
gaining market share. They achieved this through the practice of *kaizen*,
which means continuous, incremental improvement; doing things better
and better – a never-ending pursuit of perfection. They apply *kaizen* not
only to the quality of products and services, but also to the reduction of
manufacturing cycle times.

Generally speaking, time is money; save time and you save money. The quicker a product can be made, or a service rendered, usually the less it costs in labour hours. However, saving time itself can have a greater intrinsic value than its labour or cash equivalent. For example, in manufacturing the time for 'cutting metal' accounts for only about 5 per cent of the order fulfilment cycle time, but this 5 per cent is the tip of the iceberg. Now you can begin to understand how a concerted attack on the other 95 per cent can lead to such examples as the five-day automobile and the next-day pager (see Chapter 1). Think of the competitive edge this can give to companies. Similarly, being first to market an innovative product can reap superior profits compared with being second, or third or worse.

Organizations are now beginning to understand that customers who are dissatisfied with the quality or timeliness of the product or service they've bought will vote with their cheque books, credit cards or purchase orders the next time. As a result of this stark lesson, one of the fastest-growing areas of management focus has been the pursuit of total customer satisfaction and, in some cases, total customer delight. One manifestation of this is that a growing number of enterprises are seeking to gain a competitive edge by achieving the International Organization for Standardization 9000 (ISO 9000) accreditation for the quality of their quality management systems (QMS). Many organizations find that this places them on a list of favoured suppliers; indeed, some companies will only trade with suppliers that are ISO 9000 qualified. This isn't altogether surprising; organizations striving to improve the quality of their goods and services are more likely to prefer doing business with suppliers who are trying to do the same.

However, customers do not buy an organization's matchless QMS; they buy an organization's goods and services. And much to some companies' surprise, the quality of their QMS does not automatically generate a similar quality in their end products. Product and service quality improvement require a separate and altogether larger effort than attaining ISO 9000. Thus, many organizations are implementing a further quality programme, focusing on a regime of continuous improvement to reduce cycle times and product and service defects, and are underwriting these efforts through business process reengineering (BPR). Those organizations which have progressed well up the 'quality learning curve' are now aiming at what they believe to be the ultimate in customer satisfaction – total quality management (TQM). They have set their sights on achieving prestigious quality awards such as the Malcolm Baldrige National Quality Award in the USA, the European Foundation for Quality Management (EFQM) award in the European Union and the British Quality Foundation (BQF) award in the UK.

But what has this to do with training? Training is embodied in the qualifying criteria for every one of these awards and, for an organization to be considered for any of them, it has to demonstrate an ongoing commitment to the training and development of its people. People are positively encouraged to learn new skills and knowledge: perhaps new attitudes and behaviours as well. For example, clause 4.18 of the ISO 9000 guidelines deals specifically with training. In essence it says that the training of personnel should give them all of the skills to perform their job. In the case of a customer-facing employee in the service sector, for instance, personal skills training as well as detailed product knowledge is essential. A recruit or a transferee should attend appropriate courses or seminars to learn the new core skills and knowledge. Furthermore, all employees' performance should be regularly appraised and recorded. The main point here is that ISO does offer guidelines about the type of training required for different kinds of employees. Whilst the 'training system' is only one of the management systems taken into account by ISO assessors, compliance with all of the guidelines is essential if an organization is to achieve ISO 9000 accreditation.

In the United States the Baldrige Quality Award is held in very high esteem, and being awarded it is considered an outstanding achievement. Category 4 of the Baldrige guidelines concerns human resource development and management, and item 4.3 relates to employee education and training. It addresses the skills and knowledge needed by employees to meet their objectives as part of the organization's performance plans. Items within categories are further refined by 'areas to address', which give greater detail about what needs to be covered in an assessment. These include the following criteria:

○   Address the relevance of education and training to company plans. Training needs should be derived from analysing the company's business goals, determining the required skills to meet those goals and assessing the current skills. This follows very closely the needs analysis phase of SATE as described in Chapter 3.

○   Address the methods for the delivery of education and training. It is important to explain not only the different delivery vehicles, but why and how they are matched to specific subjects and audiences. These points are covered in Chapters 5, 6, 7, and 8.

○   Describe what and how key indicators take into account (1) education and training effectiveness, and (2) on-the-job performance improvement.

These criteria close the loop that began with the company's business goals and the subsequent needs analysis. They are designed to answer the question, 'This is what we planned; what have we achieved?' The Baldrige assessors are looking for results on four levels.

1.   Reaction
2.   Learning

3.   Behavioural change
4.   Results

These are close to the SATE feedback levels 1, 2, 3 and 4 introduced in Chapter 1 and discussed further in Chapters 10 and 11.

The European Foundation for Quality Management award is Europe's equivalent to Baldrige. Every year it awards the European Quality Award (EQA) to the most successful exponent of TQM in Western Europe. Just like Baldrige it includes the 'people factor' in its assessment criteria. Category 3 is concerned with people management. It asks for evidence to show how the organization releases the full potential of its people to improve its business or service continuously. In item 3b the criteria include: show how people's skills are classified and matched with the organization's requirements; training needs are identified, plans are established and implemented; the effectiveness of training is reviewed. As in the case of the Baldrige award the principles behind these criteria align well with SATE's approach to needs analysis and measurement and evaluation as discussed in Chapters 3 and 10 respectively. The BQF guidelines are modelled on EFQM and include the same criteria.

INVESTORS IN PEOPLE

Another national award that emphasizes the role of training in its guidelines is the UK's Investors In People initiative. This programme lays down comprehensive guidelines relating to employee training and development. In addition, the roles and responsibilities of management in the development of their people are made equally clear. An organization wishing to gain the Investors In People award must show that it has followed these guidelines. Additionally, the organization is expected to show increased employee morale and satisfaction, and the achievement of significant business objectives.

The Investors In People guidelines are based on a national standard reflecting four principles. These are:

1.   An Investor In People makes a public commitment from the top to develop all employees to achieve its business objectives.
2.   An Investor In People regularly reviews the training and development needs of all employees.
3.   An Investor In People takes action to train and develop individuals on recruitment and throughout their employment.
4.   An Investor In People evaluates the investment in training and development to assess achievement and improve future effectiveness.

What are known as assessment indicators expand on each of these principles to underline the purpose of the relevant principle and to offer guidance on how it will be assessed. The assessment indicators include:

○   The plan identifies broad development needs and specifies how they will be assessed and met. The key is to establish that the written plan links broad development needs to business objectives and that a process exists to assess and meet those needs. Closely allied to this is:

○   Training and development needs are regularly reviewed against business objectives. This establishes the link between the changes in direction of the business, and training and development plans. Chapter 3 discusses the needs analysis aspect of the first of these, and the curriculum development model discussed in Chapter 8 addresses the second point.

○   The organization evaluates how its development of people is contributing to business goals and targets. Evaluation is a key stage in the loop – identify needs; take action; evaluate effectiveness; improve effectiveness. The starting and finishing points of this loop should be business goals and targets. This clearly follows the SATE fundamental of measurement and evaluation as discussed in Chapter 10.

The criteria for the European and British Quality Awards and the Baldrige Quality Award all encourage organizations to use the skills of their people to improve the enterprises' performance. In reviewing the submissions for these awards the assessors are particularly interested in and concerned to understand:

○   how organizations release the full potential of all of their people
○   the development and preservation of the core skills needed by the business
○   the alignment of personal and organizational aspirations
○   the empowerment of individuals and teams to achieve key business objectives
○   what plans, processes and techniques have been adopted
○   how widely they have been applied throughout the organization
○   what results have been achieved in a clearly identified cause and effect relationship.

As we have discussed, the qualifying guidelines for all of these awards contain a significant emphasis on training and development and on the key role played by management at all levels. In most of the cases there is an explicit connection made between the training and development of the employees and the attainment of corporate goals.

THE BENEFITS OF CHANGE

This emphasis on improved quality and the role played by training and development is a response by the West to arrest its decline in competitiveness during the past two decades compared with the East, in particular Japan. As a result, the pursuit of quality has probably generated more change projects than any other single cause in the past ten years. Winning quality awards is not the primary reason for an organization's existence, but there are some important lessons to be learnt from those that wholeheartedly pursue this goal as a key part of their strategy.

O   Organizations with a clear, ongoing approach to training and developing their people enjoy high recruitment success and low sickness and attrition rates. People are attracted to organizations which offer personal career development.

O   There is a very strong link between the skill of the workforce and the success of the organization.

TABLE 12.1   UK examples – Investors In People

Company	Per cent payroll	Avg. hrs. trng. p.a.	Comments
The Rover Group Automobile manufacture 34 000 employees	3.0	56	30:1 return on training investment Sales increased 9% – 1993 Productivity increase 46% 1989–94 £100 p.a. each to spend on learning UK Quality Award in 1994
Center Parcs Hotels & leisure 2 000 employees	4.9	84	Average occupancy level at 95% Productivity up by 5% 1992–93 Net turnover up by 9% 1992–93 Operating profit up by 12% 1992–93
Birds Eye Wall's Food manufacture 1 200 employees	2.5	42	Productivity up 20% 1989–93 Cost savings of 2% p.a. 1989–93 Overheads down 15% 1989–93 Stockholding down 50% 1989–93
Unilever Research Research 1 100 employees	3.0	56	Patent filings up 14% 1992–93 Publications up 12% 1992–93 Admin. savings of £650k 1992–93 Leavers down 17% to 7% 1992–93
Brooke Bond Food Food manufacture 450 employees	3.75	72	Production up 20% 1992–93 Cost per tonne down 22% 1992–93 Overtime down by 11% 1992–93 Stocks down from 10 weeks to 4.5 weeks, 1992–93
Monsanto Chemical manufacture 290 employees	6.8	66	Productivity up 67% in 5 years Absenteeism down to 3.5% No recordable accidents in 1992 Employees taught multiple skills

○ The investment in training is a good one to make, with high returns attainable.

Some of the examples we give from the UK and the USA underline these important points. The UK examples in Table 12.1 are from Investors In People literature[1] and represent a cross-section of the many organizations which are actively pursuing its principles. These are only a few of the Investors In People success stories and obviously they have a much richer story to tell than that recorded in the scant details given here. However, they indicate what can be achieved given the right leadership and motivation.

The US examples in Table 12.2 refer to some of the Baldrige Award winners.[2] The examples have been chosen so as to represent a broad range in size and industry. In both tables we show the relative spend on training in terms of the annual percentage of the payroll and the average number of training hours per employee per year; in some cases these numbers have been inferred from data in the literature. We then show both the explicit and implicit benefits that these corporations have received in return – SATE levels 3 and 4.

TABLE 12.2 USA examples – Baldrige Award winners

Company	Per cent payroll	Avg. hrs. trng. p.a.	Comments
Motorola Electronics 107 000 employees	4.0	40	30:1 return on training investment $4.5 billion cost savings 1989–93 Average price reductions 20% p.a. Baldrige Award winner in 1988
Federal Express Distribution 93 000 employees	4.5	27	People-Service-Profit creed Lowest no. of queries ever in 1992 Baldrige Award winner in 1990
IBM Rochester Computer manufacture 8 000 employees	5.0	60	Productivity up 30% 1986–89 Development time halved 1986–89 1 000 suppliers trained in quality Baldrige Award winner in 1990
Solectron Electronics 3 500 employees	3.0	95	Competes on service, quality, cost Operates at 5 sigma level, 233 defects per million transactions On-time delivery = 97.7% Baldrige Award winner in 1991
Ritz-Carlton Hotel chain 11 500 employees	4.0	120	Customer satisfaction rating of 97% Attrition rate 30% of industry average CEO sees training as critical Baldrige Award winner in 1992
Wainwright Industries Precision engineering 275 employees	7.0	120	Accidents down by 72% 1991–94 Lost time down by 85% 1991–94 Customer satisfaction at 95% 1994 Baldrige Award winner in 1994

These examples indicate that training played a large role in helping these companies achieve key business objectives. To them it would be unthinkable not to consider training as an indispensable item in any change process. It is through investment in people, especially through their training, that business objectives are met, resulting in healthy employee satisfaction ratings; this in turn begets an impressive customer satisfaction rating.

NATIONAL VOCATIONAL QUALIFICATIONS (NVQs) AND GENERAL NATIONAL VOCATIONAL QUALIFICATIONS (GNVQs)

NVQs (in Scotland SVQs) were introduced in 1986 in the UK to replace a plethora of craft and vocational qualifications. They are acquired mainly by building up credits during on-the-job experiences. Their main features are:

- they are job-specific
- 11 job areas are defined, covering some 700 NVQs
- NVQs are based on standards set by employers
- there is no final examination
- there is no time limit for completion
- assessment is done by the student's own trainer/mentor.

NVQs measure what a person can do rather than what a person knows. As they are tests of on-the-job performance, they are closest to a SATE level 3 measurement. A written or practical examination is a SATE level 2 measurement. This distinction is the cause of much confusion and disagreement among educationalists.

GNVQs are work-related qualifications gained by study and experience in schools and colleges. They are often described as 'Applied GCSEs' or 'Applied "A" levels'. (Referring to the equivalent academic qualifications: GCSE = General Certificate of Secondary Education – aged 16 approximately. 'A' level = General Certificate of Education Advanced Level – aged 18 approximately.)

Their main features are:

- based on study modules
- evidence collected in 'portfolios'
- external tests for some modules
- no final examination
- no time limit for completion
- distinction, merit and pass grades on assignments.

The approximate equivalent of these qualifications is stated in Table 12.3.

As noted, these qualifications measure performance at different SATE

TABLE 12.3   Equivalence of qualifications

Level	NVQs – Typical job	GNVQs	Academic
5	Professional Managerial		Higher Education
4	Higher technician Junior management		
3	Technician Supervisor	Advanced	2 GCE A Levels
2	Craft	Intermediate	5 GCSEs Grades A–C
1	Foundation	Foundation	Other GCSEs Grades D–G

levels. Therefore, the concept of 'equivalence' is not entirely clear. There is a mixture of on-the-job 'apples' and examination room 'pears'. It is one thing to know *how* to do something or even to *explain* how to do it; it is a different matter entirely to actually *do* it. Moreover, there are current concerns about uniform quality of assessment of NVQs (different shapes of apple?) and 'grade creep' in national examinations (different sizes of pear?). Therefore Table 12.3 should be viewed at best as a broad template of how these qualifications relate to each other.

There has been much debate over these vocational qualifications in recent years. The general feeling is that while the strategy behind them is right, the implementation is of mixed quality. Most of the concern has been voiced over NVQs, possibly since they have been in circulation longer. The first GNVQ results were announced in August 1994 when 1 236 students obtained awards, out of the 3 800 students who started. We shall therefore look in more detail at NVQs only.

A Confederation of British Industry (CBI) document[3] reported at length on experiences with NVQs to 1994. The report contains numerous case studies of companies of different sizes in many industries. It concluded that many employers have benefited from the introduction of NVQs, especially in terms of:

O   improved business performance and results
O   a more motivated and flexible workforce
O   targeted training using resources more economically while still meeting business objectives.

The report notes that the introduction of NVQs is strongly aided by:

O   the positive commitment of top management

○   the availability of expert advice and guidance
○   the active involvement of line managers.

Interestingly, from the employee's viewpoint, the value is not so much skills improvement as recognition. Vauxhall Motors' employees are reported, in an evaluation, as agreeing strongly with the statements:

> 'I feel that my skills have been recognised'
> 'I am pleased that the company made the qualifications available'
> 'I think having the qualifications is worthwhile'
> 'I think it will be easier to get another job with another company'

Some companies regard this last statement as a danger sign, as a reason not to do NVQs or even as a reason not to train their workforce at all. Yet the statements:

> 'I am better at doing the job'
> 'I have discovered I need more training'
> 'I have gained some new skills'

evoked flat or negative responses. As the NVQ system is essentially a level 3 measurement, this is not surprising. These responses indicate a perceived failing in the current NVQ system – the lack of content and final examination. Employers wish to see knowledge specifications spelt out in detail in the NVQ standards created by the Lead Bodies (each NVQ has as an owner a 'Lead Body' – a relevant vocational organization). Such knowledge and consequent understanding could be tested in external oral or written examinations. Such specification of content and external assessment are the practice in Germany, usually recognized to have a better-qualified workforce than the UK.

Other employer concerns included excessive paperwork and variable quality of assessment. As we saw in Chapter 11 when discussing our own experiences of grading marketing skills, there are no easy answers. For consistency of marking, graders need a fairly lengthy list of 'points to look out for' – see Figure 10.9 (the grading sheet). Even so, grades can vary somewhat widely. This can be overcome to an extent by careful briefing and documentation and by giving statistical feedback to the graders – see Chapter 11. We managed this for a limited number of students (1 000) and graders (20). To do something similar on a national scale would be challenging, but this does not mean that potential solutions should not be investigated.

One step towards this might be a 'core plus options' approach which employers overwhelmingly favoured according to the CBI report. This may help to overcome the problem that NVQs can be assessed by supervisors who are different from company to company, which makes adherence to a national standard extremely difficult. A more flexible 'core plus options' approach could mean less 'core' to assess nationally (possibly defined more closely as with the German model) and more 'options' to allow for individual company/job variations. 'It is quite impossible to design methodologies for drawing up qualifications that are applicable to all occupations at all levels across the country.'[4]

No doubt the discussions about assessment will carry on for some time, not least because of different perceptions of what NVQs are for. In a newspaper article in late 1994, one commentator stated, 'Modular-based, the blocks of achievement for the qualification can be acquired at the individual's own pace. As long as candidates can prove their competence, the learning route is not prescribed.' Across the same page, another commentator stated, 'There's nothing to distinguish a student who can do a task straight away from one who makes umpteen attempts at it. They all end up with the same bit of paper.' Both points are valid. Yet the second commentator read more into the qualification than exists, namely the ability to learn quickly which, as we shall see in the next chapter, is becoming a key skill in times of change. If GNVQs develop towards the acquisition of 'soft' skills that are demanded of today's workforce, it may be that we should aim at a mixture of NVQs, GNVQs and academic qualifications, in a measure appropriate to the student's short-term and longer-term job needs. Sir Ron Dearing's report[5] makes several recommendations for the future, covering the whole spectrum of job-related needs and qualifications.

Finally, some encouraging and revealing comments from two NVQ students, who chose vocational qualifications rather than continuing along the academic route:

> Student A, during work experience at a High Street store: 'It makes you realize how important it is to be able to do things like maths.'
> Student B: 'Working for something vocational makes you realize there is merit in gaining academic qualifications.'

These students spotted the link between performance needs (level 3) and training needs (level 2). The sad thing about the ongoing debate about vocational and academic qualifications is that few commentators regard them as parts of a whole. For any given person and job, the need for one might outweigh the need for the other, yet both are required. They are not in competition. In the next chapter we will see how the rapid change that most organizations are experiencing in the 1990s makes a linked approach absolutely vital.

THE KEY MESSAGES

○   To comply with ISO 9000, the Baldrige Award, EFQM and BQF criteria, organizations have to demonstrate an ongoing commitment to the training and development of their people. No people development – no award.

○   The Investors In People and Baldrige examples indicate that training played a significant role in helping some companies achieve key business objectives. To them it would be unthinkable not to consider training as a key item in any change process.

○   NVQs measure what a person can do, not what a person knows.

○   'Working in a store makes you realize how important it is to be able to do things like maths.'

FOOD FOR THOUGHT

The armies of the doers and knowers are ranged against each other in battle. Who will win? We do not know. But an army that has both doers and knowers will beat either of them. And an army who all know and can do will beat everyone.

PART IV

LOOKING AHEAD

❖

13

ORGANIZATIONAL TRENDS

YESTERDAY'S COMPANIES have different messages for different audiences (for example to providers of capital, employees are labour costs to be cut, while to the employees 'you are our greatest asset').

Tomorrow's Company: An RSA Inquiry,
Gower, Aldershot, 1995

BACKWARD LINKS

O   Preface
O   The framework for change (Chapter 1)
O   Managing change (Chapter 2)
O   Organizing learning (Chapter 9)
O   SATE at work – II (Chapter 12)

FORWARD LINKS

O   Implications for management and workers (Chapter 14)
O   Implications for educators (Chapter 15)

AIMS

By analysing current global trends in business, to make the reader aware of:

O   The changing nature of work
O   Some of the approaches being adopted by leading-edge organizations
O   The lessons to be learned from them.

INTRODUCTION

In this chapter we look at some of the ways in which organizations are responding to today's world of intense competition, increasingly demanding customers and rapidly shrinking timescales. Sadly, some of the responses have been purely reactive, almost panic-stricken attempts to preserve the bottom line by cutting broad swathes through that most precious of assets – employees. Other companies, the ones which saw the need to change long before they were forced to, have made more measured and proactive responses, and have genuinely tried to make their companies more effective as well as more efficient. A great many of them have done this through the elimination of waste – mainly time – rather than the elimination of jobs and the people who filled them.

It is these latter organizations that are approaching change in a different and more socially responsible way – more evolutionary than revolutionary. They are seeking sustainable growth through continuous incremental change – what the Japanese call *kaizen*. We discussed *kaizen* in Chapter 12 in relation to the quality movement and TQM. There it applied to the continuous improvement of a company's products or services. Here, however, it applies to the continuous development of a company's workforce: it is the continuous development of people that generates a better and better organization. This process eventually produces the self-generative or learning organization. This is one of the outcomes of the third generation of training and development – the enabling of continuous learning and improvement.

WHAT ARE ORGANIZATIONS DOING?

DOWNSIZING AND ITS AFTERMATH

Being caught unexpectedly on the losing end of a competitive battle usually forces companies to respond in the first instance by cutting costs, a relatively quick exercise but a painful one for those who are victims of it. As people are liquid assets, redundancies and lay-offs become the order of the day. Ironically, downsizing is usually greeted in the financial markets by a rise in the company's share price. In the most blatant of cases the executives award themselves more stock options or a large pay rise or both. A rising share price is fine for the shareholders but does little for the morale of those laid off or, for that matter, those who remain. For the surviving employees there is the fear that they may be the next ones to go. As fear never sustains increased productivity, which is what is now needed in the face of a reduced headcount, it is imperative that executive management allays any fears of further lay-offs. Furthermore, as a sustainable increase in productivity is best achieved through an increase in the skills of the remaining employees, the training that accomplishes this will be better absorbed in a climate of relative job security.

Downsizing is a short-term expedient; it is not a panacea for long-term survival; few companies grow by shrinking. As we have implied, the down-sized organization now has to achieve more with fewer people if it is to maintain its market share. This entails giving the remaining people extra skills, that is, multi-skilling. At its simplest this means they have to learn the skills of the people who have just left. Provided the downsizing has not been too severe, this can be realized reasonably easily. However, if the scale of downsizing has been large, it would be impossible for the remaining workforce to do the work of the previous one (see the worked examples in Chapter 4) and further measures have to be applied. These can include eliminating non-core jobs altogether and outsourcing them to a growing band of willing suppliers, many including ex-employees.

Downsizing also affects management. Fewer employees mean fewer managers and it is not unusual for layers of management to be stripped out of an organization along with the people they once managed. The remaining managers must also take on board additional skills if they are to lead the productivity drive.

Sometimes multi-skilling is not enough. Endowing people with the same skills which have been lost through downsizing is insufficient if the competition are winning market share through new skills and unprecedented levels of customer care. The telephone banking service is a good example of this, where the combination of new skills and the competitive use of information technology is forcing the High Street banks to follow suit at the same time as they are downsizing, so far with very little success.

At present, downsizing still appears to be as prevalent as ever, with weekly if not daily announcements of redundancies, lay-offs or, the most demeaning expression of all, 'saves'. But there is also a rising groundswell of opinion among some companies that downsizing has gone far enough in its present form and that a company's long-term survival will be in doubt if taken to extremes. One American company is trying a different approach.[1]

After a round of particularly expensive redundancies, AT&T decided it made more sense to retain the better performers whose jobs were being eliminated and lease them out elsewhere in the organization where their skills were needed, albeit on a piecemeal basis. This can be cheaper than hiring in those skills from a consultancy or sub-contracting agency (where many a redundant employee has found a more exciting and lucrative career).

The people in AT&T's 'talent pool' are given training commensurate with their career aspirations. Their performance is appraised annually and those who are doing well receive a salary increase and perhaps a bonus. Those who are not placed for a period longer than 135 days (just over half of a working year) are reluctantly 'let go'. Despite this somewhat sad end to some people's careers, it seems more humane than the corporate blood-letting that has taken place over the past decade.

In some exceptional cases even middle managers are making something of a comeback after often being in the front line of the redundancy stakes. Not in their former role as the filter or amplifier of information, depending on whether it was going up or down the company hierarchy, but as a coach or mentor. This role can be fulfilled with one or more senior executives, with a group of employees or with an entire team. On the face of it, this role makes sense as middle managers have a balanced view of the company, positioned as they are (or were) neatly half-way between the boardroom and the shopfloor. Because of their experience, usually obtained in working their way up through the hierarchy, they know what works, and what doesn't, and the difference between a minor glitch and the first sign of an impending crisis. This kind of experience is proving to be attractive again – even on a part-time consultative basis.

All told, there is a growing role for training and development, whether it be in rolling out a multi-skilling programme, helping better performers to develop into broader roles or teaching ex-middle managers the fundamentals of coaching, mentoring and facilitating. Standing back and taking an impartial view of downsizing and its after-shocks, it seems to us that more, not less, training is required.

OUTSOURCING

Outsourcing is sometimes seen as an extension of downsizing. It accomplishes many of the same things; it disposes of people (a company's most priceless assets?); it reduces direct costs (pleasing the accountants); it boosts the value of the company's stock (a 'reward' from the financial markets). It does one other thing that downsizing may not do – it eliminates not just people but their jobs too. It means sub-contracting to a third party one or more functions that a company no longer wants to do.

There is a variety of reasons why a company might choose to outsource:

○   Through extensive downsizing there may no longer be the necessary capability to perform these functions adequately.

○   Few companies can afford to be good at everything and, with (presumably) a finite budget, preference ought to be given to investing it in their core competencies, not shoring up non-core functions.

○   To be able to handle periods of peak demand. Although this is transient in nature, it doesn't make sense for a company to sustain a capacity sufficient to meet maximum demand.

○   For developing technologies such as IT, it may be cheaper to out-source the function than continuously maintain the expertise in-house.

If you are contemplating outsourcing find a company that's better at certain non-core things than yours. It may even be the best at one particular function in your local area. For example, if the company down the road is far better than you are at controlling debt, then why not farm out accounts receivable if it significantly improves your cash flow? If your sales force is equipped with company cars, do you really need a fleet management department or can you hand it over to someone else? Do you really need to maintain your own training and development? Property development? Health and safety? Catering? Cleaning? Security? Information technology? If these functions are not part of your core business it may make good business sense to outsource them. As with most business decisions, there are pros and cons to be weighed up first and, to help you, here are a few to consider.

Benefits of outsourcing

○   the requisite expertise can be hired at a time and level to suit you
○   the commitment is for a finite contractual period and price
○   the expenses cease at the end of the contract
○   if the specification is drawn up correctly the onus for compliance resides with the supplier
○   if the work is performed on-site, some of the supplier's expertise may transfer to your people, possibly rendering future contracts less expertise-dependent
○   time, effort and money which can be diverted to the business's core functions are saved.

Disadvantages of outsourcing

○   jobs and people are lost and the company shrinks, possibly losing status
○   the company loses knowledge and skills which will not be available to fall back on
○   no matter how watertight and detailed the contract, you are at the mercy of your supplier, whose people may not be prepared to 'go the extra mile' when necessary.

Outsourcing is one of the fastest-growing businesses there is today, with some companies reporting growth rates in excess of 30 per cent.

BUSINESS PROCESS REENGINEERING – BPR

Hammer and Stanton define reengineering as 'The fundamental rethinking and *radical redesign* of business *processes* to bring about *dramatic* improvements in performance'.[2] (Their italics.) BPR is unlike the pursuit of incremental continuous improvements to products and services which is the bedrock of TQM. There have been significant benefits for companies which follow the TQM principles. Table 12.2 in Chapter 12 which summarizes the experiences of some of the Baldrige winners testifies to this. In most cases these benefits have been accrued over a number of years of relentless improvements. Does BPR take this long? No. While the definition of BPR makes no reference to timescale, Hammer and Stanton argue that a BPR project should be delivering tangible results within a year, otherwise support and momentum will be lost.[3] BPR is not concerned with modifying existing processes, but rather, as the definition says, with 'fundamental rethinking and radical redesign'. Thus, if TQM is evolutionary, BPR can be considered revolutionary.

However, BPR is not new. We first came across it in the late 1960s, although it didn't have such a grandiose title then; in fact, it didn't have a title at all. At the time, we were working with a select group of engineering companies in the English Midlands. These companies were upgrading their computer systems to run on the recently announced IBM general purpose computer system, System 360 (named after the number of degrees in a circle). During a survey with user departments to find out what kind of application solutions they wanted, given the range of hardware and software announcements that accompanied System 360, one particular company went further than the rest. They asked themselves, 'What are the top five issues facing our business right now?' From this came answers such as:

1. 'The inordinate amount of time, effort and cost needed to turn a potential product from the initial design to the prototype stage.'
2. 'The inordinate amount of time, effort and cost to turn . .'
3. 'The inordinate amount of time . . .', and so on.

Even three decades ago this company realized that 'time to market' and its associated cost was a basic competitive metric and that it needed to give it an increased focus if it wanted to stay ahead of the game. As a result they were one of the first companies outside of the aerospace-dominated west coast of America to install computer-aided engineering and manufacturing systems. Thirty years on, they still compete effectively at the highest levels worldwide.

In following the BPR approach world-famous names such as American Express, AT&T and Texas Instruments have achieved staggering results.[4] Lesser-known ones such as Vortex Industries of California, who repair and replace warehouse doors, and IVI Publishing, Inc. of Minneapolis have reaped commensurate rewards.[5] Sadly, not every venture into BPR results in benefits and, at present, the failures outweigh the successes. However, the reasons for success may well be implied in the statement by Frank Everett, the president of Vortex:

> We, those few of us who remained at headquarters, became coaches, showing people how to do things like repairing unusual doors, and providing training and expertise ... As branch managers became team leaders, our installers became customer service reps rather than foremen and helpers. We wanted the guys in the field with tools in their hands to become service oriented. They did. It worked.[6]

It can be easy to overlook the fact that not only are processes reengineered but, to a certain extent, so also are employees and managers. The implications of this are spelt out in the next chapter.

TEAMS AND EMPOWERMENT

To us these two elements go together: the concept of teams does not make sense unless it is allied with the reality of empowerment; otherwise why have teams? In fact they really would not be teams, merely groups of people that, while having a common purpose, did not have the authority to implement any of its own decisions. One of the best illustrations of this is that offered by quality circles, which were all the vogue in the 1970s and 1980s. Most quality circles failed to deliver what was required of them for three reasons:

1.   The additional skills they were taught were mainly limited to basic statistics and problem-solving techniques; there were no team skills.
2.   The conventional hierarchical command and control structure meant that the teams had no real authority.
3.   They were not given the total commitment at the highest levels that projects of this importance needed.

In contrast, the team approach as practised by the leading organizations of today is successful in terms of increased productivity and of the timeliness and quality of decisions. They achieve results because they are not bedevilled by the deficiencies of the quality circles, thanks to executive management who:

1.   have committed to the team approach and put in place the new structure and broad *modus operandi*
2.   have persuaded line management to 'let go of the reins', leaving the teams to make their own decisions – sometimes quite significant ones. Managers have become team leaders offering direction, guidance and advice

3.   have made sure that all of the skills and techniques needed to trans-
form a group of individuals into a highly effective team were available to be learnt when they were needed.

This results in a workforce operating as a collection of empowered, self-
directed work teams (SDWT), planning and executing projects which contribute directly to the overall business plans. An example from our own
experience, and one that has already been introduced in this book (see the
IBM case in Chapter 1), is discussed in detail in Chapter 14 under the heading of 'teamwork'.

LEARNING ORGANIZATIONS

There are numerous definitions of what a learning organization is and,
depending on which one you read, you either obtain an organization's or an
individual's perspective. We prefer the latter, so for your consideration we
offer the following: 'A learning organization is one which recognizes the
importance of the people within it, supports their full development and
creates a context in which they can learn.'[7]

In our view it is the leading-edge organizations, those at the forefront of
change, that are assuming the mantle of learning organizations. These
organizations are quite experienced in the ways of change and have probably survived its ramifications for a decade or more. There are certain hallmarks which distinguish these kinds of organizations from the rest and,
while not all companies exhibit all of them, the majority have most of them.

1.   The organization must have a strategy, with a vision of where it
wants to go, so that it can determine what it needs to learn in order
to get there. This is absolutely paramount.

2.   The organization must encourage multi-skilling, especially among
team members in a team-based organizational structure. Some companies do this quite formally, with specific courses and/or reading
assignments. Others prefer to let the skilled team members teach
the others. In fact, some companies recognize this teaching role as
being one of the signs of mastery of the subject – that is, a subject
matter expert. None of the learners are expected to exhibit the same
degree of mastery, but everyone in the team would have a good
grounding in each other's skills, knowledge and techniques. Also,
the ability to speak one another's language leads to better communications and understanding, and results in everyone making a
fuller contribution to the team's plans, projects and reviews. The
increased versatility also allows easier movement of people
between teams and there is not the same reliance on experts being
required all the time.

3. They encourage their workforce to go back to school. Some of them offer employees an annual allowance to take classes in whatever subject they like. Rover is one example of companies that do this (see Chapter 1), Motorola, Ashton Photo, Johnsonville Foods (all US) are others. The objective is to get people used to learning again; for many learning stopped when they left school or college.

4. Increasingly employees are being encouraged to take responsibility for the planning and acquisition of their own training and development. While their manager may have a say in what should be learnt and practised, the individual carries a large responsibility for its achievement.

5. This leads to the next factor – that employees can have two training or learning plans. The first concentrates on the core skills of the job, that is, those which must be developed over time if the employee is to progress within that role. The second is much wider, usually more demanding, certainly more personal than the first, and is aimed at the acquisition and development of lifetime or soft skills (see the previous section on SDWTs). Lifetime skills are the ones that a person can usefully employ as they move from job to job. They add value to a CV, as well as adding to that person's employability, and are discussed briefly in Chapter 14.

6. A further hallmark is a passion to innovate and a willingness to accept the consequences of innovations which don't work – in other words, failures. Punishing failure only stifles innovation, and people will spend so much time checking that their ideas won't fail that competition will leapfrog past them.

7. People who have been encouraged by their employers to use their intellect and vitality are precious social assets. Not only do they benefit themselves and their organization, but also the community and society outside their working environment. Thus the investment made by an organization in unlocking the true potential of its workforce will indirectly underwrite that organization's contribution as a good corporate citizen. This unexpected bonus generates considerable local goodwill, the ability to attract recruits, favourable publicity and a host of other intangible benefits.

In light of the foregoing, the phrase 'a job for life' now takes on a new meaning. Most people will have a job for life, but the chances are that it will be with several companies rather than just one.

THE KEY MESSAGES

O   Most companies don't grow by shrinking.

○   Downsizing means more training, not less.

○   Middle managers may have a new role to play, that of coaches or mentors.

○   Good project management alone does not guarantee success; there has to be excellent teamwork.

○   Just as important are 'soft skills' and personal attributes.

FOOD FOR THOUGHT

As the world business climate changes, so the rules of the competitive race are being rewritten. The effect is to make people and relationships more than ever the key to sustainable success. Only through deepened relationships with – and between – employees, customers, suppliers, investors and the community will companies anticipate, innovate and adapt fast enough, while maintaining public confidence.

Tomorrow's Company: An RSA Inquiry,
Gower, Aldershot, 1995

14

IMPLICATIONS FOR MANAGEMENT AND WORKERS

The process of acquiring 'add on', 'top-up' or totally new skills cannot be viewed as a one-off exercise. Indeed the time is close upon us when, for the most part, skills enhancement must become an ongoing process in the normal course of employment ... The continuing need for re-skilling, or whatever other label we may choose to attach to the acquisition of fresh or additional skills, is not confined to manual workers, technicians, office support staff or people in specialist employment. In industry and business this need extends also to managers.

> Mr (now Sir) Graham Day,
> then Chairman, Rover Group
> 1987 Annual Convention,
> The Institute of Directors

BACKWARD LINKS

○   Managing change (Chapter 2)
○   Skills and skills management (Chapter 4)
○   Organizational trends (Chapter 13)

FORWARD LINKS

○   Implications for educators (Chapter 15)
○   Skills and the human balance sheet (Chapter 16)

AIMS

Taking into account the global trends outlined in the previous chapter, to help the reader be aware of:

O   How management needs to change its approach to training of staff
O   The importance of culture
O   The growing need for individual ownership of learning
O   The importance of personality typing in a work context.

WHAT DOES THIS MEAN FOR NEW MANAGEMENT AND NEW WORKERS?

When society moved from agricultural employment to manufacturing, life changed for managers and for workers. Management moved from local command of a small workforce with strong human contact to more distant command of larger workforces used as adjuncts to expensive machinery. For workers, instead of open air work with hours dictated by the seasons, life changed to indoor work with hours dictated by machines which had to be kept working. Alvin Toffler[1] predicted a similar step change from the industrial society to a new techno-information society. He stressed the faster speed of this change compared with the change from agriculture to manufacturing and he foresaw its global nature.

The net result is that we now live in an environment with certain clear patterns and influences which new managers ignore at their peril.

O   Most workers in the Western world no longer operate machines but provide services, either face-to-face or via technology
O   Mass communications are swift and global
O   Information technology is all-pervasive
O   Competition is everywhere and is sudden in its effect
O   As a result of the above factors, customers are demanding, informed and fickle, and worse . . .
O   . . . what succeeds today is out of date tomorrow.

The important threads running through these trends are speed, adaptability, responsiveness and communications ability in the widest sense. These all depend decisively on people and their relationships with each other: manager/worker, worker/customer and worker/worker. The emphasis is on the person handling the transaction. Managers need to plan their own learning and their staffs' accordingly.

WHAT DIFFERENTIATES BUSINESSES?

In the recent past, entry barriers to markets were created by several factors: capital, availability of equipment, industry knowledge, personal contacts, experience and knowledge of staff, unique products, and so on. Toffler's 'Third Wave' has destroyed most of these. An 'alco-pop' drink appears on the UK market and takes a share from traditional products for the late-teens drinks market. Within months, there are half a dozen lookalike competitors, some from the other side of the world. The pub that serves these drinks gains a temporary trading advantage over its own local competitors by installing a satellite TV sports channel. Within weeks its competitors do the same. What then differentiates businesses? Capital strength is an obvious differentiator, yet the strongest companies can stumble or even fall into oblivion. Increasingly what differentiates businesses is the *sum value of the service or product they deliver.* For a car it is its image, its appearance, its performance, its reliability, the knowledge and sensitivity of the sales staff and the care and efficiency of the service staff. For a metropolitan light rapid transport system it is its frequency, reliability, cleanliness and convenience of route. We have not mentioned price yet; of course price is important and it has to be right. Yet the factors determining customer choice are much wider. The customer chooses on value and what provides this value is usually people. Technical features and building to a price can increasingly be copied. Selling to price can be counterproductive. Service levels fall, quality of service drops and rote-training substitutes for proper learning. What cannot be copied easily, or trained by rote, is the quality of staff designing, manufacturing and delivering your products to your customers.

WHAT SORT OF WORKERS DO WE WANT?

To raise the entry barrier to your market, think in terms of people. You, your management, your customers, your suppliers and your staff. If the differentiator is value, how can you make this higher than your competitors? As far as your staff are concerned, by enhancing teamwork, by making it easy for them to serve customers, by enhancing their sense of fun and loyalty, by rewarding them properly, and by releasing their natural resources, imagination and problem-solving ability. By recruitment, training or both, you need staff with:

○   sufficient basic skills of literacy, numeracy and 'skills for the job' (competencies in NVQ terms)
○   the right attitudes to customers, fellow workers, management and their company
○   teamwork skills
○   communication skills
○   interpersonal skills, used externally and internally
○   goal-directed or project skills, because clarity of objectives should be pervasive
○   willingness to accept authority
○   open-mindedness and adaptability
○   IT skills.

WHAT SORT OF MANAGEMENT DO WORKERS WANT?

In today's delayered organization, if staff are to take on more responsibility, work among themselves to objectives and answer a customer complaint and not just re-direct it, they require certain things from management. Here are some of the questions they might ask.

○   Values – what sort of an organization are we working for? What represents success round here?
○   Information – is it easy to find out what I need to know to do my job properly?
○   Resources – have I got the tools and systems I need to do the job, or if not, will management help me to get them or put obstacles in the way?
○   Communication – is it easy to talk without restraint with my managers, and do they listen?
○   Objectives – do I know clearly what I am supposed to achieve and how it fits in with the company's goals?
○   Measurement – is there a good feedback system so that I can agree with management how good a job I'm doing?
○   Reward – if I do a good job, do I get rewarded properly, promptly, fairly and visibly?
○   Training/support – if I need help to do my job better, will management help?
○   Understanding – how does my job fit in with the rest of the organization and what do the others do that helps everything to work?

It is the New Manager's job to anticipate these questions and to be pro-active in answering them. Company values and goals need to be stated prominently. At the factory visitor centre of 'Ben and Jerry's' – the highly successful ice-cream manufacturer in Vermont, USA – these are proudly displayed in the entrance hall; as you enter you cannot miss them. They include giving a percentage of profits to charity.

Information and resources need to be on tap. Management policy needs to reinforce this. The US consultancy Strategic Decisions Group adds to staff salaries a sum of money to spend on educational resources of their choice to help them in their job. The New Manager will keep staff fully informed of company objectives and will set staff their own objectives in line with these. The New Manager will ensure that communication is not just one-way and will have many ways of receiving suggestions. The New Manager will measure results and reward success, supplying support, coaching and training to enhance job performance.

REENGINEERING MANAGEMENT

Following the mixed success of reengineering referred to previously, James Champy investigated the reasons and presented his conclusions in *Reengineering Management.*[2] In a nutshell, he concluded that unless management itself is reengineered, the corporation cannot be. He listed the key questions that the actual practice of reengineering had thrown up, dividing them into four broad issues:

O   Purpose (What is this product for, this process, this task . . .?)
O   Culture (Can reengineering succeed in a culture of fear and mistrust?)
O   Process and performance (How do we get the desired processes and performance from our people? What is today's 'good manager' like?)
O   People (Who are the right people for us? How do we know? How do we find them, train them and motivate them?)

The rest of Champy's book expands on the needs of a reengineered management in these four areas, with plentiful case studies. Champy's four issues overlap some of the conclusions of our own experiences: objective setting, the importance of communicated aims, measurement, training and learning linked to business needs, and the importance of understanding people. The New Manager needs to address these areas.

CULTURE

Training is not learning. It may not even result in learning. You learn all the time, from everything around you, including the behaviour of your managers and your colleagues. We can call this the 'culture' of the organization. If this is one of blame and punishment, this engenders fear in the workforce. This makes it easier to obtain compliance and, if jobs are well specified and documented with good competence training provided, this can give the appearance of a well-run organization. But what if a worker makes an error in such an organization? It is swept under the carpet. If it involves several people, they collude to hide it. The ones who are the best at hiding mistakes are seen to make the fewest errors and get promoted. Staff perceive that it is good to be able to hide errors. Even worse, staff holding key information deliberately withhold it so that others make errors. Thus errors persist and progress stops.

Contrast this with a more open organization where there is trust. Management trusts staff and staff trust each other. Sharing information and teamwork are natural. If a mistake happens, there is no blame, but a joint focus on how it can be eradicated for the future. There is natural *kaizen*. In T. J. Watson's time at IBM, the story goes that a senior manager made a decision that cost the company $10 million. 'I suppose that means I'm fired then?' he asked. Watson replied, 'No way – we just spent $10 million educating you' . For the New Manager, a mistake is something natural that can happen. The important thing is to unearth it and stop it happening again. The opposite – a 'cover-up and blame' culture – stifles creativity and progress.

Risk

In an open environment, there is risk – risk that the mistake could be cata-strophic. Therefore there will need to be reasonable controls and proce-dures to guard against undesirable exploitation of on-the-job freedom. A passenger airline is operated under very stringent rules to avoid potential disasters, and risk is minimized almost to zero. Yet in some areas of busi-ness, the pace of change, the demands of customers and competition are such that risks need to be taken. In a large corporation there might be ten possible projects that should be undertaken, because five of them are going to work and increase business. What about the other five failures? We don't know which they are. If ten different managers each owned one of the pro-jects, five are likely to lose their jobs. Put yourself in the position of one of those managers. Are you going to risk your career at 50/50 odds?

New Managers will create a culture that not only tolerates risk but allows and calculates for it, even trains its staff about it. In Chapter 2 we advised project managers to list and manage project risks, like any other aspect of the project that needed managing. New Managers will do more than tolerate risk. They will see that their people understand it. Few people do, hence the column-miles of newsprint about food scares. It is sad that today's media and politicians make such issues black and white rather than explaining the risks properly. As a result, most of our population does not understand risk. If they did, they might never buy a National Lottery ticket again. They have a far greater chance of sudden death in the next 24 hours than winning the lottery. (For a current exploration of risk in our society, with a financial emphasis, see Peter L. Bernstein.[3])

How will New Managers train their workers?

The fundamental principle New Managers will adopt is that you do not train people; they learn. They learn about the company's culture, its risk tolerance and they absorb 'the way we do things round here' without going on courses. But can you train staff in company culture? Of course you can. Champy gives examples.[4] In IBM, 'company attitude and behaviour' was part of the entry marketing training programme. In our business practices sessions we used war stories to explain what to do and what not to do in customer situations. Cultures are different. One day after a 'what not to do' session, a trainee just recruited from a software competitor said, 'You've just described how I used to do my old job!' 'Why did you leave?' asked another.

New Managers should use the wider resources of their company and beyond to train staff. An assignment in another department, especially in the early days, can be a benefit to all. The learner understands first-hand what it's like on the other side; the other department gets fresh eyes and new ideas. An assignment outside the company can be even better. Apart from new ideas, the assignee may see jobs done a different way or not done at all. Anyone with a questioning mind will return ready to ask some fundamental questions.

Another form of training is the reward system. We explained earlier the link between reward and motivation. If the only reward is a monthly pay cheque, independent of job performance or value added to the company, it is not a motivator. The psychologist Herzberg found that pay was a 'dis-satisfier'. The New Manager will link reward to desired behaviour in a con-gruent fashion. Champy gives examples,[5] and the story of Julian Richer later in this chapter illustrates this.

As well as financial feedback, people are motivated by appraisal feed-back. Because pay is often a highly charged emotional issue, it is wise to keep development and appraisal feedback separate from pay rises. Imagina-tive *ad hoc* reward systems can combine both, as long as the emphasis is not wholly financial. The reward can have cash value, but may be in kind – short-term use of a prestigious car, a dinner for two or a home PC.

INDIVIDUAL RESPONSIBILITIES FOR LEARNING

Given enlightened new management, what of individuals within the organi-zation? How should they react to change? By responding in kind, by adding value to their organization, by cooperating, by accepting responsibility and exercising authority fairly, by trusting where trust is offered, by being flexible and imaginative, and by gaining more skills every day that passes: skills not only for performing their jobs better, but softer skills of focusing on customers, continuous improvement, understanding better the people around them and improving their two-way communication; and improving their basic skills of numeracy and literacy, as well as learning and using information technology skills. Each individual needs to keep a constant eye on their CV and not let it stagnate. In this they have a common aim with management, which is increasingly coming to the fore in the form of a personal development plan.

THE PERSONAL DEVELOPMENT PLAN – PDP

When organizations downsize, rightsize, delayer, empower or all four at once, there are two outcomes: skills and experience have shrunk and the people left have more to manage. Before long, work previously done by employees is sub-contracted, often to erstwhile employees. These no longer have the same psychological contract with the employer. Since they left, the better ones have gained fresh experience, they have paid for re-skilling and now they want to charge for it, in some cases substantially more than in their previous employment. The costs of learning from experience and upskilling cannot be hidden. They do not disappear when a company downsizes; they are a negative entry in the skills balance sheet. All in all, is there a gain or a loss from downsizing? The current fashionable theory is that downsizing has gone too far and what matters is competitive edge. We are back to people again and their development. And it rings true.

The interests of employees and of the organization merge in the personal development plan. Like any planning exercise (see Chapter 2) this needs an A-point, a case for action, a B-point and a monitored way to get there. Management should analyse the development needs of their staff in the light of business needs and plan the route with them. Part of the plan might be formal training, part of it on-the-job experience with monitoring, part of it might be experience outside the job or outside the company. *Fifty Ways to Personal Development*[6] gives a variety of ideas for such a plan. The role of the manager moves from command and control to that of a coach. A good coach will first assess the *status quo* and the requirements with the students, produce an action plan, measure the results, compare with the plan and adapt if required to produce the desired improvement. The skills needed from a good coach include empathy, analysis, facilitation and psychological support. Compare these with the traditional management skills of yester-year, of instilling obedience (even fear), 100 per cent control, a one-way command structure and a tidy ship for all outsiders to see.

TRAINING THE TRAINERS

Of all the different parts of the organization, the training department (if one still exists) needs to change most. The days of packaged vanilla-flavoured courses which the students are 'sent on' are over. This is why many organizations have closed training departments and outsourced training. In doing so they have discarded the baby with the bathwater. Training, when done properly and linked to the business, is a powerful source of change. One of us recently ran a short, tailored one-company training course for some computer engineers to improve selling skills. We prefaced it by a brief training needs analysis (TNA) to understand how the training was planned to improve business results. The first interesting thing was that business results started to improve before the course started. The mere act of asking questions focused effort on the company's desired objectives. Perhaps one way to cut training costs is not to deliver the course at all – merely to do the analysis. However, in this case we ran the course. During the TNA it emerged that some individuals were concerned about poor teamwork and some individuals harboured desires to enter sales. The course therefore had as part of its content some team exercises and it also presented selling as an honourable profession. Within a few days of the end of the course, the general manager remarked on the noticeable improvement in teamwork and one of the engineers transferred to sales.

Training can affect the business. It is not a useful-to-have that can be sub-contracted. When expressed more subtly as learning, it is absolutely fundamental to the organization. In the next chapter we shall investigate in more detail how organizational trends affect the training and development department, but for now, we shall spend a little time on the psychology of people, personality and teamwork. Of all aspects of the individual's development, these are increasingly becoming the most important factors. Let us start with a current trend – psychometric testing.

PSYCHOMETRIC TESTING AND PERSONALITY TYPES

Psychometric testing is becoming increasingly popular, often as a means of selection of staff, along with other tests, interviews and assessments. We have some reservations about the use of these tests for selection, but when used honestly, they have value for personal and team development. Psychometric testing aims to analyse a combination of fitness for job and personality type. There are various types of test, with roots going back to the psychologists Carl Jung and Raymond B. Cattell.[7]

Jung defined two attributes: extroversion and introversion, concepts that are now in wide currency, and four functions in opposing pairs: the rational functions of *thinking* and *feeling*, and the irrational functions of *sensing* and *intuiting*. The eight possible combinations of attribute and function define eight different personality types.

Jung recognized that such a simple model could not represent reality. His theory allowed for further distinctions, depending on the relevant dominance of certain functions or attributes. There are qualifications in two important aspects: first, 'pure types' represent extreme cases and there is wide variation within any one type; second, no single type is better than any other. Whilst Jung's models have been developed by later workers, notably Myers and Briggs who are well known for the Myers-Briggs Type Indicator (MBTI), the basic concepts and qualifications still stand. See, for instance, Thurbin[8] for a discussion of MBTI in the context of personality self-analysis in a learning organization. For another interesting view of Myers-Briggs techniques as related to native American Indian mysticism, see Loomis.[9]

Cattell took a different approach – the 'trait approach' – again one built on by later workers such as Gordon Allport. It has been developed for use as another type of personality test, often called '16PF' (16 personality factors). It can also be used in psychiatry to describe abnormal mental states such as chronic anxiety, as we shall see below. The traits in 16PF are listed in a bipolar form, each factor being scored by a set of self-analysis questions. The extremes are:

Reserved	—	Outgoing
Less intelligent	—	More intelligent
Affected by feelings	—	Emotionally stable
Humble	—	Assertive
Sober	—	Happy-go-lucky
Expedient	—	Conscientious
Shy	—	Venturesome
Tough-minded	—	Tender-minded
Trusting	—	Suspicious
Practical	—	Imaginative
Forthright	—	Shrewd
Self-assured	—	Apprehensive
Conservative	—	Experimenting
Group dependent	—	Self-sufficient
Casual	—	Controlled
Relaxed	—	Tense

Second-order composites can be derived, such as anxiety. A person with chronic anxiety would score high on the poles of:

O   affected by feelings
O   suspicious
O   apprehensive
O   tense

Besides applying such tests to individuals, they can also be applied to teams. One such set is the Team Management System.[10] Though there are some similarities with the Myers-Briggs approach, their methods are rather more directed to how people behave in a work situation and how much they enjoy doing what they do. TMS defines a set of nine key work functions common to all teams. These are:

Advising	Organizing
Innovating	Producing
Promoting	Inspecting
Developing	Maintaining
	Linking

The last function (linking) is usually the main responsibility of the team leader, but in a well-functioning team can, indeed should, be shared.

TMS then defines four key work preference factors, with bipolar ends. These are described in terms of how people:

form relationships	....	Extrovert	–	Introvert
handle information	....	Practical	–	Creative
make decisions	......	Analytical	–	Beliefs
organize work	....	Structural	–	Flexible

A series of questions then places a person at some point on each scale. The resulting combination can be compared to job preference. Margerison and McCann found a correlation between TMS types and job preference. For instance, someone who scored 'ECAF': extrovert, creative, analytical and flexible, correlated strongly with the 'promoting' function. Such a person might be at home in a marketing role, for instance.

This form of analysis has many uses. Apart from the obvious one of fitting round pegs into round holes, it can be used to examine the make-up of an existing team. By better mutual understanding, team members can improve working relationships. A promoter, for instance, does not always see eye-to-eye with an inspector. Their whole approach to work is different, yet a successful team needs both. Sometimes a team may be too unbalanced. A team of promoters would have a great time and be fun to be with but would never produce anything. A technique such as TMS can identify gaps in team members' work preferences. The team could fill these gaps by searching for people different from the existing team norm. Too often the opposite happens. 'Like' recruits 'like' when what is needed is the opposite.

INTERPERSONAL STYLES

In teams and in any dealings with colleagues, suppliers or customers, every-one shows a certain interpersonal style. Versatile people can vary theirs according to the situation and people they are dealing with. The Wilson Learning Corporation developed a simple model that has numerous uses.[11] The model has two dimensions that describe independent interpersonal characteristics: assertiveness and responsiveness. The dimensions have extremes of:

○   ASK vs TELL in the case of ASSERTIVENESS – do you assert yourself over others by asking or by telling them to do something?

○   CONTROL vs EMOTE in the case of RESPONSIVENESS – do you tend to be poker-faced, low response or animated, high response?

These two dimensions form the sides of a square, which can be divided into quadrants describing four basic interpersonal styles. These are:

ASK	+	CONTROL	=	ANALYTIC
ASK	+	EMOTE	=	AMIABLE
TELL	+	CONTROL	=	DRIVER
TELL	+	EMOTE	=	EXPRESSIVE

Each of the four styles displays certain characteristics. The Analytic likes facts, is systematic, but is reserved and slow to decide. The Driver likes results, is decisive, wants to be in charge, but can appear autocratic. The Amiable gets on with everyone easily, but is not pushy. The Expressive is the life and soul of the party, full of energy, but is often as well directed as a loose cannon aboard ship. All styles have their virtues and drawbacks.

Individuals and team members can gain greatly from an understanding of their normal interpersonal style, its strengths and drawbacks. By understanding the style of the person they are dealing with and using as much versatility as they possess, they can get on with others better and achieve better results. If the Analytic meets an Expressive, the Analytic needs to relax, wind down and have fun a bit more. The Expressive in return will approach the Analytic's style and value the Analytic's orderliness and attention to detail. This has obvious application to marketing situations. It can also be applied to other human contact, especially with teams. It can be used further as part of a selection process. For example, you would not recruit an Expressive as a bomb disposal officer.

The beauty of this model is its simplicity. It can easily be kept in the head. An individual's position within the square can be derived from questionnaires. It is possible, after some training and practice, to pinpoint the other person's position on the square by a few quick observations, even from a telephone call, by analysing the tone of voice, pace, level of detail, ask/tell statements, and so on. We would recommend the use of this model, or similar, as a basic skill requirement for anyone in an organization who deals with others. These days, that means just about everyone.

BRINGING IT ALL TOGETHER – TEAMWORK

An illustration from our own experience of how we brought management direction and teams to work together

THE CLASS A PROJECT

When we implemented a totally new Entry Marketing Education curriculum in IBM UK (see Chapter 1) we had less than three months to do it. The USA version had already been implemented at IBM's Education Centre in Atlanta, Georgia, so there was some experience available in running it. It was early January and a team of ten instructors and four administrative and support staff was in place. Although this was in reality a new team, some of its members had worked together for two years or more beforehand, so there was a certain degree of comfort with each other. The first class, imaginatively called 'Class A', was committed to start in the UK before the end of March. Class A was four weeks long and needed tailoring to UK needs. All of the material was totally new to us. It was seen to be, in the language of the time, a 'challenge'. The whole team rose to the challenge and succeeded. There are some powerful messages for project management in this story, but many more for teamwork.

THE PROJECT MANAGEMENT OF CLASS A

The first thing the team did was to meet for a project definition workshop (PDW) facilitated by an internal consultant (see Chapter 2). There were some voices which said that this would be a wasted day and that we needed to 'get on with it'. There was a sketchy plan of record involving trips to Atlanta late on to see Class A first-hand. But by clarifying our *specific* objectives for the UK Class A and then working out what *exactly* needed to happen by when, we realized that most of us needed to be in Atlanta within the week. The class had a complex structure of interrelated events and the priority was to understand this first-hand.

During the PDW the key step was to agree an overall definition of success; this was, 'To run an acceptable UK version of Class A between 28 March and 23 April, within budget'. 'Acceptable' was further defined as:

1.   producing student overall evaluations better than 2.5 (where 1 = best, 5 = worst)
2.   producing student learning gains comparable with those found in the USA
3.   acceptable in the opinion of the UK sales director (the sponsor) using feedback from line managers.

These tests mapped the first three levels of SATE evaluation and, furthermore, meant we could evaluate priorities. To take one example – course materials. First, Class A and its pre-course preparatory work made use of USA video and multi-media materials. There was clearly no chance of modifying these for UK use in the time. In any case the cost would have been enormous. Second, Class A made extensive use of a case study with many American names and places. The effort to turn this into a UK case study would have been prohibitive. We agreed to leave it as it was and explain the reason to the students. Despite fears that they would struggle with American geography, they completely accepted the explanation. If anything, they complimented us on making a sound business decision. The priority was to run the class. Some changes, however, were very necessary. Several terms in business law and accountancy differ between the USA and the UK, so these were changed. Some computer products were available in the USA but not yet in the UK. These changes had to be made, otherwise the content would have been incorrect. In this way, we analysed early on in the project what in generic terms definitely needed changing and what could be left alone. Event owners (see Chapter 9) made changes to materials as they went along, as part of the process of familiarizing themselves with the content.

These two examples of the use of good project management techniques, now being termed 'goal-directed project management' by some, will show why we devoted Chapter 2 to this topic. Without such an approach, the first Class A run in the UK would have been a disaster. As it was, it met all the evaluation criteria. Furthermore, because the PDW process is top-down and concentrates on milestones, key deliverables and clear responsibilities, the entire project plan fitted on to one sheet of paper. This plan was on every team member's desk and in their briefcase throughout.

TEAMWORK IN CLASS A

Good project management alone does not guarantee success. There had to be excellent teamwork. The full team had not met before the start of the project and, at first, rules were somewhat vague. On the other hand, the overall goal was abundantly clear and the project was reasonably well financed and resourced. The resources included, for example, an extensive refit to two floors of an existing building to make it suitable for back-to-back classes of 48 students each, with enough syndicate rooms for one-to-one role plays and enough PCs for immediate student access when needed.

The PDW did a great deal to enhance teamwork. Even though the agreed plan meant that half of the team had to stay in the UK and miss the delights of early spring in Georgia, all knew and accepted their roles and responsibilities at the outset. The six who went to Atlanta worked very hard. During the day they attended events; in their spare time they worked on the UK version of their own events. Every night the whole team met to compare notes and raise issues. Although the two authors of this book were the senior people in the team, each person took it in turn to chair the meetings and a different person took the minutes each night. Weekends were sacrosanct. We departed to various spots in Georgia according to personal interests. The team worked better than any we have worked with in our respective careers. Why?

LESSONS FOR TEAMWORK

This project showed us most of the key lessons for successful teamwork:

1.   As stated, the *goals were clear.* The PDW refined and agreed them.
2.   The project was *backed by management* and *properly resourced.*
3.   The team had authority – to get on with the job.
4.   The team members were willing to accept this authority.
5.   The team members had a variety of specialist skills (and person-alities) which complemented each other.
6.   Those skills were current, so that every team member had the respect of the others.
7.   All team members had basic skills of self-organization, the ability to chair meetings, to take minutes and to get on with others. Their personal IT skills varied, but the stronger readily helped the weaker when needed.
8.   Communications with management, within the team (separated as it was by the Atlantic) and with our US colleagues were open and excellent at all times.
9.   The team members displayed consistent personal qualities of trust, flexibility, integrity and resourcefulness.

The above list has very little to do with specific hard job skills, apart from items 5 and 6. At least as important in the list were project skills, and personal attributes and skills. We detect from our discussions with other organizations that this is a fast-increasing trend. This has a fundamental impact on how organizations train their own people, on how individuals look after their own careers, and on national education systems.

   Successful teamwork needs:

○   Clear goals
○   An agreed breakdown of goals into personal objectives and tasks
○   Management backing
○   Proper resources allocated
○   Authority delegated to the team
○   Acceptance of this authority by the team
○   Variety of current skills
○   Complementary personalities
○   Respect by the team for every member
○   Team members possessing basic organizational and IT skills
○   Open, fast and frequent communications within the team and with the outside world, including management
○   Strong personal qualities of all team members.

Meet all of these requirements and your team will work extremely well.

THE KEY MESSAGES

○   To raise the entry barrier to your market, you now need to think in terms of people.

○   Training, when done properly and linked to the business, is a powerful source of change.

○   Understanding people's styles, what motivates them and how they react under pressure is a little-practised but very powerful skill.

FOOD FOR THOUGHT

Julian Richer – the New Manager

Julian Richer has created a £50 million group of businesses from nothing.[12] The best known is 'Richer Sounds', a chain of hi-fi retailing shops – said to be the most profitable in the UK, with the highest sales per square foot of any retailer in the world. The way he created and manages this company is a good example of James Champy's 'Reengineered Manager' at work.

Richer has two obsessions – customer service and looking after his staff. One per cent of his profits go into a 'hardship fund' for unexpected staff crises. After five years of service, his staff can use his country home for holidays. Richer reasons that if businesses expect staff to be loyal, they in turn should be loyal to, and care for, their staff. Too often we hear contrary reports of staff who are demoralized and demotivated by cuts and down-sizing exercises, poorly thought out and badly communicated and implemented.

Richer blends his aims for high customer service and staff morale with competitions where the best branches have temporary use of a prestigious car. His simple motivational philosophy is, 'If you want good service, then reward good service'. He uses 'mystery shoppers' who call on stores anonymously and ask four questions. If staff get them right, they are rewarded with £50. Thus staff look forward to 'mystery shopper' visits. Contrast this with 'mystery shopper' schemes where branches are called on or phoned anonymously, with subsequent collection of branch statistics on comparative waiting times, courtesy and quality of information. The ones at the bottom of the table are punished and 'mystery shopper' visits are dreaded.

Richer makes extensive use of suggestion schemes to support mission statements that might seem ethereal. He stresses the importance of:

○   making schemes easy to use
○   replying to all suggestions quickly
○   encouraging groups to meet to implement good suggestions
○   giving small but frequent rewards

○   avoiding too much concentration on purely financial impact
○   putting the ideas to use
○   measuring and publishing the results.

He gets some 20 ideas a year for every employee – a phenomenal outcome in what is apparently a simple, even mundane, business. Not only does this 'get the ideas out of the heads of all employees' as Japanese practice under-lines, but it makes them feel valued and listened to. Too many companies think of their staff as financial objects to be used rather than as positive sources of information and ideas that can help and develop the company.

Another source of input, this time on attitude, is Richer's employee survey. This is anonymous, aimed at improvement and reinforcing the culture of a fair management that looks after its people. Richer can thus measure not only business results but morale. He also measures customer complaints, even encourages them. How many organizations brush them under the carpet? The number of complaints at Richer Sounds are few, yet interestingly, frequency of complaint correlates negatively with good branch morale and success. The better branches get fewer complaints.

Richer is passionate about communications, not only by surveys and idea schemes, but by peer get-togethers, including training sessions and simply 'management by walking about'. We know from direct experience how valuable 'MBWA' can be. Yet the manager who does it must be credible, sincere and must *listen*. However good an ideas scheme or opinion survey, there is no substitute for direct contact with staff at all levels, provided there is the *trust* that permits frank feedback.

Richer is passionate about values. We mentioned trust above. He stresses too the need for senior managers to show humility, to admit errors, most of all to show integrity – 'the bedrock of our culture'. If asked for a 'business case' for his values and practices, he refers to the theft rate in his shops which at 1 per cent is half the industry average. On a turnover of £30 million, this is a saving of £300 000 a year. In addition, there is low absenteeism and tremendous staff loyalty. He claims only one unwanted leaver in 18 years of operation.

As well as creating and communicating values, and caring for staff and customers, Richer stresses the need for an effective manager to show leader-ship and to be commercial. He shows a healthy attitude to some currently fashionable views of empowerment. He is sceptical about the need for, and the possibility of, 'every cashier becoming a manager'. He says that for most jobs, there is only one best way to do it, and the trick is to have a way to find it and then to do it all the time. By contrast we have heard managers claim 'My people are empowered' when what they really mean is 'My people have no direction from me, no specific personal or work objectives (until after the event, when someone has to be blamed for failure or error) and, if they need anything, they have to ask me for it.' This is not empowerment, it is MBA, 'management by abdication'.

In summary, Richer's style addresses most of the implications of the key issues to be faced by Champy's 'Reengineered Manager':

    Purpose
    Culture
    Process and performance
    People

It blends values with care of its people and customers in a way that constantly improves performance across the business. It is small wonder that Richer is developing a second career consulting to chief executives of some of Europe's largest organizations. They want to know how he did it.

15

IMPLICATIONS FOR EDUCATORS

The only way we can beat the competition is with people. That's the only thing anybody has. Your culture, and how you motivate and empower and educate your people, is what makes the difference.

Robert Eaton, CEO of Chrysler,
Fortune, 13 December, 1993

BACKWARD LINKS

○   The framework for change (Chapter 1)
○   Managing change (Chapter 2)
○   Analysing learning needs (Chapter 3)
○   Skills and skills management (Chapter 4)
○   Organizational trends (Chapter 13)

FORWARD LINKS

○   Skills and the human balance sheet (Chapter 16)

AIMS

The aims of this chapter are to help the reader to:

○   Appreciate the changing role of the training function in supporting the organization's plans
○   Recognize the emergence of a learning culture and the individual's responsibility for self-development
○   Understand how secondary and higher education can affect the role of training and development.

INTRODUCTION

In Chapter 13 we looked at how some of the organizations are responding to today's competitive environment, and the moves they are making to survive or give themselves an advantage in their market sector. In Chapter 14 we developed our views about the implications of these trends for managers and workers, in terms of new expectations, relationships, and what can be called 'personal reengineering'. In this chapter we look at the implications for educators, initially for training and development, and then for schools and universities. How schools and universities provide education has a profound effect on the future role of training and development.

Most of the trends we discussed previously – reengineering, teamwork, learning organizations and so on – have an impact on T & D. The exception seems to be downsizing which, on the face of it, does not appear to impact T & D at all. However, this is not the case. The aftermath of downsizing can have a considerable effect, as we showed in Chapter 4. The additional training is 'business as usual' – replacing the skills that have just walked out of the door by further training of the remaining employees. Thus, T & D has not had to develop any new courses or learn any new skills.

It is when we consider the other trends that the need for T & D to broaden its horizons becomes obvious. The trends discussed in Chapter 13, and developed in Chapter 14, have introduced phrases such as 'business process reengineering', 'empowerment', 'time-based competition', 'learning organizations' and so on. T & D has to understand this new world if it is to support the organization's plans and play an active role in achieving them. The question that T & D needs to answer is – how?

HOW CAN TRAINING AND DEVELOPMENT SUPPORT THE NEW WORLD?

Needs analysis begins with executive management articulating the primary business objective; typically one such as, 'Implement a time-to-market (TTM) reduction programme, saving at least 25 per cent in the first year.' This follows the 'SMART' principle for objectives (see Chapter 2): specific, measurable, achievable, realistic and timed. Furthermore, it implies an ongoing effort beyond the first-year checkpoint. Translating a business objective such as this into a corresponding performance objective poses some interesting questions for management, such as:

1.   What exactly is time-to-market?
2.   In your particular market sector, what is the shortest TTM?
3.   Where are you by comparison?

4.   If competition have an advantage, how have they achieved it?

5.   What could you do to begin to close the gap?

The answers are equally intriguing. Question 1 really demands a definition that is as precise and unambiguous as possible. The answers to questions 2 and 3 are purely numeric; hence the need to be precise about the definition of TTM, so that when the organization is comparing its TTM with others it is comparing like with like. This comparison will show how far behind it is, if indeed it is behind. This is useful information, but it does not indicate what should be done. This comes from the answers to questions 4 and 5, 'How do they do it?' and 'What could we do now?', for these help to formulate the learning requirements. The answer to question 4 could include, for example:

○   Teamwork; in a manufacturing company this could mean that engineering, production, suppliers, marketing and the customers are all involved with bringing a product to market, operating as a cohesive group. This team approach saves time by reducing the delays and confusion caused by the normal sequential hand-offs from one department to another in the standard end-to-end TTM cycle.

○   Reengineering; teamwork can help shorten the TTM cycle as we have explained in Chapter 13, but time can also be saved by examining and reengineering key, internal processes. For example, if only 5 per cent of the time is actually spent 'cutting metal' in a manufacturing order fulfilment cycle, what is the other 95 per cent of the cycle time spent on? Attacking these areas can result in significant outcomes, such as Toyota's 'five-day car' and Motorola's 'one-day pager', discussed in Chapter 1. Chapter 12 has other examples of what can be achieved in this area.

○   Benchmarking; the American Productivity and Quality Center described benchmarking as 'The practice of being humble enough to admit that someone is better at something, and being wise enough to try to learn how to match and even surpass them at it'.[1]

As T & D weighs up these answers it will realize that it does not offer courses in teamwork, BPR, benchmarking and the like. In fact, if it was to conduct a benchmark of the T & D functions in other companies, it may be surprised at the range of topics that are being offered, such as:

problem-solving	brainstorming	teamwork
time management	effective meetings	effective leadership
presentation skills	basic statistics	project management
budget planning	networking	understanding interpersonal styles
benchmarking	BPR	writing skills

We would consider some of these subjects as skills, whilst others can best be described as tools or processes. For example, making effective presentations is a skill. The basics can be demonstrated, explained and learnt via a normal, two-day experiential classroom course using skilled instructors and video equipment. On the other hand, basic statistics is a tool used extensively in quality systems and can be learnt from a book. Brainstorming is a process, not a skill, and it has to be approached differently. To appreciate T & D's role calls for an understanding of the process itself.

BRAINSTORMING

Brainstorming was first used in the 1930s for developing a group's creativity and is a method for generating a lot of ideas in a short period of time. It sounds easy. Give a group the objective of, say, developing new ways of improving customer satisfaction and put them in a room big enough for them to relax and cogitate in. Without guidance, what happens? Usually a certain amount of chaos, puzzlement, resentment, impatience from the ones who want to complete the task in the shortest possible time, silence from those who are the quiet thinkers and hate being in the spotlight, and so on. Eventually, and it could be later rather than sooner, some semblance of order might emerge from the chaos and there may well be a number of suggestions put forward to improve customer satisfaction. However, this is not a particularly effective process and the chances are that the group fumbled their way fairly inefficiently towards a solution. In contrast, they could have run it as a brainstorming session.

Brainstorming is a process comprising a series of linked steps, which should be gone through in a specific sequence. Certain ground rules apply at each step and to the entire process, and these must be accepted and adhered to by all of the participants. Because of the need to follow the rules, and because of the number of participants – any number from, say, 6 to 16 – there is a need for an independent guide, cum adjudicator, cum coach, cum leader. Such a person is called a facilitator and a competent one can get a group of people to generate good, solid ideas in a relatively short space of time. One of us ran such a session for a golf club, the objective being to develop ideas to raise extra income. The group were the members of the council and, as they were elected on a yearly basis, were far from being a team. However, in half an hour 27 ideas had been suggested and logged. One hour later these had been reduced to a shortlist of five, and within a further 30 minutes they had been whittled down to two solid ideas. These two were simple to action, could be implemented without delay or significant resource and were deliberately aimed at 'low-hanging fruit' – that is, easily attainable results. The council had the goal – extra income; they also had in their heads the possible solutions; it was the job of the facilitator to bring the two together.

ELECTRONIC BRAINSTORMING

The development of information technology (IT) has seen it applied to brainstorming to give what we call electronic brainstorming (EB). EB is a suite of computer programs that link desktop personal computers (PCs), or laptops, to a master terminal operated by a facilitator. The participants sit at the PCs, which may be in the same room, different rooms or even on different continents. At any time the facilitator can display on all of the PCs the agenda, or a statement defining the issue under discussion, or a consolidated list of all suggestions grouped by theme, or the results of a voting round, and so on. The main advantages of EB over a conventional brainstorming session are:

○ the group does not have to be in the same room in order to participate in a session

○ the participants do not even need to be on-line at the same time. The power of the software and networking allows the participants to log-on at a time that suits them, alleviating the impact of different time zones across the world

○ the computer software takes care of minutes, suggestion lists, voting results, action lists, and their like

○ in a 60-minute meeting everyone can 'talk' for 60 minutes without interruption, and the keyboard speedster (who may not be very effective in face-to-face situations) gets to 'say' the most.

Solutions such as these are used in government, commerce, industry, healthcare, and their like, not only for brainstorming but also for negotiating, teambuilding, strategic planning, needs analysis and Baldrige self-assessment, to name but a few. Former US President Jimmy Carter is reputed to have remarked at the 1993 Higher Education Conference that, 'This kind of tool (EB) was the best tool for conflict resolution that he had ever used, and that he wished he had had such a tool when he was in the White House.'

To run an effective EB session the facilitator needs the additional attributes of being computer-literate, to have good keyboard skills and to possess a clear and concise writing style, as this may well be the prime mode of communication with the various members of the team.

TRENDS IN TRAINING

From the foregoing discussions we can begin to see one of the emerging roles for today's training department – facilitating group or team sessions. This is not training in the accepted sense; after all, what have the participants learnt? As it happens, something very important. Together they can be very creative and productive, and the next time they have a team problem to solve they will use a facilitator. But what is facilitation, and what does a person need to be a facilitator?

Facilitation and facilitators

Facilitation can be described as, 'Providing a structure to help teams (and individuals) develop *their* solutions to *their* problems by directing and channelling *their* knowledge, skills and expertise'. Or put another way, 'Taking a team from where they are, to where they want to be'. Nowhere in either of these descriptions is it implied that the facilitator knows of, or has any vested interest in, either the problem or the potential solutions. In fact it is best if the facilitator knows nothing about either. Facilitation does not enforce or impose anything on to teams, or their individual members. Neither does it require the team to be trained in, or be familiar with, the techniques used by the facilitator.

The key point is that a brainstorming session – note that it is not called a course – is organized and run by a person called a facilitator, not by someone called an instructor or trainer. The participants are not called 'trainees'; there is no end-of-course report. The facilitator is working with a peer group and all of them are striving for a positive outcome.

Can anyone be a facilitator? This is a little like asking can anyone conduct an orchestra? The answer is 'Yes, but . . .'

What are the characteristics of an effective facilitator? An effective facilitator must:

○   have credibility within the organization
○   be willing and able to persevere against the odds
○   understand group dynamics and the importance of personal styles
○   be willing to accept, even promote, a certain degree of chaos
○   revel in the success of the session and the group
○   be comfortable dealing with all levels within the organization (the highest-level team could be the board of directors)
○   exhibit leadership qualities
○   be flexible
○   be impartial
○   have a sense of humour
○   learn from the experience.

What does a facilitator do? Depending on the type of session a facilitator will:

○   use a preferred process or structure
○   lead the group through the various phases
○   ensure effective time management
○   record the key points, including actions arising

○   use a decision-making process based on consensus or democracy
○   set expectations and focus on results.

What are the benefits of facilitation?

○   sessions can be run on-site as and when needed, with the minimum
         of equipment; only the facilitator need travel
○   increased productivity of the group and the individual
○   increased morale by completing a potentially difficult task effec-
         tively
○   better understanding of each other's *modus operandi* and personal
         style
○   increased synergy, and a 'can do' outlook.

There are certain types of people who are better suited to this role than
others. One of these is the experienced instructor who is already aware of
the role of group dynamics and the group's need for fairly formal procedures if chaos is not to reign supreme. Line managers, general managers
and executive managers can also prove effective facilitators. In general,
though, facilitators have tended to come from one of two sources: internally
from the T & D function or externally from specialist agencies. Which one of
these is the most appropriate for an organization will depend to a great
extent on how many facilitated sessions will be requested. The more the
word spreads about the effectiveness of such sessions the greater the
demand will be.

Learning and learners

At the individual level there is a trend for employees to have two development objectives, as mentioned in Chapter 13. The first relates to the
development of the core competencies needed by employees to progress
within their jobs; that is, to progress from 'apprentice' to 'expert'. This
is business as usual for the training function, the employees and line
managers. The second relates to the development of the non-core lifetime
skills such as presentation, writing, demonstration, and face-to-face skills,
time management, effective meeting skills, project management, networking
and so on. These objectives will have been developed jointly by the
employees and their line managers, and result in a mixture of requirements,
together with an expectation of 'training on demand', or 'just-in-time training'. This all adds up to a wider spread of training requirements, delivered
increasingly at the individual level, at a time and place to suit each person.
These conditions can be met in a variety of ways, including:

○   learning centres, organized to accept *ad hoc* bookings for a range of
         topics

O   interactive multi-media computer packages for PCs, possibly using CD-ROM
O   external training sources, especially those offering accreditation or certification. This 'proof of satisfactory completion' can earn credits towards academic or vocational qualifications, as well as adding value to an individual's CV.

For individual members of self-directed work teams there is the need for specific team skills. These include teamwork, problem-solving, BPR, benchmarking, budget planning and management, and so on. Teams will also need just-in-time training, and it is up to the training function to ensure that the relevant expertise and delivery vehicles are available when needed.

Trainers themselves have development plans and initially they will almost certainly be seeking external courses that result in accreditation, in order to give them credibility when being a facilitator for their peers. A few of them, again probably experienced trainers, will be seeking accreditation to train others within their own organization to facilitate events – 'Teach the teachers' accreditation.

And it should go without saying that measurement and evaluation procedures should be established to ensure that all of these learning events, whether directed at the individual, teams or trainers, are contributing to the organization's plans.

IMPLICATIONS FOR SECONDARY AND HIGHER EDUCATION

SCHOOLS

Organizations are changing; schools prepare children for life in organizations, so they need to change too. In the UK, the publication of league tables of test results at first created consternation. Quite rightly, teachers pointed out that these tables measured quality of output, without regard to quality of input. The concept of 'added value' gained currency. By 1996, four 'Key Stages' were defined, corresponding to ages 5–7, 7–11, 11–14 and 14–16, with national tests and assessments at the end of each age range. In 1996, a further move was announced to provide for a national 'baseline assessment' for five-year-olds. This will complete the picture for today's formal academic education system and will allow for a much better evaluation of added value. So some changes are already under way.

Even with only partial evidence available of progress throughout the age ranges, some UK schools made notable progress following publication of 'league table' results. It is interesting to see what led to this progress. An Essex school improved its GCSE A–C grade results from 4.5 per cent to 18 per cent over a three-year period. Neither are startlingly high figures, but half the school's 11-year-old intake typically had a reading age of nine or below. The progress was the significant fact and was due to several initiatives. A mentoring scheme was introduced, with a teacher assigned to every GCSE student, providing both pressure and support, and maintaining close parent contact. Students had goals and action plans with dates and regular reviews. Staff gave up out-of-school time for study sessions; homework was emphasized; examination techniques were taught.

A Northern England school in a deprived housing estate achieved similar success by adopting a plan that involved staff, pupils and parents more closely and set clear targets. There was strong leadership from the headteacher and a lucid school development plan, communicated to all staff and laying out specific targets for every staff member. There was homework every night and a work log for every pupil, out-of-hours classes overseen voluntarily by staff, new school rules and the re-introduction of school uniforms. In addition, school management, supported by the governors, brought a £200 000 budget deficit into balance in three years, and increased pupil numbers from 620 to 840. By mid-1996 there was a waiting list for entry to the school.

A school in the English Midlands in a similar industrial area increased its GCSE A–C grades from 14 per cent to 24 per cent over five years. The driving force was the raising of expectations. It was 'OK' for a teacher to say to the pupils 'Those of you who go to university will come across Chomsky'; pupils learned that higher education was an entirely appropriate route. This school also introduced 'academic tutoring' – provision to each GCSE pupil of a mentor who was a staff member, providing advice and monitoring coursework. Parental involvement was secured by a signed promise to attend parents' evenings and check on homework completion. Pupils had a written record of achievement, covering not only homework, but attendance, punctuality and meeting targets.

The threads that run through these and other examples of successful schools are:

O   raising expectations of pupils, parents and staff
O   clear targets for pupils and teachers
O   school, pupil and parent involvement
O   a mentoring system
O   strong leadership by the headteacher
O   shared vision, values and goals
O   monitoring of progress
O   an orderly, positive and purposeful learning environment
O   positive reinforcement
O   staff continue to be learners themselves.

Do any of these themes sound like echoes from earlier parts of this book? How many schools could provide a similar list of their own?

SCHOOLS AND WORK

We have seen how what is basically good, enlightened modern management can improve the success of schools in quite unpromising environments. But what about the content of what is taught? What about the pupils' personal qualities? What do employees need? Increasingly, employers cry out for improved basic skills of literacy and numeracy. They also ask for imagination and skills of communication and influencing. Yet schools are in danger of training their pupils merely to pass examinations. University admission tutors look for 'A' level passes, because that is their predictor of degree success. But these level 2 tests – 'A' levels and university degrees – are inconsistent with level 3 needs – employers' work requirements.

In the 1996 UK National Curriculum, 20 per cent of the time is in theory unallocated ('options time'?) and can be used at will by schools. How can schools use this time to provide the right sort of 'mulch' to encourage their pupils to grow beyond the narrow confines of exam topics? For surely, it is the duty of any teacher not just to take pupils through examinations, but to kindle sparks of curiosity into flames of passion for knowledge and use of imagination. In terms of de Bono's d-lines, the more d-lines etched on the memory-surface of the brain, the more possible connections between them, the more surprises, the more fun. Knowledge builds on itself. The more you learn, the easier it is to learn more. If, as an English speaker, you know French, it is that much easier to learn Spanish. If you have in addition a little Italian, you can read Catala (Old Menorcan) with minimal effort. You may be amused by the Catala word 'boinder', when you find it means 'bow-window', an architectural feature found outside the UK almost only in the Menorcan capital of Mahon (which incidentally lent its name to 'mayonnaise'). But why are English architectural features found in the Balearic Islands? When were bow-windows first popular? What were the English doing then in Menorca? Why? We soon move from linguistics to history. All it takes is basic knowledge, making connections and curiosity, attributes which employers increasingly prize. This is a significant factor behind the pressure to widen the narrow three-subject 'A' level system. But in the meantime, what can schools do?

The obvious move is to encourage any steps to link school life with work. The simplest is a short spell of work experience, typically two weeks. Organizations such as Business Education Partnerships work with local Training and Enterprise Councils (TECs) and local authorities to provide school pupils with such assignments. A 14-year-old boy recently learned that a misplaced decimal point could cost nearly £50 000. He should have entered £500.00 into the calculator and almost lost his employer £49 500. Another reported back, 'You get treated as an adult. You get respect. They really listen to what you have to say'. A low achiever turned out to be a wonderful primary school assistant and, in helping difficult children, at last found something she could excel at. Such links with business can be exploited further. Teachers can be seconded to businesses, and business managers seconded to teaching. Business people can help with coaching school pupils in interview skills, CV preparation and career planning. The interview can be made lifelike by asking the pupil to turn up at the business's address for an imagined post. Even if pupils learn only that they need to telephone in good time for directions and to arrive promptly, appropriately dressed, they will have learnt something significant from an apparently simple experience.

Schools need not rely on outside businesses for work experience. In the USA, a growing number of schools are being run by private firms, which have to meet agreed targets such as test scores or attendance. In one such private sector scheme, the Edison Project, students will run the cafeteria and administration, and will clean the school. In this scheme, children can start school in daycare facilities soon after birth, progressing via kindergarten and high school, to finishing college on the same campus. The scheme challenges most assumptions concerning conventional education.

A scheme in the UK, the planned 'Optimum Primary School' in Manchester, turns pupils into teachers. There are no set classes or class teachers in its design; children learn from projects. The teacher checks that the project is reasonable for the child, then provides initial teaching or resources as required. The child can learn from a peer who has more knowledge or experience, or can go back to the teacher for help. There is no set school day; no bell rings at the end of a lesson to interrupt concentration; there need be no school holidays. If this school is turned into reality, it will have reengineered primary education in the UK.

CHANGE IN SECONDARY EDUCATION

Sir Ron Dearing's report[2] recommends some changes in secondary education in the UK, especially in the 16–19 age group, but with implications for earlier years. Besides proposing a unified framework for vocational and academic qualifications, it proposes the relaunch of the National Record of Achievement (NRA). This was introduced in 1991 as a recording and planning vehicle for personal learning – a form of personal development plan as in Chapter 14. The NRA links readily into the workplace and can be linked to an Investors In People programme. It could have a major impact on developing skills via planning and managing the student's own learning.

In addition to basic achievement in literacy and numeracy, including mental arithmetic, the needs identified by Dearing from employers and higher education authorities included:

○   competence in IT as a lifetime skill
○   skills in working with other people
○   presentational skills
○   problem-solving skills
○   self-management of lifelong learning.

These all imply and lead to positive progress in learning. Yet the current examination system is designed as a set of hurdles. Many fall at each one and their education ends there; only the best survive. The system needs to be altered to one where the basic assumption is that learning is continuous.

Learning is also broad. Dearing proposes wider use of the GNVQ/NVQ structure to improve performance across the range of all pupils in the three key skills of communication, application of number and information technology. All relevant teaching institutions should provide opportunities for pupils to develop these skills and have them recognized. Universities and employers should look for formal evidence of attainments in these skills at the selection stage. Finally, teachers themselves need development in order to teach them. For the personal and interpersonal skills also demanded by employers, institutions need to provide opportunities for practice, by oral presentations to peers, structured discussions, and projects and group work that will also develop teamworking ability.

In summary, the school system needs a wider definition of 'achievement'. The days are over when the brightest people rose to the top and the rest, under-educated and unambitious, had a job of some sort. The world was stable; there was enough income around for all to enjoy life. For most, this enjoyment came outside work. The world has changed; jobs are no longer there for the untrained, less able people. Even the bright ones have little job security. Dearing's proposals will do much, if accepted, to provide youngsters with a wider set of skills and a better base for improving them as their lives go on.

PATHWAYS TO ADULT AND WORKING LIFE

The pattern is set even earlier than the 16–19 age group. The drop-out rate at age 16 is frightening and so are the social consequences. Most schools would agree that a significant aim is to 'release the potential' of their pupils. Yet they would be hard pressed to define what this actually means in specific terms. In 1993, a pilot project 'Pathways to Adult and Working Life' was started with the aim of addressing this. It was led by businesspeople and funded by the Department for Education and Employment. Its starting point

1. Learners achieve full potential within the whole curriculum by having:
   o a range of qualifications at appropriate levels
   o a current Record of Achievement and Individual Action Plan
   o the ability to apply knowledge, skills and understanding gained to familiar and unfamiliar situations
   o competency in numeracy, literacy and oracy in the contexts of daily transactional use and technical use
   o the ability to store and retrieve information

2. Learners have knowledge, skills and understanding in relation to adult and working life, which include:
   o valuing lifelong learning
   o awareness of necessity to be adaptable in a rapidly changing world
   o self-motivation
   o knowledge and understanding of further and higher education, training and job pathways, qualifications, assessment procedures, different culture systems and routines
   o knowledge and understanding of the economy, wealth creation, the organization and culture of industry and business
   o ability to accurately recognize and record achievement and weaknesses and to plan accordingly
   o knowledge of where to seek advice and assistance
   o understanding that with rights go responsibilities

3. Personal and interpersonal skills:
   o awareness of strengths and weaknesses
   o can record and evaluate own achievements and preferences
   o can review and plan accordingly
   o well presented, knows how to take care of oneself
   o enthusiastic and determined
   o well-developed ethical code
   o be enterprising
   o knowledge of the range of learning styles which are most effective for them
   o can work on one's own
   o plan and manage time and energy
   o think independently
   o carry through an agreed responsibility
   o make decisions
   o set targets
   o appreciate the importance of teamwork and the value of contributions from self and others, at home, at work and in the community

4. Socially confident:
   o has developed self-esteem
   o understand and work with other people's strengths and weaknesses
   o can ask appropriate questions
   o can work with people in authority and act appropriately for the common good when in authority
   o can contribute to teamwork

FIGURE 15.1   Student outcomes at 16

was to define the outcomes a school wants its pupils to achieve at age 16. From this, a framework can be drawn up to facilitate improvement, with 'Key Stage' statements within each age group. The eventual student outcomes at age 16 are shown in Figure 15.1

The pilot is in operation at three schools. The schools like it because it tells them what to do and why in a manageable way. There is more emphasis on tutoring and guidance. Teachers look for a wider menu of achievement than before. Much of this is new to them, so they need their own skills to be updated, in mentoring, assessing and communication. Sadly, other schools say, 'We think this is right, but we haven't time to do it. There is no space in the curriculum and it could detract from our academic results.' If the aim is 'A' level points in the league table and university places, who can blame them? These are *their* level 3 and level 4 objectives after all.

UNIVERSITIES

If the only significant record of achievement is a set of academic examination grades, what can universities do except use these? There is some emphasis on the interview, if it actually happens, but the main criterion is 'A' level grades. After 14 years of education, the hopeful undergraduate's future depends on a few capital letters. Small wonder that 'A' level results time is highly stressful for such students (now a third of the age group) and their families. These few letters are the linkage between secondary and higher education. This tenuous link typifies the lack of a SATE-type structure in the UK's current education system. Each part of the system operates on its own, when what is needed is a cohesive whole, with clarity of objectives and assessments leading through to entry into working life and beyond. It will not be easy to reach this, but it should be the aim, and any pilots in this direction or initiatives such as Sir Ron Dearing's deserve attention and support.

But what about the final step, from university to working life? We have seen sad examples, time and time again, of graduates who have excellent academic qualifications but cannot talk. They are ill presented at interview, lack character and have no sense of responsibility for their own future. A business could take on such candidates and train them in life skills, but time is short and such training is expensive. Should the universities be doing more? There are no government league tables for universities' success in placing their graduates into work, so what incentive is there? Besides that, the raw material they take in has been produced by a system that currently places little emphasis on non-academic strengths. Yet, against these odds, there are positive signs.

A study by the Quality in Higher Education Project at the University of

Central England found that employers rated new graduates high in the skills of:

○   willingness to learn
○   cooperation
○   commitment
○   desire to achieve
○   self-motivation
○   reliability
○   ability to use computers
○   drive/energy
○   teamwork
○   flexibility.

However, oral and written communication skills came in the lower half of the employers' rating of skills, and in the bottom 10 (out of 62) were:

○   negotiation skills
○   financial knowledge
○   commercial awareness
○   leadership ability
○   decision-making skills
○   influencing skills.

Whilst this says little for the graduates' possession of the soft skills wanted by employers, it says a great deal about the same graduates' personal qualities and potential. The raw material is there to work on and today's competitive environment is bringing it to the fore. What can universities do to help? There are many examples.

○   The Department of Employment's Enterprise in Higher Education (EHE) initiative funds projects to introduce personal transferable skills and work experience into university education. Many UK universities take advantage of this scheme.
○   Following an initiative by the Science and Engineering Research Council (SERC) to provide to Ph.D students intensive one-week graduate schools to draw out transpersonal skills, the government proposed a one-year MRes (a research masters degree) to train graduates, including potential Ph.Ds, in research techniques and transferable skills such as teamwork, communication and business know-how. There is some reservation that this could deplete Ph.D funding as a result, but it is at least a positive recognition of the issue.
○   In 1992, University College London (UCL) initiated the UCL Graduate School to provide formal training in the skills needed to conduct

successful research, together with presentational and other transferable skills.

O   UCL also launched in 1995 a management centre in response to industry's needs for employees to have not just excellent specialist skills, but to be able to manage a project, a team, or a budget. 'Management Studies' can be taken as a minor subject of several full degree courses, so that management skills become integrated with physics, law or medicine.

STEP

Work experience is the best way for a student to discover the needs of the workplace and the differences from academia. Short work experience spells are common in schools, but not for undergraduates. Yet there is at least as much reason and potential benefit.

One scheme we have several years' experience with is promoted by Shell UK, Shell Technology Enterprise Programme (STEP). It aims to place undergraduates into business for eight weeks in the summer vacation prior to their final year of study. The emphasis is on placements in small to medium enterprises, on well-defined projects with a technical flavour, either due to the industry or the application. Smaller companies benefit particularly from such placements because they gain access to skills they do not possess and cannot afford at consultancy rates. Students benefit particularly because in a small company they can see the whole breadth of the operation and can talk directly to the top managers to understand their perspective. They can see the importance of their project for the business in a manner which would not be obvious in a large business, where a project is swallowed up in the corporation.

We asked students at one STEP induction meeting what benefits they thought they would bring to the business. Their list was interesting:

DIRECT BENEFITS
Academic specialist knowledge
Prior experience of the application
Cheap labour
INDIRECT BENEFITS
Fresh eyes
Initiator of change
Imagination
PERSONAL QUALITIES AND SKILLS
Teamwork
Interpersonal skills
Character

Willingness to accept responsibility
Problem-solving skills
Project skills.

The reader might compare this with the list of graduate qualities as perceived by employers provided earlier in this chapter.

What did the students hope for from their project? Again, an interesting list:

○   do a good job
○   get a bonus
○   project success
○   find a job via developing skills and gaining experience
○   exceed the employer's expectations
○   learn about small businesses
○   learn how small businesses compete against large ones
○   transfer academic skills to real business
○   make contacts
○   create career opportunities
○   work in a different environment
○   enjoy the work.

This variety shows how motivation can vary widely by person.

They had fears as well as hopes:

○   practical problems (fitting a holiday in)
○   not 'my usual area'
○   new situation
○   into deep end
○   9–5 office environment
○   might not like the work
○   might not meet employer's expectations
○   failure
○   into the unknown
○   short of required skills
○   consequences to the business of project recommendations.

Many of these are 'comfort zone' problems which face a new employee in any situation. This underlines the need for a good induction programme and close management attention for any new employee in a company to minimize fears which could affect performance.

The STEP programme encourages employers to recognize the need to induct their students properly, to set clear documented objectives and to review performance against these regularly. A by-product is that it gives the company some basic management training in a subtle way.

Students have private documentation to complete. STEP aims to concentrate on core skill areas of the UK Management Charter Initiative (MCI) model of personal competencies:

○   teamwork
○   communication and presentation
○   focus on results
○   information search skills
○   confidence and drive
○   ethical perspective
○   influencing others
○   self-management
○   strategic perspective
○   thinking and decision-making.

STEP students demonstrate and list in a weekly skills review evidence of progress in the top five skills, and observe their work colleagues in the host company for evidence of the others. At the end of the placement, the student writes a report summarizing experiences, conclusions and performance against objectives. We will close with some comments from some recent reports – the words of the learners themselves as they experience one of life's fundamental changes, the change from formal education to work.

> 'Computer scientists often fall into a stereotype. Although extremely proficient technically, they often lack the interpersonal skills that are so vital to succeed in today's world.'
> 'I have become much more relaxed and purposeful when dealing with clients and people in general.'
> 'The important thing to the partners was the solution, not necessarily the method used.'
> 'I have learned a great many new skills which will stand me in good stead in the "real world". These skills include a better grasp of the fundamental business principles and that you sometimes have to be an accountant, a salesman, an administrator and many other people if you are to succeed. I have learned that aggression doesn't always get things done; the diplomatic approach is often much more effective. I feel I can now "read" people better too. I have discovered the importance of networking. I now know how vital useful contacts are.'

The above quotations are from one student's report on a very successful eight-week project. Setting project success apart, in what other way could that student have learned what he did in such a short period, or understood the need for and acquired new interpersonal and interdisciplinary skills in that time?

Some more quotes:

> 'I was in charge of everything from the research to the naming and pricing of the product. All decisions were made by myself alone. All this responsibility was fearsome at first, but in no time it became a blessing. I truly enjoyed it.'
> 'Being the interface between company and clients instilled in me a real sense of purpose. I knew that the business implications of a mistake in this role could be serious. This factor significantly developed my commercial acumen.'
> 'Having to maintain order and productivity in a meeting at which both the managing director and sales director were present was no easy task. Through this experience, however, I developed my skills of tact, diplomacy and organisation. A vital skill which I have developed is to treat each person with whom I come into contact in the most appropriate way.'

THE KEY MESSAGES

O   One of the new roles of T & D will be the facilitation of group or team exercises on demand.

O   An experienced facilitator can begin to unlock the total potential of a team.

O   Because of the new requirements T & D will have to act increasingly as a broker rather than a provider of development.

O   International 'league tables' are making governments aware of the need for secondary and higher education to better prepare pupils for their role in the workforce.

O   This is manifesting itself as proposals for a cohesive and unified framework for vocational and academic qualifications.

O   The messages of 'A Learning Approach to Change' of

> clarity of expectations, goals and targets
> good communications
> mentoring
> leadership
> measurement
> a positive learning environment
> lifetime learning by teachers too

apply to academia just as much as to business.

O   Academia needs to supply students to the world of work with soft skills as well as examination certificates.

O   Student learners have enormous potential but often are not given the chance to show it. We need to find ways out of the current system to release this potential for the good of all.

FOOD FOR THOUGHT

Two final observations by STEP students:

> 'I realized what would be expected of me regarding my project but I was given absolute freedom to undertake my tasks in whatever way I considered best. This was a motivating force as it enabled me to make my own decisions, make use of my initiative and ideas, and manage my own time. In addition to this, my capability to undertake this project successfully was always assumed, which made me feel trusted and useful.'
>
> 'The working environment in the company is nice and friendly. I see it as a big team in which all of us play an important role and are encouraged to make a contribution.'

These relate to a company founded in 1992 by one person with £3 000. In 1996 it employed 50 staff and turned over £3 million per annum. Perhaps the management style, with its emphasis on empowerment, trust, responsibility and teamwork, has something to do with its success.

16

SKILLS AND THE HUMAN BALANCE SHEET

Intellectual capital is at least as important as financial capital in providing an accurate picture of an enterprise's true worth.

Leif Edvinsson, Skandia,
Fortune, 9 September 1996

BACKWARD LINKS

O The previous chapters of this book, and especially the quotations at the beginning and end of each one.

FORWARD LINKS

O The future, and to the practice, as well as the concept, that people really are the most valuable asset an organization can possess.

AIMS

The aims of this chapter are:

O To make the reader appreciate the implications of training and learning from the individual's point of view
O To introduce the reader to the concept of intellectual capital and the progress that two leading organizations are making in turning the concept into reality
O To engage the readers' enthusiasm to pursue their interest in the subject and perhaps make a contribution that can be shared with others.

THE HUMAN ASPECTS OF SKILLS MANAGEMENT

So far in this book there has been very little discussion about the employees' view of change, training and skills management. Most of the discussion has centred on the organization's perspectives and interests. But *people* are the organization, so the first part of this chapter is written from their point of view. The middle part of the chapter introduces the concept of intellectual capital, what it means to those organizations which lead the way in its development, and how it is being used as an additional indicator of corporate health. The final part brings the two topics together in a fictitious, but conceivably real, Annual General Meeting.

WHAT'S IN IT FOR ME?

Where training is involved this has to be the most obvious question in the world that an employee can ask. The answer has to be just as obvious: training means more than just attending a course. The fact that training is being offered, with the opportunity for the employee to learn something new, demonstrates an organization's commitment to growing its people. It is an investment that it is keen to make so that both the employee and the employer will benefit. The employees gain extra skills, knowledge and experience and hence become more valuable, not only to their current employer but in the marketplace in general. The employer gains when these new skills, knowledge and experiences are directly applied to the company's products, services and key business processes.

As a good illustration of this message the Investors In People standard looks for enterprises that develop their employees':

- skills, knowledge and qualifications
- motivation, commitment and loyalty
- confidence
- job satisfaction
- career prospects.

Another example is provided by Motorola, considered by many to be one of the leading benchmark companies for training in the USA. According to Bill Wiggenhorn, president of Motorola University (the in-house training facility), the company has a philosophy that goes something like this:

> When we hire you we hope you will be a part of our community for forty years. But it's a two-way street. Our obligation is to provide you with the opportunity to learn the skills you need *today* and *tomorrow*. It's your responsibility to learn and apply those. If either of us breaks the [implicit] contract, then our investment in education won't work.[1]

Nowadays any reference to a job for life, even forty years, must be treated with caution. Nevertheless, we have to admire the sentiments behind the statement and the action behind the words. The average amount of training that every Motorola employee gets is about 40 hours a year. Motorola hopes to quadruple that by the year 2000, which would equate to about five weeks of training a year. Motorola feels that the way to stay ahead of competition is through an ever-increasing amount of training and hence a workforce that grows in capability and value continuously.

THE ULTIMATE LEARNING ORGANIZATION – ME INCORPORATED

In some of the leading-edge organizations the evidence is growing that once people acquire a taste for learning again they cannot get enough of it. When a company ties status and financial compensation to the acquisition and application of extra knowledge and skills, then stand back and prepare to be amazed at the rate of progress – not just of the company but also the workforce. Ironically, the evidence has been around for a long time. According to an article entitled 'Companies That Train Best',[2] the Corning organization in the US spent 3.0 per cent of its payroll costs and gave each employee an average of 92 hours of training in 1992. This was in excess of two weeks' full-time training each, most of which was given by ordinary employees, not professional educators. The rewards for the factory workers undergoing this training was direct and tangible; their pay rose with each new skill that they learnt. As a result of the training Corning's product defects fell by 38 per cent, with productivity up and waste down. A similar scheme operates at General Motors' Delco-Remy plant in Fitzgerald, Georgia. There, amongst a host of other innovative schemes, the *average* worker 'participates in a pay-for-knowledge program (for learning almost every job in the plant)'.[3]

Some people argue that the term 'learning organization' is a misnomer, that the knowledge, skills, experience and attitudes reside in the individual employees, not in the corporate body. That is why downsizing is seen as a dilution of a company's capability by everyone except the financial markets, who usually 'reward' a downsizing exercise with an increase in the company's share price.

INTELLECTUAL CAPITAL (IC)

Hamel and Prahalad[4] put a much more positive view on an organization's capability in relation to its share price. Taking the end of 1993 figures they show that some companies have a ratio of market value to asset value well in excess of 1.0. They cite Cisco Systems with a ratio of 11.7, Oracle Systems at 7.8 and Microsoft at 5.7 (in excess of 15 in 1995), and suggest that the difference between asset value and market value is core competence – the skills and ideas embodied in the employees' limbs and brains. While there are very precise and elaborate techniques for measuring, allocating and accounting for financial assets in the balance sheet, there are seldom any equivalent measures for accounting for the remaining three-quarters, nine-tenths or whatever of the market value. This difference in worth is accounted for in no small measure by the value of all of the individuals in the organization.

There are encouraging signs that some enterprises are becoming increasingly aware that the collective skills, expertise, knowledge and experience of their workforce can be a key competitive differentiator in their chosen market. The companies in the vanguard of this movement are striving to discover ways of measuring what they have labelled 'Intellectual Capital' (IC), in which the collective wisdom of their workforce plays an important part. In this section we will take a look at two of the leading lights in the intellectual capital movement. This is not to imply that no other companies are actively engaged in this arena, but these particular two are extremely willing to place their thoughts and experiences in the public domain, and for this we should all be very thankful.

CANADIAN IMPERIAL BANK OF COMMERCE

In the early 1990s the Canadian Imperial Bank of Commerce (CIBC), North America's seventh largest bank, fretted over their inability to make good lending decisions.[5] Banks had become, in the words of Senior Vice President Rob Paterson, '...such crummy lenders ... we don't understand what we're lending against anymore'. CIBC's analysis led them to believe that 'soft' assets, such as the programming skills of a software company, the information technology infrastructure of a telephone-based insurance organization or the creativity and experience of a firm of architects, could be a much better credit risk than, say, the 'hard' assets of an out-of-town shopping complex. But how do you measure this intellectual capital, and how do you grow it; in other words, how do you actually manage it? Enter Hubert Saint-Onge, whose business card proclaims him as 'Vice President, Learning Organization and Leadership Development' for CIBC.

In the CIBC model that he has helped to develop, intellectual capital is seen as being created from three key elements:

O   individual skills needed to serve the customer – its human capital
O   organizational capabilities needed to operate in the market – its structural capital
O   the strengths of its business – its customer capital.

For example, CIBC's customer base of six million people represents a significant piece of customer capital and is worth immeasurably more than the computer disks on which it endlessly spins around. As regards human capital, Saint-Onge abolished training *per se* and replaced it with learning. CIBC operates on the understanding that 'for learning to really take place, individual employees have to have full ownership of their development, and full responsibility and accountability for their performance'. To aid measurement of the human capital, quantitative competency models have been developed that describe the various skills and knowledge that customer-facing employees should have. There are about four dozen in all, including: a knowledge of accounting, expertise in credit analysis, communication skills, selling skills and so on. Assessing themselves against this list, employees are responsible for learning what they don't know and building on what they do know; not in preparation for their next job, but in doing their current one better.

CIBC uses a range of indexes to measure the growth of intellectual capital, arguing that, just as no one number shows a company's financial health, IC needs to be tracked in a variety of ways. Some indexes measure the employees' creativity and innovation in terms of the number of ideas generated, and the number that are implemented as new products or services. Others then measure the take-up of these products in generating new revenue streams and what percentage of the total revenue these represent. (As an example of this, in the very fast-moving and competitive world of information technology, especially PCs, a company lives or dies by its innovative ability. Consequently, an increasing amount of a company's total revenue comes from products that were not available twelve months previously. And if you want to be number one in the market this 'lag' needs to be reduced to nine, six or perhaps even three months to keep ahead of the more nimble competitors.)

For CIBC the end result has to be better management of its intellectual capital, and in understanding, applying and developing these practices in its own business first, putting it in a better position to judge its corporate customers similarly – the days of 'crummy lending' could be over for this bank.

THE SKANDIA GROUP

In 1991 this Swedish international insurance and financial services company appointed Leif Edvinsson to the position of Corporate Director of Intellectual Capital, a rather unique position. Skandia defines intellectual capital (IC) as the gap between the market value and the book value of a company's shares. Furthermore, they see intellectual capital comprising the human capital that goes home at night, plus the structural capital that remains in the office. Structural capital is seen as the strategies, systems, software, databases, manuals, trademarks, structure, culture, customer files and so on – in other words, organizational capability.[6]

Skandia was convinced that its future prosperity depended greatly on its ability to grow its IC, and at a rate faster and more targeted than its competitors. But, how to measure it, and how to manage it? This was the job that Edvinsson was being asked to do. In 1994 the first tangible results of this work were seen when a major unit of Skandia, Assurance & Financial Services (AFS), issued a 'Balanced Annual Report on Intellectual Capital 1993', a supplement to Skandia's annual report for 1993. This initial version was presented as a 'project in process', with unaudited figures, and mainly as a prototype to invite comment and criticism. There have been annual and interim supplements to all of Skandia's annual reports ever since, each of them charting the startling progress being made. In the supplement to Skandia's 1994 annual report entitled 'Visualizing Intellectual Capital in Skandia', the President and CEO of Skandia, Bjorn Wolrath, announced the extension of the project to other units and introduced the Skandia Navigator.

THE SKANDIA NAVIGATOR

It was called Navigator to underscore the concept of the need to know the enterprise's position, its direction and velocity – to help it navigate into the future.[7] The Navigator is a reporting model used in a consistent manner across all involved Skandia operating units and, to some extent, it is still evolving. The design of the Navigator stemmed from considering that the success of a business depended on a set of critical success factors (CSFs). CSFs could typically be:

- competent and committed employees
- proficient fund management to give good customer yield
- loyal customer base
- low costs to maintain competitive edge
- and so on.

From these can be developed a set of indicators that would testify to the future strength of the business and which can be measured and managed.

The CSFs and their associated indicators are not the same for every unit in Skandia; what might be appropriate in banking may not be in aviation insurance, for example. Therefore, one of the earliest tasks was for each unit to devise its own set. Although these vary from unit to unit they can all be grouped into major focus areas: the financial focus, the customer focus, the process focus, the human focus and the renewal and development focus. Where indicators are common across units, the sharing of relevant knowledge and the implementation of best practices is encouraged and expected. The indicators used in the renewal and development of intellectual capital are pointers to the business's future health and growth. Appropriate training would fall into this category, as we shall show in the following examples of the various focus areas taken across a variety of units.

Financial focus

- ○ Fund assets per employee
- ○ Income per employee
- ○ Amount invoiced per employee

Customer focus

- ○ Market share
- ○ Number of accounts
- ○ Customers lost – percentage
- ○ Satisfaction index

Process focus

- ○ Administration expense as a percentage of total revenue
- ○ Administration expense per employee
- ○ Processing time for outpayments
- ○ Applications filed without error – percentage
- ○ Personal computers per employee
- ○ IT expense as a percentage of administration expense

Human focus

- ○ Number of employees
- ○ Number of managers
- ○ Employee turnover
- ○ Average length of service
- ○ Empowerment index (the results of a survey conducted by the Swedish Institute of Public Opinion Research that measures employees' motivation, support within the organization, awareness of quality demands, responsibility versus authority, competence and so on)

Renewal and development focus

- ○ Competence development expense per employee
- ○ Training hours as a percentage of total hours
- ○ Training expense as a percentage of administrative expense
- ○ IT expense as a percentage of administrative expense
- ○ Employee satisfaction index

FUTURE ACTIVITIES

Skandia continues to develop its work on IC. Among the activities planned are:

○   developing the role of IC controllers (the first was appointed in 1994)
○   more systematic comparisons, such as benchmarking
○   cooperation between the accounting and HR functions to develop indicators and capital ratios that pertain to human capital
○   systems for the creation of structural capital through IT.

The years ahead are exciting ones indeed for the Skandia group, and for all those interested in the concept of intellectual capital. In this next section we consider the skills content of IC and discuss its possible inclusion in what we have chosen to call the human balance sheet.

THE HUMAN BALANCE SHEET

We have ranged over many aspects of needs and skills in this book, including the not so obvious ones of vitality, brainstorming, creativity and their like. Training and the learning of new skills and knowledge is not restricted to the domain of the classroom or corporate university. Those organizations which are at the forefront of helping their workforce to realize their full potential know that learning happens all the time, not just on scheduled courses.

At the Annual General Meetings of shareholders CEOs proudly announce that, '*Our people are our most valuable asset.*' Indeed they are. Yet in times of a recession we see just how liquid an asset people can become. If people are indeed the most valuable asset an organization has why can't they be shown on the balance sheet in some way? After all, other assets are. So is depreciation – the decrease in the value of assets. So for that matter are items like goodwill, and the value of intellectual property and patents. So why not people? Why can't we make an effort to show the shareholders and other interested parties some form of value of the organization's human assets, just as Skandia are doing, but in a slightly different way? It should be possible to show how the skills of the workforce have grown since the last reporting period and over the past five years, say, so that year on year comparisons can be made. If we can show the number of people employed year on year over the last five years, then we ought to be able to show their skill value.

What we have in mind is something that is easy to implement, simple to understand, and meaningful to everyone. However, it does rely on the availability of a skills management system to provide an aggregate skills value by individual, department, function and organization. In the absence of an SMS, a stock check of skills has to be carried out to size the skills inventory and value it, just as a company carries out its normal annual stock check and valuation. The organization can then adjust the growth in its skills value on attaining, say, ISO 9000, the UK Quality Award, achieving Investors In People status and so on. These are corporate achievements and, in adding to the overall skills value of the organization, would appear in the SMS at the corporate level. What would also appear in the SMS would be individual achievements, such as first and second degrees, recognized institutional diplomas, vocational qualifications, such as NVQs and SVQs in the UK, and similar awards in other countries. All of these would have rational and acceptable numerical values (as explained in the notes to the human accounts). One intriguing aspect about an organization's skills is that they actually increase in value with usage, as the employees progress up their learning curves and gain experience. (Table 4.1 in Chapter 4 shows this in terms of increasing skills levels.) This is in complete contrast to inanimate assets, which are assumed to gradually wear out in the course of producing goods and services.

There would need to be some accounting for the 'depreciation' of dormant or redundant skills and knowledge. Like radioactivity, skills, knowledge, techniques and expertise all have a limited half-life if unused or unrefreshed, or overtaken by technology. To ensure that important skills are kept refreshed and razor sharp, airline pilots undergo regular training in flight simulators to hone their skills in handling emergency situations that they hope will never arise in normal operations. This part of human accounting might be trickier than accounting for growth. Nevertheless, HRM should be able to devise an acceptable solution. And considering this, perhaps we should now call this function human resource accounting (HRA).

One accounting method would be the financial one of writing-down the book value of certain skills by 50 per cent of their residual value each year, thus making the point about the half-life of unused or outdated skills. This would have to be with the agreement, and hopefully the initiative, of the employees and their management. In other words, it cannot be decided by HRA in isolation.

Downsizing now takes on a new aspect, that of organizational anorexia. Not only does the organization cut its costs, it also loses part of its skills inventory. This is the part of human capital that walks out of the door at night, but doesn't come back the following morning. Unless an enterprise has an apprentice scheme, a graduate recruitment policy, or some form of replenishment strategy, it can do itself irreversible damage. In the United Kingdom this has already happened to commercial shipbuilding, and has almost happened to motorcycle manufacturing. Some of the precious skills that are being lost are design skills, which were built up over decades, and are not easily or rapidly replaced. At least, not apparently so.

Some companies, perhaps more far-sighted than others, are offering a severance package to their employees in exchange for a mandatory 'brain dump'. This entails the employees being as precise as possible in explaining how they use their skills, expertise, experience and logic to perform the complex aspects of their job. This information is then used to generate computer-based 'expert systems'. If these programs are written correctly the results obtained by a novice should match those of the departing expert. In fact these expert systems should become valuable, if somewhat intangible, 'human' assets, qualifying for inclusion somewhere in the company's skills balance sheet.

It would be easy from here to move on to analogies equivalent to cash flow, the sources and usage of funds, and so on. However, financial accounting is difficult enough as it is to laypeople, and human accounting should be kept as simple as possible at this stage if it is to be understood by all the organization's stakeholders. Then perhaps, at some future Annual General Meeting, the CEO might be able to say with conviction,

> These robust financial results are due as ever to our people, who remain our most valuable assets. This year I am proud to report a record increase in our corporate skill level for the fourth successive year. Our skill level now exceeds three thousand units, greater than either of our two largest competitors. This has been achieved with a relatively stable headcount and a workforce that once again has demonstrated that it is able to surpass its own superb record of achievements. I am forever amazed at their ability to grow their capabilities year on year without faltering. In the three key areas of customer commitment, output per employee and value added per employee they have surpassed all existing records. It augurs well for the future that our order book – no, their order book – has never been stronger.
>
> Personally, the highlight of the year was our annual awards ceremony, when a record number of our employees, including I might add, two senior board members, received public recognition from their colleagues for their outstanding progress during the year.
>
> Running this a close second was the pride I felt when we were voted Learning Organization of the Year (LOFTY) by our peers. Not only is this company one of the most skilful and knowledgeable in the industry, it also manages to scoop most of the industry's training and achievement awards each year as well.
>
> As sure as night follows day this growth in our skills is followed by achievement, and our benchmark studies have shown us to be the national best-of-breed in three key aspects of our business. We are gaining on the best-in-the-world quite rapidly, and we have set ourselves the demanding target of displacing them within three years.
>
> You may be surprised to learn that we also take a great deal of interest in the human assets of our major suppliers. Their skills levels and the environ-ments they have fostered to encourage growth within their own company

are important to us. We seek out kindred organizations and form an affinity with them so that we both may prosper. By working closely with them we can influence the quality of the goods and services they provide us. We are extremely fortunate to be able to work with some of the best suppliers in the business. They, in their turn, may feel that they are equally fortunate to have us as their customer.

Ladies and Gentlemen, this is an excellent state of financial and human affairs I report to you and one that foretells a bright future. We are well placed to take advantage of any shifts in the marketplace and to lead events from the front. And we are the envy of our industry.

It is now five long years since I stood before you and said that this company had to face up to a period of unprecedented change if it was to continue as an independent organization. I warned that it would not be easy, that there would be doubters and setbacks. We have all had to go back to school again to take on board new skills, new knowledge, and above all else, new attitudes. You may be interested to know that this week I have agreed that your company should host a delegation from the Far East who wish to study our methods in depth. Ladies and Gentlemen, what better testimonial to our people could there be? I think we can safely say that we have turned the corner and are on the right track.

Thank you for your continued support. I know that none of us will let you down.

Yes, we know it's simplistic and perhaps a little too far-fetched. But why shouldn't we contemplate something like this? How else are we going to demonstrate the human worth of the organization? If you were an investor or a potential recruit how would you know which company was best-of-breed, even with a hundred company reports in your hands?

The financial press regularly publishes performance tables of unit trusts and equity funds. These, in general, reflect the skills of their management. The tables are readily accepted as valid and informative. They enable any interested observer to reach an unambiguous conclusion about the abilities of the funds' management. In the UK the government compiles and publishes (much maligned) 'league tables' of hospitals and schools. Respectively, these tables are based on criteria for service and achievement. In that respect they reflect the skills, knowledge and expertise of the workforce in providing that service and facilitating that achievement. Patients and parents therefore have a degree of choice and some information, however basic, at this early stage on which to make a decision.

There is a very strong relationship between the success of an enterprise and the strength of its human assets. We see examples every year in the performances of football, hockey, baseball, basketball and other team sports. Each team member is not necessarily the best-in-the-world in that particular position. But because of the synergy generated by the right philosophy, vision, leadership, training and willingness to learn, the team becomes the best-in-the-world in their sport. It is also relatively easy to spot the skills gaps. There are teams whose skills are growing and who are destined for eventual glory. There are others whose skills are declining and who need to increase their skills, either through training or acquisition, or both, to avoid finishing last.

We should be able to apply a similar yardstick to the value of human assets in industry, commerce and the public and voluntary sectors, except in this case it should be easier to use. The sooner we tackle this issue the quicker we will appreciate the human value of an organization as easily as we do its financial worth. And at that point competition will take on a whole new dimension.

THE KEY MESSAGES

○   As far as training is concerned every employee is entitled to ask, 'What's in it for me?' The answer has to be obvious and personal – 'It makes you more valuable.'

○   This is a two-way contract. The employer's obligation is to provide the opportunity to learn; the employees' is to seize it.

○   The evidence is growing that once people get a taste for learning again they can't get enough of it.

○   The difference between a company's market value and its asset value reflects the value of its workforce; what some have called intellectual capital.

○   There is a very strong relationship between the success of an enterprise and the strength of its human assets.

FOOD FOR THOUGHT

Those who are in love with learning are in love with life. For them change is never a problem, never a threat, just another exciting opportunity. It does, however, require what you might call a positive mental attitude.

Charles Handy, *The Age of Unreason*,
Random Century Hutchinson, London, 1989

EPILOGUE

The show ain't over till the fat lady sings.

Anon

INTRODUCTION

On 25 May 1997, just as we were finalizing this book with Gower Publishing, the following headline appeared in the *Sunday Times*: 'Small firms fail to profit from training'. The article below the headline went on to quote a report[1] by the Foundation for Manufacturing and Industry, the University of Warwick Business School and Coopers & Lybrand. The substance of the report was that small firms waste money on training because neither do they link it to their business strategy nor measure its effectiveness. We felt that we had to follow this report up. The Foundation for Manufacturing and Industry kindly provided a review copy, and the University of Warwick provided us with a Working Paper,[2] written by the same authors, that supplies much of the statistical analysis and references to earlier work.

This Epilogue summarizes the report's conclusions, and adds our own observations.

THE 'MIDDLE MARKET'

The first observation we noted was that the report does not in fact relate to 'small firms'. It relates to 'Middle Market' companies as reported in a 1994 Coopers & Lybrand study: companies turning over between £8 million and £500 million per annum, employing about one third of the UK workforce

289

and contributing about 30 per cent of GDP. The comparable 'Mittelstand' in Germany, long recognized as the backbone of German industrial success, turns over between £10 million and £100 million per annum, employs two thirds of the workforce and accounts for 50 per cent of GDP.

PURPOSE OF REPORT

As stated by its authors, the purpose of the current report was to focus on the education, training and development of 'Middle Market' employees from boardroom to shopfloor and to review:

> How much attention is paid by companies in the 'Middle Market' to the education, training and development of the workforce at all levels, and in particular at Board level?
> How far are the principles expressed by senior executives in relation to the capabilities of the workforce carried through into practice?
> Can we trace any connections between better-performing companies and their education, training and development principles and practices?

The Working Paper notes that what little research existed hitherto had been focused primarily on the relationship between the provision of training and the benefits for the trainees. The authors' concern in writing the paper, however, was rather with the relationship between training provision and corporate performance in the Middle Market. In SATE terms (see Chapters 1, 11 and 12), this is the link between level 2 and level 4 outcomes. The report's authors are unaware of any previous study with such a focus. They note that there is 'a presumption of a direct link between national economic efficiency and high levels of Education and Training'. But is it valid? Can it be proved? We note in Chapters 11 and 12 the difficulty of measuring outcomes at level 4 (business results) that can be linked directly to training.

EDUCATION, TRAINING AND DEVELOPMENT

The report defines these as follows:

Education:	The formal process of learning including pre-school, primary, secondary, tertiary, graduate and post-graduate education.
Training:	Skill-based programmes used to enhance efficiency where tools and techniques can be applied – e.g. a marketing course, learning word-processing etc.
Development:	Exposure to experiences (formal and informal) which develop character, self-awareness, confidence etc. which complement basic job skills.

METHOD

A survey was made of 308 'Middle Market' companies from all regions of the UK, via questionnaires to board directors (65 per cent of sample) or to senior managers. The replies were correlated statistically with performance measures of two types:

'INTERMEDIATE' OUTCOMES

- Percentage of customer complaints
- Quality of raw materials or other bought-in supplies
- Level of defects
- Productivity
- Delivery lead time
- Percentage of orders delivered in full and on time
- Absenteeism
- Staff turnover

These relate directly to SATE level 3 'performance results', or to 'specific' objectives in terms of our discussions on project thinking in Chapter 2.

'FINAL' OUTCOMES

- Return on sales compared with industry average
- Return on capital employed
- Cash flow
- Overall cost per unit of output

These relate directly to SATE level 4 'business results', or to 'global' objectives in project terms.

CONCLUSIONS OF STUDY

Many general findings emerge. We note particularly the following.

ON PERFORMANCE

Productivity is not improving rapidly in many of these companies. In fact 45% of the sample report that productivity is static or declining.

ON EDUCATION

There is common agreement that continuing education is important, but less than 50% of companies regularly assess the educational needs of staff and provide on-going support for further education.

Managing Directors are better educated, in terms of academic and professional qualifications, than Board Directors who in turn are better educated than managers.

ON TRAINING

There is overwhelming support that training is 'a good thing', but the majority of companies treat training in isolation rather than as part of the business plan. 66% do not have a formal training plan which is linked to the overall business plan, and only 53% of companies have a regular and formal appraisal system for employees which identifies their training requirements.

70% of companies have a department responsible for training with only 43% of companies having a department which also takes responsibility for the training of Board Directors.

Taking an alternative view of this last finding, imagine a group of companies in which only 70 per cent had a payroll department. Imagine further that in this group only 43 per cent had a payroll department responsible for paying Board Directors . . .

ON DEVELOPMENT

Most respondents believe that staff development is important to the individual and to the performance of the business as a whole. However, considerable discrepancies exist between the importance which respondents attach to development *in principle* and the limited opportunities which they provide for staff development *in practice*.

55% of companies regularly assess staff development.

Only 40% provide staff with internal and external development opportunities.

LEADERS AND LAGGERS

The report uses the 'intermediate' and 'final' outcome measurements to calculate an aggregate performance score. 'Leaders' are defined as those companies in the top 10 per cent of scores. 'Laggers' are those in the bottom 10 per cent. The study goes on to link their performance with education, training and development (ETD) efforts. The results are these:

Education and performance

> While the better performing companies – the 'leaders' – place more empha-
> sis on the importance of education to competitiveness and Board Directors
> and Managers are better qualified in the leading companies, there is only
> weak evidence in the study that higher qualifications lead directly to
> improved company performance.

This is not surprising. Qualifications are a SATE level 2 measure. Company
performance is level 3 or level 4. There is no *a priori* reason why improvement in qualifications should automatically lead to improvement in performance. One of the authors of this book has a Ph.D in Astronomy. It isn't the
slightest use for advising owners of small businesses how to improve sales
of their goods. What really matters is the linkage between qualifications and
performance needs. It is not simply the *level* of qualification which provides
value, but rather the *relevance* of that qualification.

Training and performance

> 61% of 'laggers' – the worst performing companies – have a training
> department responsible for the training of all staff including Board
> Directors compared with 32% of 'leaders'. However, 'leaders' are more
> likely to have a Board Director as the most senior person responsible for
> training, and to provide training plans specifically for Board Directors.
> 'Leading' companies provide more training days for all levels of staff includ-
> ing Board Directors. 40% of 'laggers' provide no training for Board
> Directors at all.
> 'Lagging' companies spend more on employee training than do the 'lead-
> ers'.

This last point is perhaps the one that caught the eye of the *Sunday Times*
headline writer. Put into context, it becomes easier to rationalize this.

First, there is not just training; there is development. We shall see below
that 'leaders' place heavier emphasis on development than 'laggers'. They
also delegate more – a powerful way to develop people.

Second, although 'leaders' spend less on training than 'laggers', they get
more for their money! Perhaps this is an example of the better use 'leaders'
make of their cash resources generally – a sign of better management overall. How often have we seen trainees who have been 'sent' on courses, without briefing or knowledge of where the course fits their job, their personal
objectives (if they have any) or their development plan (if they have one).

Third, having a board director as the most senior person responsible for
training demonstrates high-level sponsorship, underlining our remarks on
sponsorship of change projects in Chapter 2. It also serves to demonstrate
that directors will act as role models for personal and business development
throughout the organization.

Development and performance

> 'Leading' companies are more likely to have a development plan for Board Directors, which is aligned to their own personal objectives and the company business plan.
>
> 'Leaders' are more likely to encourage staff to get involved in activities external to the firm, such as involvement in TECs, Trade Associations and schools.
>
> Board Directors in leading companies have more international experience than those in the lagging companies, and have found that this international experience has been important to their own development.

'Alignment to personal objectives and the company business plan' now begins to emerge. Well! Perhaps this is part of the secret . . .

Furthermore, external and international experiences seem to help development! We hope our readers will begin to appreciate our reasons for dwelling in earlier chapters on human psychology, cognition and the need to encourage changes of perception and attitude.

OUTCOMES

The study finds some linkage between ETD and performance as partly exemplified above. It notes that the better-performing companies concentrate on all aspects of ETD and incorporate ETD policy within the overall company strategy. However, it adds:

> But, on the whole, there is limited evidence that the rhetoric employed in relation to the importance of people, their education, training and skills, is being put into practice. There is little connection between skills formation and the business plan – in fact insufficient evidence of people skills lying at the heart of the business. Given the fact that the majority of respondents were Board Directors themselves and in a key position to influence recruitment and development practice, this indicates a general lack of focus on people skills at the top level.
>
> We hoped and expected to report that this research would show that 'Middle Market' companies which invested heavily in their human resources – what we call ETD – clearly performed better than those which did not. It would be even better to have demonstrated that investment in ETD 'caused' better performance of Middle Market companies.
>
> Unfortunately we were able to provide only weak support for the first statement and no support at all for the idea that the individual items of education or training or development are clearly linked to performance. We therefore certainly cannot show from our research that ETD investment causes better performance.
>
> To some this may come as a shock. In many British companies training is seen to be a 'good thing' bringing benefits both to the company and the

economy in general. Government has vigorously promoted this notion. For example, in its 'Investment in People' leaflets it encourages the belief that investment in training leads to improvements in a company's 'bottom line'.

Our research, based on more than 300 Middle Market companies, demonstrates that it is currently difficult to make that link. This is certainly not to say that either there are no associations or to imply that, in principle, ETD cannot influence company performance. However, to move discussion forward we believe it is imperative to explode the simple-minded assumption that additional expenditure on either education, training or development will lead semi-automatically to an enhanced performance on the part of the firm.

So Why Is The Link So Weak?

This research provides three insights into why the link is weak:

1. The first is that for many businesses ETD policy has only recently been introduced, and so may not necessarily have had its full impact at the time of the survey.
2. In many Middle Market companies ETD policy was not clearly linked to the business plan. We gained the strong impression that ETD was an 'add on', rather than 'at the heart of' Middle Market companies' competitive strategies.
3. Frequently very top people in Middle Market companies were not taking their own personal training and development strategies seriously. Whilst fine phrases were being used about the importance of people within the organisation, the practice was often less impressive than the rhetoric. For example, a key finding is that of all the occupational groups in a business, it was Board Directors who undertook the least number of training days.

INFERENCES

The authors of the report conclude further that investment in human resources, although viewed as 'a good thing', is not monitored and appraised as carefully as other investments. The authors surmise that, although high-quality management is at the heart of competitiveness, this is seen as a 'soft' skill that is hard to justify. Part of this problem is a lack of measurement scales, which the study goes some way to address, via the intermediate and final outcome measures listed above. We would commend to the reader the Skandia Group's approach to human capital as discussed in Chapter 16, as another constructive approach.

The report adds, and we fervently agree:

> In short, it may even be wrong to regard ETD as inherently desirable. Instead there has to be a change in the 'mind set' of companies to viewing expenditure in ETD as requiring clearer justification based on quantifiable

performance impact. In this way ETD will become more clearly linked to enhancing the competitiveness of Middle Market companies.

Whenever we are asked to perform training, we ask in return why the client wants it. The reply is usually quick but unclear. Then we ask what performance improvement is expected. This is a difficult question for the client to answer. There is probably little, if any, performance measuring being done, so how can it be possible to say what improvement is wanted? The client just wants a course on X, as though it were a slimming pill.

LINKING ETD TO BUSINESS NEEDS

One of the key findings of the report (p. 18) was that, of all the companies surveyed, *only 33 per cent link training to the business plan.* We hope by now the reader will need no more convincing that if there is one message we want to leave with the reader on closing this book it is the supreme need to

LINK ETD TO THE BUSINESS PLAN.

This is especially true at a time of change. The message is simply put, but has many implications:

O   the need to define the change, to commit to it, to communicate it and to manage it.
O   the need to create and organize education, training and development (or in one word: Learning) according to how adults generally learn and to individual learning styles
O   the need to relate learning to business and performance needs in a systematic way such as via the SATE model
O   the need to evaluate outcomes just as with any other investment or business activity.

We have provided examples of how other organizations have done all this. We have illustrated the SATE processes, showing how some current UK government initiatives like Investors In People potentially match the SATE model. Finally, we have called on this recent report of the Middle Market to provide a status report of the position one significant market sector has reached.

There is clearly some distance to go, and there are some misconceptions concerning the role of ETD, but we hope this book will point the way forward and encourage these and others along the route ahead.

NOTES

CHAPTER 1   THE FRAMEWORK FOR CHANGE

1. Ghoshal, Sumantra (1993), 'Scandinavian Airlines System', in J. Hendry & A. Eccles (eds), *European Cases in Strategic Management*, London: Chapman & Hall.
2. Ibid.
3. *The Compendium: Developing Education To Meet Business Requirements* (1991) (First Edition), IBM International Education Centre, La Hulpe, Belgium.
4. *The Bolton Evening News*, Newsquest (Bolton) Ltd., 31 January 1994.

CHAPTER 2   MANAGING CHANGE

1. Eccles, A. (1994), *Succeeding with Change*, Maidenhead: McGraw-Hill.
2. Handy, C. (1989), *The Age of Unreason*, London: Hutchinson.

CHAPTER 3   ANALYSING LEARNING NEEDS

1. Waterman, R. (1994), *The Frontiers of Excellence*, London: Nicholas Brealey.
2. *Investing in People* (1992), Ref No. IIP28 Revised, Employment Department, Sheffield.
3. Henkoff, R. (1993), 'Companies That Train Best', *Fortune*, Time Inc., 22 March.
4. 'Reinventing the Factory with Lifelong Learning', *Training*, May 1993.
5. 'No Train, No Gain', *Information Week*, 26 July 1993.
6. 'On Their Own', *Wall Street Journal*, 27 June 1994.

CHAPTER 4   SKILLS AND SKILLS MANAGEMENT

1. Hammer, M. and Stanton, S.A. (1995), *The Reengineering Revolution*, London: HarperCollins Publishers.

CHAPTER 5   WHO ARE THE LEARNERS . . . ?

1. de Bono, E. (1969), *The Mechanism of Mind*, London: Jonathan Cape Ltd.
2. Ibid.
3. Edelman, G. (1992), *Bright Air, Brilliant Fire*, London: Penguin.
4. Eysenck, M.W. (1993), *Principles of Cognitive Psychology*, Hove: Lawrence Erlbaum Associates Ltd.
5. Pryor, K. (1985), *Don't Shoot the Dog*, London: Bantam.

CHAPTER 6   . . . AND HOW DO THEY LEARN?

1. Lovell, R.B. (1982), *Adult Learning*, London: Croom Helm.
2. Senge, P. (1990), *The Fifth Discipline*, New York: Doubleday.
3. Covey, S.R. (1989), *The Seven Habits of Highly Effective People*, New York: Simon & Schuster.
4. Peoples, D.A. (1988), *Presentations Plus*, New York: John Wiley & Sons, Inc.
5. Covey, *The Seven Habits of Highly Effective People*.

CHAPTER 7   PUTTING ADULT LEARNING CHARACTERISTICS TO WORK

1. Hair, J.F., Erffmeyer, R.C. and Russ, K.R. (circa 1989), *Traditional Versus High-Tech Training Methods: A Sales Perspective*, USA: a study report.
2. Janis, I.L. and King, B.T. (1954), 'The Influence of Role Playing on Opinion Change', *Journal of Abnormal and Social Psychology*, 69.
3. Covey, S.R., *The Seven Habits of Highly Effective People*.
4. Bagley, D.S. and Reese, E.J. (1988), *Beyond Selling*, Cupertino, Calif.: Meta Publications.
5. Wilde, O. (1995), *Lady Windermere's Fan and Other Plays*, London: The Penguin Group.

CHAPTER 8   DESIGNING AND DELIVERING LEARNING

1. U.S. Congress, Office of Technology Assessment (1995), *Worker Training: Competing in the New International Economy*, Government Printing Office, Washington DC. (Research from the U.S. Office of Technology Assessment provides these comparisons of a variety of delivery methods for workplace learning. Surveyed firms were Fortune 500 and private companies with sales of $500 million or more.)
2. 'Interactive Technology: Rising Star on the Training Stage', *Workplace Training News*, USA, March 1994.
3. Knight-Ridder Press Release, 14 April 1994.
4. Advertisement in *CompuServe Guide For New Members*, CompuServe Inc., Columbus, 1996.
5. 'Electronic Service Manual', *Workforce Training News*, USA, November/December 1993.

CHAPTER 10   MEASUREMENT AND EVALUATION

1. *Managing Best Practice – Training Evaluation*, The Industrial Society, July/August 1994.

CHAPTER 11   SATE AT WORK – I

1. *Training*, Reed Business Publishing, London, March 1996.
2. The Industrial Society, *Managing Best Practice*.
3. The notes accompanying the diagram of the Carousel of Development shown in Figure 11.4 were kindly provided to the authors by Mr Andrew Forrest, Human Resources Director, The Industrial Society, London, 1997.
4. Ibid.
5. ibid.
6. The Industrial Society, *Training Trends*, No. 16, January/February 1996.
7. The Industrial Society, *Training Trends*, No. 22, January/February 1997..

CHAPTER 12   SATE AT WORK – II

1. *INVESTING IN PEOPLE: The Benefits of Being an Investor in People* (1994), REF No. IIP 37 (rev), Investors In People UK, Sheffield.

2. Much of the original information was gleaned from articles entitled 'Companies That Train Best', *Fortune*, 22 March 1993, 'Putting On The Ritz', *Training and Development*, December 1993, and updated whenever possible from a range of newspapers, magazines and Internet articles.
3. Confederation of British Industry (1994), *Quality Assured – The CBI Review of NVQs and SVQs*.
4. *Training*, Reed Business Publishing, London, March 1996.
5. Dearing, Sir R. (1996), *Review of Qualifications for 16–19 Year Olds*, London: SCAA Publications.

CHAPTER 13   ORGANIZATIONAL TRENDS

1. *The Sunday Times*, Times Newspapers Ltd, London, 8 December 1996.
2. Hammer and Stanton, *The Reengineering Revolution*.
3. Ibid.
4. Ibid.
5. Ibid.
6. Ibid.
7. O'Connor, J. and Seymour, J. (1994), *Training With NLP*, London: HarperCollins.

CHAPTER 14   IMPLICATIONS FOR MANAGEMENT AND WORKERS

1. Toffler, A. (1980), *The Third Wave*, New York: Random House.
2. Champy, J. (1995), *Reengineering Management*, London: Harper-Collins.
3. Bernstein, P.L. (1996), *Against the Gods*, New York: John Wiley & Sons.
4. Champy, *Reengineering Management*.
5. Ibid.
6. Forrest, A. (1995), *Fifty Ways to Personal Development*, London: The Industrial Society.
7. Schultz, D. (1976), *Theories of Personality*, Belmont, CA: Wadsworth Publishing Co. Inc.
8. Thurbin, P.J. (1994), *Implementing the Learning Organisation*, London: Pitman.
9. Loomis, M.E. (1991), *Dancing the Wheel of Psychological Types*, Wilmette, IL: Chiron.
10. Margerison, C. and McCann, R. (1989), *TMS: An Overview*, TMS (UK) Ltd.

11. Wenschlag, R. (1989), *The Versatile Salesperson*, New York: John Wiley & Sons Inc.
12. Richer, J. (1996), *The Richer Way*, London: EMAP Publications.

CHAPTER 15   IMPLICATIONS FOR EDUCATORS

1. Zairi, Dr M. (1994), The Benchmarking Forum, Stratford upon Avon, November.
2. Dearing, *Review of Qualifications for 16–19 Year Olds*.

CHAPTER 16   SKILLS AND THE HUMAN BALANCE SHEET

1. Waterman, R. (1994), *The Frontiers of Excellence*, London: Nicholas Brealey.
2. Henkoff, R. (1993), 'Companies That Train Best', *Fortune*, Time Inc., 22 March.
3. Peters, T. (1989), *Thriving On Chaos*, London: Pan Books.
4. Hamel, G. and Prahalad, C.K. (1994), *Competing For The Future*, Boston: Harvard Business School Press.
5. Stewart, T.A. (1994), 'Your Company's Most Valuable Asset: Intellectual Capital', *Fortune*, Time Inc., October.
6. Advertisement (1996), 'Competing on knowledge', *Fortune*, Time Inc., September.
7. The Skandia Group, (1996), 'The Navigator', Supplement To Skandia's 1996 Interim Report, Sweden.

EPILOGUE

1. Amos, E., Spiller, J., Storey, D. and Wade, R. (1997), *The Middle Market – How They Perform: Education, Training and Development*, Foundation for Manufacturing and Industry, London.
2. Amos, E., Spiller, J., Storey, D. and Wade, R. (1997), *Working Paper No 48: The Impact of Board Director Education, Training and Development on the Performance of Middle Market Firms in the UK*, Research Paper produced by the Centre for Small and Medium Sized Enterprises, University of Warwick.

BIBLIOGRAPHY

Amos, E., Spiller, J., Storey, D. and Wade, R. (1997), *The Middle Market – How They Perform: Education, Training and Development*, London: Foundation for Manufacturing and Industry.

Amos, E., Spiller, J., Storey, D. and Wade, R. (1997), *Working Paper No. 48: The Impact of Board Director Education, Training and Development on the Performance of Middle Market Firms in the UK*, Research Paper produced by the Centre for Small and Medium Sized Enterprises, University of Warwick.

Bagley, D.S. and Reese, E.J. (1988), *Beyond Selling*, Cupertino, Calif.: Meta Publications.

Champy, J. (1995), *Reengineering Management*, London: HarperCollins.

Confederation of British Industry (1994), *Quality Assured – The CBI Review of NVQs and SVQs*, CBI.

Covey, S.R. (1989), *The Seven Habits of Highly Effective People*, New York: Simon & Schuster.

Dearing, Sir R. (1996), *Review of Qualifications for 16–19 Year Olds*, London: SCAA Publications.

de Bono, E. (1969), *The Mechanism of Mind*, London: Jonathan Cape Ltd.

Eccles, A. (1994), *Succeeding with Change*, Maidenhead: McGraw-Hill.

Edelman, G. (1992), *Bright Air, Brilliant Fire*, London: Penguin.

Forrest, A. (1995), *Fifty Ways to Personal Development*, London: The Industrial Society.

Hair, J.F., Erffmeyer, R.C. and Russ, K.R. (circa 1989), *Traditional Versus High-Tech Training Methods: A Sales Perspective*, USA: a study report.

Hamel, G. and Prahalad, C.K. (1994), *Competing For The Future*, Boston: Harvard Business School Press.

Hammer, M. and Champy, J. (1993), *Reengineering the Corporation*, London: Nicholas Brealey.

Hammer, M. and Stanton, S.A. (1995), *The Reengineering Revolution*, London: HarperCollins.

Handy, C. (1989), *The Age of Unreason*, London: Hutchinson.

Henkoff, R. (1993), 'Companies That Train Best', *Fortune*, Time Inc., 22 March.

Janis, I.L. and King, B.T. (1954), 'The Influence of Role Playing on Opinion Change', *Journal of Abnormal and Social Psychology*, 69.

Loomis, M.E. (1991), *Dancing the Wheel of Psychological Types*, Wilmette, IL: Chiron.

Lovell, R.B. (1982), *Adult Learning*, London: Croom Helm.

Margerison, C. and McCann, R. (1989), *TMS: An Overview*, TMS (UK) Ltd.

O'Connor, J. and Seymour, J. (1994), *Training With NLP*, London: Harper-Collins.

Peoples, D.A. (1988), *Presentations Plus*, New York: John Wiley & Sons.

Peters, T. (1989), *Thriving On Chaos*, London: Pan Books.

Pryor, K. (1985), *Don't Shoot the Dog*, London: Bantam.

Schultz, D. (1976), *Theories of Personality*, Belmont, CA: Wadsworth Publishing Co. Inc.

Senge, P. (1990), *The Fifth Discipline*, New York: Doubleday.

Stewart, T.A. (1994), 'Your Company's Most Valuable Asset: Intellectual Capital', *Fortune*, Time Inc., October.

Sumantra, G. (1993), 'Scandinavian Airlines System', in J. Hendry and T. Eccles (eds), *European Cases in Strategic Management*, London: Chapman & Hall.

Thurbin, P.J. (1994), *Implementing the Learning Organization*, London: Pitman.

Toffler, A. (1980), *The Third Wave*, New York: Random House.

Waterman, R. (1994), *The Frontiers of Excellence*, London: Nicholas Brealey.

Wenschlag, R. (1989), *The Versatile Salesperson*, New York: John Wiley & Sons Inc.

FURTHER READING

THE BRAIN, THE MIND AND PERSONALITY

1. E. de Bono, *The Mechanism of Mind* (1969), Jonathan Cape Ltd. De Bono explains in detail three models of the mind and relates them to a wide range of human phenomena, such as insight, learning, humour, self and the four types of thinking: natural, logical, lateral and mathematical. He explains how, although the brain can be highly effective, it gives rise to inevitable defects such as polarization, myth-making and adherence to rigid patterns of thought.

2. Michael W. Eysenck, *Principles of Cognitive Psychology* (1993), Lawrence Erlbaum Associates Ltd. A clear and accessible overview of cognitive psychology. It covers sensory systems and perception, attention, memory, language and thinking, including problem-solving, reasoning and decision-making. There are extensive references to original experimental evidence and balanced views and summaries of the key approaches and theories in this large and expanding area of modern psychology.

3. Karen Pryor, *Don't Shoot the Dog* (1985), Bantam (by arrangement with Simon & Schuster). An immensely readable and useful book based on practical applications of the Skinner school of behaviourist psychology. Dolphin-trainer Pryor gives numerous examples of the use of behaviourism in training and retraining humans and animals, including eight ways of changing undesired behaviour in ten different situations, including work and domestic situations.

4. Richard D. Gross, *Psychology – The Science of Mind and Behaviour*, (1992), Hodder and Stoughton. A thousand-page, clear and readable introductory text to the entire subject of psychology. Extensive references and case studies. Undergraduate level.

5. Malcolm Hardy and Steve Heyes, *Beginning Psychology* (1979), Weidenfeld and Nicolson. Briefer and less detailed coverage of psychology than Gross (4), yet a suitable introductory guide for interested laypeople. High school/pre-university level.

6. Alan Rogers, *Teaching Adults* (1986), Open University Press. A superb, readable handbook covering the issues faced by any teacher of an adult group. This book set us examples of the way forward, and its content and guidance will last for some time.

7. R. Bernard Lovell, *Adult Learning* (1982), Croom Helm Ltd. Similar in coverage to (6) but with a theoretical slant. Full of ideas, especially on the learning environment, including age, social context and personality differences.

8. D. Schultz, *Theories of Personality* (1976), Wadsworth Publishing Co. Inc. A historical view, theorist-by-theorist, of the main personality theories. Covers Freud, Adler, Horney, Fromm, Sullivan, Jung, Murray, Erikson, Allport, Rogers, Maslow, Kelly, Cattell, Skinner, Bandura and Walters, and ending with Limited-Domain Theories, with a background to each investigator (for this can be of relevance to each theory), and a final commentary to each chapter.

9. J. O'Connor and J. Seymour, *Introducing NLP: or Neuro Linguistic Programming* (1990), Mandala. An introductory text to the recent theories mainly originated by Bandler and Grinder as to how consciousness, language and behaviour come together. NLP can be used to understand learning, perception, system thinking, language, personal influence, therapy and thinking strategies. It may be a significant way forward for our self-understanding.

10. R. Bandler and J. Grinder, *The Structure of Magic* (1975), Science & Behaviour Books Inc. 'A Book about Language and Therapy'. See (11) for comments.

11. J. Grinder and R. Bandler, *The Structure of Magic II* (1976), Science & Behaviour Books Inc. 'A Book about Communication and Change'. NLP is something that we cannot afford to ignore.

12. Dan S. Bagley III and Edward J. Reese, *Beyond Selling* (1988), Meta Publications. An application of NLP to selling. It maps closely the techniques and ideas we have fruitfully followed over the years. It is nice to know there was some theory behind it, and theory that may be of use in areas beyond selling.

PERSONAL DEVELOPMENT

1. Andrew Forrest, *Fifty Ways to Personal Development* (1995), The Industrial Society, London. An excellent book, small enough to fit in your pocket, to be taken out and browsed through any time you have a few spare moments.

INDEX

and NVQs 222
responsibility for performance evaluation 50
and shared responsibility for training 156–7
as team leaders 235
line management's involvement with training 210
at Barclays Bank 207
at UK Customs and Excise 208
at Scottish & Newcastle 209
link between training and business plan 295–6

Malcolm Baldrige National Quality Award (Baldrige) 52, 215, 216–17
assessment of 216–17
examples of winners of 220
guidelines for 216
see also Baldrige Quality Award
Management Charter Initiative (MCI) 274
management-training relationship 156
managers as coaches and mentors 11, 157, 232, 246
see also coaches, mentors
manufacturing cycle times 214–15
Margerison and McCann
and Team Management System (TMS) 249
Maslow, Abraham 102
mass customization 4
Matsushita 11
measurement and evaluation 19–20, 50
commitment to 205
coordinator 168–9
dangers in interpretation of level 1 feedback 175–6
lack of evaluation outside classroom 206
of role plays 185–92
of SATE levels 1 to 4 138–9
measurement, evaluation and feedback (of delivery systems) 144
memory 88–91
long-term memory 89
sensory memory 88
short-term memory 88–9
mentor 164, 167
see also adviser
mentoring in secondary schools 265

methodology for measuring return on investment (ROI) 57
see also return on investment
Microsoft 279
Middle Market companies 289–90, 294, 296
lack of top level focus on people skills 294
leaders and laggers: performance link to ETD 292–4
link between ETD and business results 290–92
see also education, training and development (ETD)
mind-set 91, 295
mission statements 51
Mittelstand 290
modelling
of the brain 79
of the human psyche 80
of the mind 80–82
of the Universe 80
moderation of subjective marking 196
module 140
module owner 159
'money off the bottom line' 58
morale after downsizing 230
Morton, Tom 88
Motorola (Baldrige winner) 5, 15, 56, 237, 259, 278–9
average amount of training per employee per year at 220, 279
learning philosophy of 278
University 278
multi-choice tests 184–5
multi-media 153, 163, 164
Performax, positive effect on learning of sales skills 200–202
see also Performax
multi-media personal computer 151–2
multi-skilling 231, 236
Myers-Briggs Type Indicator (MBTI) 247
use in a learning organization 247

national and international initiatives 214
National Health Service (NHS) 9
National Record of Achievement (NRA) 267
National Vocational Qualification (NVQ) 221–4, 268
benefits of 222

Change and the Bottom Line

Alan Warner

A Gower Novel

- How do you plan organizational change?
- How good are you at managing change?
- How do you monitor progress?
- How can you identify resistance - and deal with it?
- What concepts and techniques are available to help?

These are some of the questions addressed in Alan Warner's business novel. He takes the characters already established in his two earlier books - *The Bottom Line* and *Beyond the Bottom Line* - and sets them in a new context. Phil Moorley has become CEO of a family firm in the North of England, where his main task is to change its culture so that it can meet the challenges ahead. Once again he enlists the aid of Christine Goodhart, now a training consultant.

We follow Phil's attempts to create allies and pacify enemies, and we share with him the pains and the triumphs involved. We learn about some of the methods that can be used to bring about change and we see how they work - or fail - when put to the test.

Change and the Bottom Line is another highly effective case study, given life by the fictional treatment. An added feature is the detailed commentary provided by the author, drawing on his personal experience of working closely with change specialists. The result is an entertaining introduction to one of the key areas of management responsibility.

Gower

Diary of a Change Agent

Tony Page

Tony Page is a 40-something management consultant, wrestling with the conflicting demands of a growing business and a growing family. For three years he kept a diary to which he confided his hopes and fears, his triumphs and setbacks. With painful honesty he analysed his working and business relationships as he strove to add value to his clients' businesses and to improve his own abilities.

The diary captures a unique personal journey and by including further commentary, analysis and exercises Tony Page both challenges the reader and emphaizes the human component in managing change.

Tony Page's book:

- introduces diary-keeping as a method for continuous professional and personal learning
- demonstrates ways of gaining control over personal performance
- shows how to conduct conversations that empower other people to change and learn
- provides an example and a direction for leaders who want to 'walk the talk'
- uncovers why corporate change programmes fail and how to mobilise people in an organization.

This honest account will have immediate appeal for anyone serious about business performance improvement, change and learning.

Gower

Facilitating

Mike Robson with Ciarán Beary

How to manage change, and how to ensure continuous
improvement: these are perhaps the two most important
challenges confronting businesses today. And increasingly
facilitating is being seen as the best way to deal with both.

Facilitators - and managers operating in a facilitative style - work
on helping individuals, groups and organizations to enhance their
performance. This book shows how that can be done. The first part
deals with the nature of facilitation and why those involved need
to understand the basis of human behaviour. The second covers
the management of change at different levels. The third provides
practical guidelines on the relevant skills. The fourth looks at the
kinds of situation where facilitators can be effective and includes
case studies from a wide variety of settings. The final part deals
with facilitative styles of management.

For any manager or trainer determined to release the unfulfilled
potential of their organization and the people in it, this book is the
ideal starting point.

Gower

Facilitating Change

Ready-to-Use Training Materials for the Manager

Barry Fletcher

This is a manual designed to help managers to help their staff, using a range of techniques borrowed from the training professional's armoury, with full explanation of how any manager can use them in a team development context. Introductory chapters describe the principles and methods involved in developing people to cope confidently with change. There are questionnaires and suggestions for diagnosing learning needs and recognizing learning opportunities.

At the heart of the manual is a collection of thirtyfive learning activities. Each is self-contained but can be combined with others within the collection to form a more extensive programme of development. All activities start with a brief description and a note of potential benefits, guidance over who it is suitable for and the time and resources required. This is followed by a step-by-step guide to running the activity. Ready-to-copy masters are supplied for any material to be used by participants. The activities are indexed by subject to make it easy for managers to identify the most appropriate for their own needs.

For any manager who'd like to unlock the full potential of his or her team, *Facilitating Change* provides an excellent starting point.

Gower

The Facilitation of Groups

Dale Hunter, Anne Bailey and Bill Taylor

Group synergy is a source of power that has scarcely been tapped. Facilitation offers a way of unlocking that power. This book reveals the secrets of the art of facilitation and shows how to use it to initiate group empowerment.

Developing facilitation skills means first fully understanding the facilitator role: that of a guide helping a group or individual towards a conclusion, without steering the decision. To become an effective group facilitator you need to understand the principles of self-facilitation and the facilitation of individuals, as well as that of a group.

The authors, all experienced facilitators, begin by fully explaining the skills required and the benefits to be derived. The Toolkit which follows includes practical activities, designs and processes, and includes a model facilitation training programme.

This combination of personal experience and practical advice will have wide appeal for facilitators, trainers and group members.

Gower

Gower Handbook of Management Skills

Third Edition

Edited by Dorothy M Stewart

'This is the book I wish I'd had in my desk drawer when I was first a manager. When you need the information, you'll find a chapter to help; no fancy models or useless theories. This is a practical book for real managers, aimed at helping you manage more effectively in the real world of business today. You'll find enough background information, but no overwhelming detail. This is material you can trust. It is tried and tested.'

So writes Dorothy Stewart, describing in the preface the unifying theme behind the new edition of this bestselling *Handbook*. This puts at your disposal the expertise of 25 specialists, each a recognized authority in their particular field. Together, this adds up to an impressive 'one stop library' for the manager determined to make a mark.

Chapters are organised within three parts: Managing Yourself, Managing Other People, and Managing Business. Part I deals with personal skills and includes chapters on self-development and information technology. Part II covers people skills such as listening, influencing and communication. Part III looks at finance, project management, decision-making, negotiating and creativity. A total of 12 chapters are completely new, and the rest have been rigorously updated to fully reflect the rapidly changing world in which we work.

Each chapter focuses on detailed practical guidance, and ends with a checklist of key points and suggestions for further reading.

Gower

A Manual for Change

Terry Wilson

Change is now the only constant, as the cliché has it, and organizations who fail to master change are likely to find themselves undone by it.

In this unique manual, Terry Wilson provides the tools for planning and implementing a systematic organizational change programme. The first section enables the user to determine the scope and scale of the programme. Next, a change profile is completed based on twelve key factors. Finally, each of the factors is reviewed in the context of the user's own organization.

Questionnaires and exercises are provided throughout and any manager working through these will have not only a clear understanding of the change process but also specific plans ready to put into action.

Derived from the author's experience of working with organizations at every level and in a wide range of industries, the manual will be invaluable to directors, managers, consultants and professional trainers battling to help their organizations survive and flourish in an increasingly turbulent environment.

Gower

A Real-Life Guide to Organizational Change

George Blair and Sandy Meadows

'Management ideas may change with fashion, but the underlying concepts do not lose their validity. We offer you prepared food for thought for your organizational microwave, rather than exotic dishes that are very difficult to copy.'

George Blair and Sandy Meadows - themselves battle-hardened veterans of the change process - take a refreshingly different approach to most of the new books, videos, seminars and gurus emerging to tell managers how to cope with change. They encourage the reader to start from the reality of his or her own organization and have the courage to design the programme that will work in real life.

Drawing both on proven systems and their own extensive experience, they chart the way forward from strategy to implementation. With the aid of checklists, illustrations and case studies, they show how to diagnose existing problems, how to construct the appropriate plans and how to deal with the politics. They examine the various options, including empowerment, TQM and re-engineering, set out the criteria for selecting the best mix for your own circumstances and then explain the techniques involved in implementation. Unlike many other books on change, they pay due attention to the need for a reward strategy to support the aims of the change programme.

This accessible and often humorous book is firmly grounded in reality, and will be a welcome relief for managers trying to assimilate accepted 'best practice' in change management into their real working lives.

Gower

Takeover

Sam Volard

A Gower Novel

Over the elaborate Christmas festivities at the Human Ethicals Division of AgriBus International falls a shadow in the shape of an alarming rumour. Can it be true that the Division is being sold? And if it is true, what will it mean for the staff of HED? In particular, how will it affect the heroes of Sam Volard's novel - the assorted but loyal group of friends who we meet in the opening chapters at their traditional Christmas holiday together? Their friendship is about to be put under intense pressure...

For the one-year period covered by the story we follow the reactions of scientists Brian Curtis, Britt Berghoff and Armand Hernier and lawyer Tony Johns, together with their partners and their colleagues. We see how they survive - or fail to survive - the turmoil of redundancies and restructuring until the Division has been fully integrated into the new parent company. At the same time we come to understand the problems of the new divisional chief and his head office team as they deal with the initial trauma and then, with the help of a detailed change model, set about creating a High Involvement Workforce.

Takeover can be read for its fast-moving story and colourful characters. But as we follow the process of the takeover from initial rumour to total integration, we see it from all angles, with good and bad management practice, and all the hopes and fears brought in its wake. The author also provides a chapter-by-chapter commentary analysing the action and underlining the lessons to be drawn. Senior managers will find this a stimulating and rewarding read: one to which many will relate from their own past or current experience.

Gower